THE SLAVONIC & EAST EUROPEAN REVIEW

Volume 91, Number 2 — April 20

ARTICLES

Literature, Art and Thought
DAVIDSON, P. Aleksandr Ivanov and Nikolai Gogol′: The Image and the Word in the Russian Tradition of Art as Prophecy 157

Cinema
VAN HEUCKELOM, K. Londoners and Outlanders: Polish Labour Migration through the European Lens 210

History
TROCH, P. The Intertwining of Religion and Nationhood in Interwar Yugoslavia: The School Celebrations of St Sava's Day 235

Social Sciences
SAVELLI, M. The Peculiar Prosperity of Psychoanalysis in Socialist Yugoslavia 262

STAŃCZYK, E. Caught between Germany and Russia: Memory and National Identity in Poland's Right-Wing Media Post-2004 289

REVIEWS

Del Gaudio, S. *On the Nature of Suržyk: A Double Perspective* (A. Danylenko) 317
Sumarokov, A. *Ody torzhestvennyia. Elegii liubovnyia. Izdanie podgotovil Ronald Vroon* (C. L. Drage) 318
Aptekman, Marina. *Jacob's Ladder: Kabbalistic Allegory in Russian Literature* (V. Vinokur) 320

Kheteni, Zh., Dukkon, A. and Kalafatich, Zh. (eds). *Gogol′ i 20 vek.* (A. McMillin) 322
Torri, Stefania. *Dostojewskij in der deutschen und italienischen Literatur. Eine komparative Studie (1881–1927)* (D. Rayfield) 324
Masing-Delic, Irene. *Exotic Moscow under Western Eyes* (E. Skomp) 325
Moran, John P. *The Solution of the Fist: Dostoevsky and the Roots of Modern Terrorism* (J. Goodwin) 327
Leving, Yuri. *Keys to 'The Gift': A Guide to Vladimir Nabokov's Novel* (S. H. Blackwell) 329
Andryczyk, Mark. *The Intellectual as Hero in 1990s Ukrainian Fiction* (U. Blacker) 332
Renfrew, A. and Tihanov, G. (eds). *Critical Theory in Russia and the West* (M. Grishakova) 333
Longinović, Tomislav Z. *Vampire Nation: Violence as Cultural Imaginary* (N. Kovačevič) 336
King, David. *Red Star Over Russia: A Visual History of the Soviet Union from 1917 to the Death of Stalin* (S. Morrissey) 338
Smithgall, Elsa (ed.). *Kandinsky and the Harmony of Silence: Painting with White Border* (P. J. Kachurin) 339
Neef, Sigrid. *Die Opern Nikolai Rimsky-Korsakows*; Neef, Sigrid. *Die Opern Sergej Prokofjews* (P. R. Bullock) 341
Joseph, Charles M. *Stravinsky's Ballets* (G. Morris) 343
Beumers, B. and Condee, N. (eds). *The Cinema of Alexander Sokurov* (L. Kristensen) 345
Meinander, Henrik. *A History of Finland* (G. Maude) 348
Plakans, Andrejs. *A Concise History of the Baltic States* (M. Seppel) 349
Shore, Paul. *Narratives of Adversity: Jesuits on the Eastern Peripheries of the Habsburg Realms (1640–1773)* (D. Deletant) 351
Davies, Brian. *Empire and Military Revolution in Eastern Europe: Russia's Turkish Wars in the Eighteenth Century* (J. P. LeDonne) 353
Butterwick, Richard. *The Polish Revolution and the Catholic Church, 1788–1792: A Political History* (M. Printy) 355
Lachowicz, Teofil. *Polish Freedom Fighters on American Soil: Polish Veterans in America from the Revolutionary War to 1939* (M. J. Chodakiewicz) 357
Uyama, Tomohiko (ed.). *Asiatic Russia: Imperial Power in Regional and International Contexts* (R. Turaeva) 360
Sked, Alan. *Radetzky: Imperial Victor and Military Genius* (I. D. Armour) 362
Jianu, Angela. *A Circle of Friends: Romanian Revolutionaries and Political Exile, 1840–1859* (D. Mironescu) 363

CONTENTS

Becker, Elisa M. *Medicine, Law and the State in Imperial Russia* (C. Henze) 365
Dennison, Tracy. *The Institutional Framework of Russian Serfdom* (D. Moon) 367
Klier, John Doyle. *Russians, Jews and the Pogroms of 1881–1882* (V. Levin) 369
Kocho-Williams, Alastair. *Russian and Soviet Diplomacy, 1900–39* (K. Neilson) 372
Pinnow, Kenneth M. *Lost to the Collective: Suicide and the Promise of Soviet Socialism, 1921–1929* (S. A. Kowalsky) 374
Haynes, R. and Rady, M. (eds). *In the Shadow of Hitler: Personalities of the Right in Central and Eastern Europe* (A. Kasekamp) 376
Apunen, O. and Wolff, C. *Pettureita ja Patriootteja. Taistelu Suomen ulko- ja puolustuspolitiikan suunnasta 1938–1948* (G. Maude) 378
Rochlitz, Imre. *Accident of Fate: A Personal Account, 1938–1945* (B. Aleksov) 380
Swain, Geoffrey. *Tito: A Biography* (D. Djokić) 382
Ewing, E. Thomas. *Separate Schools: Gender, Policy and Practice in Postwar Soviet Education* (S. T. Duke) 384
Roxburgh, Angus. *The Strongman: Vladimir Putin and the Struggle for Russia* (M. Bowker) 386
Ališauskienė, M. and Schröder, I. W. (eds). *Religious Diversity in Post-Soviet Society: Ethnographies of Catholic Hegemony and the New Pluralism in Lithuania* (S. Rimestad) 387
Headley, Stephen. *Christ after Communism: Spiritual Authority and Its Transmission in Moscow Today* (K. Richters) 389
Keman, H. and Müller-Rommel, F. (eds). *Party Government in the New Europe* (S. Hanley) 391
Stewart, Michael (ed.). *The Gypsy 'Menace': Populism and the New Anti-Gypsy Politics* (A. McGarry) 393

PUBLICATIONS RECEIVED 396

ABSTRACTS 398

Aleksandr Ivanov and Nikolai Gogol′: The Image and the Word in the Russian Tradition of Art as Prophecy

PAMELA DAVIDSON

'The Slav-Russian poet should be more Asiatic in spirit, like a prophet. — He should declare faults clearly and praise virtues. — The artist echoes him.'
A. A. Ivanov, 'Thoughts Arising upon Reading the Bible', 1846–47

'[Ivanov] was the same in painting as Gogol′ in writing and Kireevskii in philosophical thought.'
A. S. Khomiakov, 1858

THE pervasive Russian image of the writer as a prophetic figure is generally regarded as a verbal construct, rooted in and developed through literary tradition. And indeed, there are ample grounds to support such a view, as the image can be traced through a chain of texts from the late eighteenth century onwards. Originating in the writings of Gavrila Derzhavin and Mikhail Lomonosov, it first became widespread during the period after the Napoleonic wars leading up to the Decembrist uprising, when it flourished in the verse of Vasilii Zhukovskii, Fedor Glinka, Vil′gelm Kiukhel′beker, Nikolai Iazykov and Aleksandr Pushkin. Its subsequent metamorphosis from an agent of social and political change into a religious, theurgic force was largely facilitated by Nikolai Gogol′. By the time it reached Fedor Dostoevskii, Vladimir Solov′ev, the Symbolists and their successors, it had already become a canonical image, embodying an uncontested literary 'truth'.[1]

Pamela Davidson is Professor of Russian Literature at the School of Slavonic and East European Studies, UCL.

[1] On the development of the image of the writer as prophet in literary tradition, see the following articles by Pamela Davidson: 'Between Derzhavin and Pushkin: The

The aim of this article is not to dispute this view, but to enrich it by considering a hitherto neglected but significant contributing factor: the role of the visual image in building up the view of the artist and writer as prophets. For this purpose I will focus on a specific case-study that marked a crucial turning-point in the formation of the tradition: the relationship between the artist Aleksandr Ivanov (1806–58) and the writer Nikolai Gogol′ (1809–52) from the time of their first meetings in Rome in the late 1830s until Gogol′'s death in 1852. Throughout this period Ivanov was settled in Rome, working on his magnum opus, 'Iavlenie Khrista narodu' ('The Appearance of Christ to the People', 1833–57),[2] while Gogol′ was toiling away on *Mertvye dushi* (*Dead Souls*, 1835–52, first part published in 1842), revising his short story 'Portret' ('The Portrait', 1835, second revised version published in 1842) and penning *Vybrannye mesta iz perepiski s druz′iami* (*Selected Passages from Correspondence with Friends*, 1845–46, published in 1847). The notion of the prophetic message of art (understood in its broad sense, encompassing both verbal and visual dimensions) is crucial to all four of these works in different ways. It is particularly rewarding to analyse the way that Ivanov's visual treatment of this theme interacted with and influenced Gogol′'s literary development of the image of the artist as prophet. While deriving considerable support from each other's ideas and artistic practice, the two men differed in their approaches to the relative value of the image and the word in creating new forms of religious art; at times they almost seemed to be competing for the role of principal prophet, leading to a growing tension in their relationship that reached a peak around 1847.

This study falls into three main sections. The first part considers the influence on Ivanov and Gogol′ of two key formative contexts — the relationship of visual and verbal elements in biblical and iconographic representations of prophecy (unified through common purpose) —

Development of the Image of the Poet as a Prophet in the Verse of Zhukovsky, Glinka, and Kiukhelbeker', in Catherine O'Neil, Nicole Boudreau and Sarah Krive (eds), *Poetics. Self. Place. Essays in Honor of Anna Lisa Crone*, Bloomington, IN, 2007, pp. 182–214; 'The Moral Dimension of the Prophetic Ideal: Pushkin and his Readers', *Slavic Review*, 61, 2002, 3, pp. 490–518; 'The Validation of the Writer's Prophetic Status in the Russian Literary Tradition: From Pushkin and Iazykov through Gogol′ to Dostoevsky', *Russian Review*, 62, 2003, 4, pp. 508–36; 'Vladimir Solov′ev and the Ideal of Prophecy', *Slavonic and East European Review*, 78, 2000, 4, pp. 643–70; 'Viacheslav Ivanov's Ideal of the Artist as Prophet: From Theory to Practice', *Europa Orientalis*, 21, 2002, 1, pp. 157–202.

[2] This title is used throughout for convenience, although Ivanov referred to his painting over the years by several different titles, including 'Iavlenie Messii' ('The Appearance of the Messiah').

contrasted with Western tradition (prioritizing difference and competition). The second part traces Ivanov's creation of a series of visual images of prophecy, culminating in 'The Appearance of Christ to the People'. The third part analyses Gogol′'s verbal responses to the artist's work and the way in which their dialogue shaped their differing views of art as prophecy. Finally, some conclusions are drawn about the importance of the visual image and its legacy to the Russian tradition of art as prophecy.

1. Contexts: Image and Word in Biblical and Iconographic Representations of Prophecy

The relationship of the visual image to the literary word in building up the tradition of art as prophecy raises several issues which first need to be set in a broader context. Some of these are addressed in the large body of theoretical literature on the relation between word and image and the hierarchy of power ascribed to both art forms at different historical periods.[3] Two specific contexts of particular relevance to Russian religious tradition deserve consideration at the outset as both were invoked by Ivanov and Gogol′ in support of their views: the representation of prophecy in Hebrew scripture and in Russian icons.

Prophecy in the biblical tradition

How was the relationship between the visual and the verbal represented in the biblical tradition of prophecy? This question is best considered with reference to two distinct stages: the reception and the transmission of the prophetic message.

The reception or original experience of prophecy in Hebrew scripture can be both visual and verbal: it may result from the revelation of an image to the prophet's vision, or of a message to his hearing. Two key Hebrew terms for a prophet both relate to the faculty of vision: *roeh* (seer), derived

[3] See, for example, W. J. T. Mitchell, *Iconology: Image, Text, Ideology*, Chicago, IL and London, 1987; Antonella Braida and Giuliana Pieri (eds), *Image and Word: Reflections of Art and Literature from the Middle Ages to the Present*, Oxford, 2003; Martin Heusser et al. (eds), *Text and Visuality: Word & Image Interactions* 3, Amsterdam and Atlanta, GA, 1999; Rui Carvalho Homem and Maria de Fátima Lambert (eds), *Writing and Seeing: Essays on Word and Image*, Amsterdam and New York, 2006. On aspects of the image-text relationship in Russian culture, see Roger Anderson and Paul Debreczeny (eds), *Russian Narrative and Visual Art: Varieties of Seeing*, Gainesville, FL, 1994 (including James West's essay, 'The Romantic Landscape in Early Nineteenth-Century Russian Art and Literature'); Maria Rubins, *Crossroad of Arts, Crossroad of Cultures: Ecphrasis in Russian and French Poetry*, New York, 2000; L. Geller (ed.), *Ekfrasis v russkoi literature: Trudy Lozannskogo simpoziuma*, Moscow, 2002.

from the root *raah* (to see), and *hozeh* (visionary), from the root *hazah* (to see a vision). Surprisingly, there is no equivalent term in Hebrew for a prophet defining him as a 'hearer', despite the fact that scripture contains many more examples of prophetic experiences received by ear than by eye, invariably introduced by the phrase 'the word of the Lord came unto me, saying'.

Of particular interest for our topic is the fact that these two forms of prophetic experience are frequently combined, usually in a particular sequence. The prophetic vision is commonly followed by a verbal message; indeed, the act of seeing is often presented as a preliminary stage, preparing the prophet to hear the voice of God. It is only after Jacob has seen the vision of a ladder connecting heaven and earth that he hears God speaking to him in his dream (Gen. 28:12–15). Joseph first has two vivid dreams (his brothers' sheaves bow down to his sheaf, the sun, moon and eleven stars all bow down to him) and then gives a verbal interpretation of what he has seen (Gen. 37:5–11). When Moses first sees the burning bush, he says: 'I will turn aside now, and see this great sight [*v-ereh et hamareh*], why the bush is not burnt' (Exod. 3:3). The narrative continues: 'And when the Lord saw [*va-iar*] that he turned aside to see [*lirot*], God called out unto him out of the midst of the bush, and said "Moses, Moses". And he said: "Here am I"' (Exod. 3:4). In this last example, the emphasis placed by the prophet on the purposeful act of seeing (while awake, not dreaming, as in the cases of Jacob and Joseph) appears to be a necessary prelude to the direct verbal communication that follows from God.

Among the later Hebrew prophets a similar pattern is repeated. Isaiah opens with 'the vision [*hazon*] of Isaiah the son of Amoz, which he saw [*hazah*]' (Is. 1:1), and then continues with the verbal message that he received from God, beginning 'Hear, O heavens, and give ear, O earth, For the Lord hath spoken' (Is. 1:2). Later, Isaiah first sees (*va-ereh*) the Lord sitting upon a throne, surrounded by six-winged seraphs; after his lips are purified by one of the seraphs with a burning coal, he is able to hear the word of God (Is. 6:1–8). This passage is of particular significance to the Russian literary tradition of prophecy because of its frequent echoes in verse, most famously in Pushkin's 'Prorok' ('The Prophet', 1826).

The book of Jeremiah, warning of the destruction of Jerusalem and the Temple, begins with an account of the prophet's calling. When the word of the Lord first comes to Jeremiah, he responds that he cannot speak for he is a child. God touches his mouth and reassures him that He has put His words into his mouth (Jer. 1:6–9). He then asks 'Jeremiah, what seest [*roeh*] thou' (Jer.1:11). When the prophet answers that he sees (*roeh*) a rod of an almond tree (*shaked*), God says 'Thou hast well seen [*heitavta lirot*]; for I watch over [*shoked*] My word to perform it' (Jer. 1:12). The play on the words *shaked* (almond tree) and *shoked* (watch over) has a deeper meaning, suggesting that what the prophet sees, translated into verbal form, reflects God's providential relation to his creation. God asks a second time what the prophet can see. This time Jeremiah describes a seething pot facing from the north (Jer. 1:13), a vision for which God supplies a verbal interpretation, a plan of action to defeat the evil threat coming from this direction. This sequence implies that the prophet's ability to 'see well' is in some sense a pre-condition of his ability to act as a conduit for the execution of God's will in this world.

As in the cases of Isaiah and Jeremiah, a series of visions prepare the prophet Ezekiel for hearing the voice of God. The account of his calling opens with the words: 'the heavens were opened, and I saw visions [*va-ereh marot*] of God' (Ezek. 1:1). His ensuing vision of the living winged creatures surrounding the throne of God culminates in the transition from seeing to hearing: 'And when I saw [*va-ereh*] it, I fell upon my face, and I heard a voice of one that spoke' (Ezek. 1:28).

These examples all appear to suggest the primacy of the visual element over the verbal with regard to the initiation of the prophetic state. Indeed, since the verb 'to see' in Hebrew also carries the more general meaning of 'to perceive' or 'to apprehend', it connects with the act of understanding — a link also suggested in Russian by the cognate verbs *videt′* (to see) and *vedat′* (to know). Accordingly, after hearing the ten commandments at Sinai, the Israelites can 'see' (*roim*) the thunderings and the voice of the horn (Exod. 20:15). Even a verbal communication can be 'seen' in this sense, as in 'the word that Isaiah the son of Amoz saw [*hazah*] concerning Judah and Jerusalem' (Is. 2:1). However, the fact that the vision rarely stands on its own and is almost invariably accompanied by a verbal communication indicates the need for a two-stage process, in which the vision first engages the attention of the prophet and deepens his understanding, but remains incomplete without the fuller verbal elucidation that follows.

When it comes to the transmission rather than reception of the prophetic experience, an interesting difference may be noted. In Hebrew scripture, since God has no likeness, he cannot be represented by any image (Deut. 4:12, 15). The prophets therefore did not have recourse to any visual aids; commanded to go forth and spread the word of God, they articulated and communicated their prophetic revelations to others through words, not images. The language of rebuke, admonishment and moral instruction must necessarily be verbal. The visual aspect occurs only in relation to the transmission of a verbal message, as in the case of the 'writing on the wall', seen by king Belshazzar and deciphered by the prophet Daniel (Dan. 5).

With the advent of Christianity, attitudes to the possibility of visual representations of the divine changed. If God had become incarnated as a man, it was argued that he could and indeed should now be represented. Although this was a point of considerable disputation during the iconoclastic controversy of the eighth and ninth centuries, generally seen as the last step towards the great schism between East and West, the veneration of icons was eventually re-established in the Greek Church. Once the visual representation of the divine was accepted in principle, the way was open for art to serve as a medium for prophecy and for artists to be regarded as sacred priests, communicating a holy message. As we shall see below, this was precisely the line of argument adopted by Ivanov in his letter to Gogol′ of 1848, in which he claimed that Russian artists were the chosen successors to the biblical prophets.

Prophecy in the Russian iconographic tradition

In such a context the Russian iconographic tradition naturally played a crucial and distinctive role in shaping attitudes towards the relationship between prophecy and its visual and verbal aspects. The iconostasis in its full, five-tier form gave considerable prominence to the Hebrew prophets. The top fifth row, known as the Forefathers Tier (*Praotecheskii*), included prophets such as Abraham, Jacob, Joseph and Moses. The fourth row, called the Prophets Tier (*Prorocheskii*), was centred on the icon of the Virgin of the Sign and displayed a range of major and minor prophets, depicted holding open scrolls inscribed with their prophecies, usually associated with the coming of Christ. In the middle Church Feasts Tier (*Prazdnichnyi*) Moses and Elijah flank Christ at the Transfiguration. The second Deisis Tier (*Deisusnyi*) places John the Baptist, the last of the Old Testament prophets, alongside Christ and the Virgin Mary. Finally, the bottom 'local' row (*nizhnii, mestnyi*) would often include icons of the popular prophets Elijah and Daniel on either side of the Royal Doors (*Tsarskie vrata*) through which the clergy could gain access to the inner sanctuary.[4]

Russian worshippers standing in front of an iconostasis found themselves facing this rather powerful, complex series of images, combining the verbal and visual aspects of prophecy. Many icons of Moses, for example, clearly

[4] Leonid Ouspensky and Vladimir Lossky, *The Meaning of Icons*, trans. G. E. H. Palmer and E. Kadloubovsky, 2nd revised edn, Crestwood, NY, 1982, pp. 60–64, 67.

point to both dimensions: he is shown next to the burning bush of his original prophetic vision, holding an open scroll inscribed with his verbal prophecies (Figure 1). Which aspect carried more significance? One could argue that the verbal aspect was more important because icons appealed to a prior tradition of written prophecy and emphasized this dependence by depicting the prophet presenting the words displayed on his scroll. Or one could take the view that the visual aspect was dominant, given the fact that the icon is an image, venerated in its own right as a holy 'spirit-bearing' object of worship. Since the first Orthodox Church Bible was not available

Fig. 1: 'Moses the Prophet' (1700–25).[5]

[5] Iconostasis of Kizhi monastery <http://commons.wikimedia.org/wiki/File:Moses-icon.jpg> [accessed 30 July 2012].

in a full Russian translation until the publication of the Synod Version in 1876,[6] and since Russian Orthodox church services did not include regular readings from the prophetic books of scripture, many nineteenth-century Russians were likely to be more familiar with the Hebrew prophets through their visual representation on icons than through their original writings.

A third approach incorporating both dimensions is also possible: the visual representation of the prophets can be regarded as a sacred gateway, which prepares the viewer for a proper understanding of verbal prophecy (in the same way as the Hebrew prophets often saw a vision before they heard the divine message). The iconostasis not only provided a visual image of the biblical prophets, it also initiated the viewer into the prophetic experience in several ways. Its composition, through its vertical hierarchy and significant horizontal juxtapositions, was designed to draw attention to the fulfilment of the prophecies of the Old Testament in the church of the New Testament. In addition, unlike depictions of prophets in Western European art, the sacred status of icons enabled the worshipper to gain direct access to the spiritual message that they conveyed. The iconostasis mediates between the sanctuary (the domain of the priest, representing the Divine world and spiritual man) and the nave (the domain of the congregation, representing the human world and physical man). It acts as a boundary, showing division, but also as a symbol of how the two worlds are fundamentally united and can be reconciled.[7] Since this symbolic representation is created by an artist, art — as well as the artist himself — can be regarded as the prophetic medium or conduit, through which this connection can be made.

According to Russian Orthodox teaching, the image and the word are on an equal footing in terms of their religious significance. As Leonid Ouspensky explains:

> the icon is placed on a level with the Holy Scriptures and with the Cross, as one of the forms of revelation and knowledge of God, in which Divine and human will and action become blended. Apart from its direct meaning, each alike is a reflection of the higher world; each alike is a symbol of the Spirit contained in them. Consequently, the meaning both of the word and of the image, their role and significance are the same.[8]

[6] Alexander I founded the Bible Society in 1812. Work on the Russian translation of the Bible began in 1816, but was delayed by the block placed on the activity of the Russian Bible Society by Nicholas I in April 1826 and only resumed in 1858. For further details, see note 79 below.

[7] See Ouspensky, *The Meaning of Icons*, pp. 60, 67.

[8] Ibid., p. 30.

The influence of different traditions on Ivanov and Gogol′

These two traditions — scriptural and iconographic — were instrumental in shaping a sense of the prophetic dimension of art. Not surprisingly, they framed Ivanov's and Gogol′'s debate about their respective roles in creating new forms of religious art and the relationship between image and word in this context. Both artists modelled their work on different aspects of Hebrew prophecy. Ivanov dedicated himself to the creation of visual illustrations of narratives of biblical prophecy, combining the aesthetic style of Raphael and Leonardo da Vinci with the religious significance of his native iconographic tradition, which was undergoing a gradual revival of interest.[9] Gogol′, as a writer, naturally drew more on the verbal tradition of biblical prophecy, but consistently sought support for his views in the power of the visual image. Both artists needed each other's backing — just as the image needs the word to explain its significance, so too the word needs the image to validate its claims and authenticity. In line with the biblical and iconographic models outlined above, they could see themselves as forming a sort of prophetic duo, working in tandem to develop the visual and verbal aspects of prophecy, following distinct but related paths of equal importance. Ivanov's artistic representations of prophecy could be seen as testimony to the authenticity of his prophetic vision, linking him to the reception stage of prophecy, while Gogol′'s literary works could be regarded as a verbal development of the original prophetic vision, associating him more closely with the transmission of the prophetic message. Although this approach might appear to give primacy to Gogol′ as the more public figure, articulating and conveying the vision to a wider audience, Ivanov's art, especially when viewed as a modern extension of iconographic tradition, gained a distinct advantage by virtue of the holy status of the image.

Ivanov's and Gogol′'s contributions to the view of art as prophecy could therefore be seen as fairly evenly balanced, reflecting the complementary, mutually supportive roles of the visual and the verbal, outlined above. So much for the theory, but what about the practice? Was their partnership always harmonious, or were there elements of tension? Although the biblical and iconographic traditions presented a model of unity, based on a common religious ideal, Western cultural tradition offered several alternative models for the relations between the arts, generally marked by a spirit of competitiveness rather than cooperation. The core issue here was

[9] On the revival of interest in iconography in the modern period, see the stimulating collection Jefferson J. A. Gatrall and Douglas Greenfield (eds), *Alter Icons: The Russian Icon and Modernity*, Pennsylvania, PA, 2010.

not how the different arts might support each other in service of a single goal, but rather how to rank them in a hierarchy based on difference. As W. J. T. Mitchell pointed out in his seminal study of image, text and ideology:

> the history of culture is in part the story of a protracted struggle for dominance between pictorial and linguistic signs, each claiming for itself certain proprietary rights on a 'nature' to which only it has access.[10]

Thus, for example, Leonardo da Vinci, while subscribing to the 'sister arts' theory associated with Horace's dictum *ut pictura poesis*, used the nature-convention distinction to underwrite claims for the superiority of images to words in the tradition of the *paragone*, or contest of painting and poetry.[11] By contrast, in *Laocoon: An Essay upon the Limits of Poetry and Painting* (1766) Lessing opposed the 'sisterly' analogy and insisted on the separateness of the arts, arguing that painting, the visual art of space, should not try to convey narrative progressions or ideas, because these can only be properly expressed in language and poetry, the verbal art of time.[12]

Such approaches emphasized division between the visual and the verbal arts rather than unity of purpose and tended to foster competition rather than collaboration. While nominally espousing the unified vision of religious tradition, in reality the prophetic partnership of Ivanov and Gogol′ was fraught with tensions reflecting the power struggle between word and image, exacerbated by personal differences of temperament. In order to reach a deeper understanding of the way these varied approaches informed the dynamic of their relations and their competing aspirations to the status of artist-prophet, we shall first look at the ways in which Ivanov drew on biblical and iconographic traditions to develop a new form of prophetic art and then examine Gogol′'s response to these visual images of prophecy in his dialogue with the artist between 1838 and 1852.

2. *Ivanov's Images of Prophecy*

Early representations of biblical prophecy (1824–33)

Biblical prophecy played a prominent role in Ivanov's *oeuvre* from as early as 1824. At the age of sixteen, he wrote to his uncle about his current work as a student of the Petersburg Academy of Arts: he had already completed

[10] Mitchell, *Iconology*, p. 42.

[11] Ibid., pp. 78, 119.

[12] Lessing, *Laocoon: An Essay upon the Limits of Poetry and Painting* (1766), trans. Ellen Frothingham, New York, 1969, p. x; cited in Mitchell, *Iconology*, pp. 40–41.

and exhibited a picture of Moses giving the law and was finishing one of John the Baptist prophesying in the wilderness, for which he hoped to receive a prize.[13] Although he also treated a conventional subject from Greek mythology ('Priam, asking Achilles for the body of Hector', 1824), the depiction of biblical scenes remained central to his work until the end of his life. An interesting note from the 1830s casts light on his possible motivation for this choice of orientation: 'For the ancient Greeks the idea was a peripheral matter — they were concerned with external form... We were made differently: our highest value is truth.'[14] An additional impetus was the assignment set for him in 1827 by the Committee of the Society for the Encouragement of Artists (Komitet Obshchestva pooshchreniia khudozhnikov): to show Joseph in prison interpreting to Pharaoh's chief cupbearer and baker the significance of their dreams. This episode took the artist into the heart of the prophetic sequence with its visual and verbal components: understanding the divine communication, imparting the message and capturing its varied impact on the recipients. The painting was judged to be a great success, earning Ivanov a golden medal.[15] Before 1829 he also drew a sketch, most probably of the birth of John the Baptist, for the iconostasis of the church of the Tauride Palace — a significant first attempt at linking the prophetic theme in art to iconographic tradition.[16]

In May 1830 Ivanov set off on a journey through Germany, Austria and Italy to take up a four-year studentship in Rome, sponsored by the Society. He was under instructions to spend the first year familiarizing himself with various works of art, in the second year to make a copy of Michelangelo's 'Creation of Man' from the ceiling of the Sistine Chapel, and in the last

[13] Ivanov, Letter to A. I. Dèmert of 16 February 1824, in I. A. Vinogradov (ed.), *Aleksandr Ivanov v pis′makh, dokumentakh, vospominaniiakh*, Moscow, 2001, pp. 30–31. Neither work has survived.

[14] Ibid., p. 106.

[15] 'Iosif, tolkuiushchii sny zakliuchennym s nim v temnitse vinocherpiiu i khlebodaru', 1827, canvas, oil, 178,5 x 213, Gosudarstvennyi russkii muzei, St Petersburg (hereafter, GRM), reproduced in L. I. Iovleva (ed.), *Aleksandr Andreevich Ivanov: 1806–1858*, Moscow, 2006, p. 31. On critical responses to the painting, see L. A. Markina, 'Aleksandr Ivanov. Ocherk tvorchestva', in ibid., p. 11.

[16] 'Rozhdestvo Ioanna Krestitelia (Rozhdestvo bogomateri) (?)', sketch of a composition for the iconostasis of the church of the Tauride Palace (?), before 1829, paper, pen, pencil, brush, 13,6 x 22,5, GRM, reproduced in Grigorii Goldovskii and Nataliia Uvarova, *Aleksandr Ivanov*, St Petersburg, 2006, p. 41. As can be seen from the catalogue's uncertain description, the subject and purpose of this sketch have not yet been definitively established. Ivanov's father, A. I. Ivanov, was one of the academicians who painted icons for the iconostasis, set up in 1829, of the Tauride Palace's church. See 'Tserkov′ Vozdvizheniia kresta Gospodnia pri Gosudarstvennoi dume' <http://www.encspb.ru/object/2804676167?lc=ru> [accessed 29 February 2012].

two years to produce an original painting of his own composition.[17] After settling in Rome in early 1831, he worked assiduously on the copy of the 'Creation of Man', while searching all the time for a suitable topic for his future painting.[18]

Over the next few years he completed several oil sketches on a wide range of biblical subjects, including 'Samson in Delilah's embraces' (1831?), 'Jacob's dream' (two versions, early 1830s), 'David playing the harp for Saul' (1831), 'David comforting Saul by singing his psalms' (seven versions, before April 1832), 'David chosen to be anointed king' (before April 1832), 'Joseph and Potiphar's wife (1831–32), 'Joseph revealing himself to his brothers' (1831–33) and 'Joseph's brothers finding the cup in Benjamin's sack' (several versions, 1831–33).[19] The choice of these subjects, while reflecting the Academy's promotion of biblical themes, highlights the painter's particular fascination with prophetic figures active in determining the history of their nation.

'The Appearance of Christ to the People' (1833–57)

Ivanov was obliged to report on his progress to the Society every two months. Early in 1833 he informed the Society that, after sending them his sketches of Joseph's brothers finding the cup in Benjamin's sack, he had completed a further twenty sketches and had sought the advice of various artists. His revered mentor, the German religious artist Johann Friedrich Overbeck (1789–1869), had pointed out to him that the subject of Joseph's brothers finding the cup in Benjamin's sack was too episodic in character

[17] 'Instruktsiia Obshchestva pooshchreniia khudozhnikov, dannaia A. A. Ivanovu pri otpravlenii za granitsu. 1830 g.', in Vinogradov, *Aleksandr Ivanov v pis′makh*, pp. 47–48.

[18] 'The choice of a subject for my future painting troubled me for a long time'. 'A. A. Ivanov — Obshchestvu pooshchreniia khudozhnikov', spring 1832 (?), in ibid., p. 82.

[19] 'Son Iakova', early 1830s, sketch, paper on pasteboard, oil, 20,5 x 32,5; sketch, paper, oil, 24,3 x 44,4, Gosudarstvennaia Tret′iakovskaia galereia, Moscow (hereafter, GTG); 'David igraet na arfe pered Saulom', sketch, paper, oil, 8,5 x 13,5, GTG; 'Iosif i zhena Pentefriia', 1831–32, sketch, paper, pencil, chalk, 43,5 x 60,4, GTG; 'Iosif otkryvaetsia brat′iam', 1831–33, sketch, pasteboard, oil, 23 x 38,5, GTG; 'Brat′ia Iosifa nakhodiat chashu v meshke Veniamina', 1831–33, sketch, canvas, oil, 49,5 x 62,7, GTG; final sketch, canvas, oil, 36 x 55, GTG. All these works are reproduced in Iovleva, *Aleksandr Andreevich Ivanov*, pp. 34–36, 137, 229. 'Samson v ob″iatiiakh Dalily', 1831?, is mentioned by M. P. Botkin, cited in Vinogradov, *Aleksandr Ivanov v pis′makh*, p. 58; 'David, uteshaiushchii Saula peniem psalmov svoikh' (7-y raz mnoiu traktovannyi)' and 'Izbranie Davida v pomazanniki' are mentioned by Ivanov in his report to the Society of 9 April 1832, ibid., p. 81. For further examples of biblical subjects, see the extensive lists of Ivanov's works in Mikhail Botkin, *Aleksandr Andreevich Ivanov: ego zhizn′ i perepiska. 1806–1858 gg.*, St Petersburg, 1880, pp. 433–65.

and advised him to choose a broader subject for his future work.[20] Ivanov had therefore renewed his search; after combing through the history of every nation renowned for its deeds, he came to the following conclusion:

> I [...] found that there existed no people more elevated than the Jews, for they were entrusted from above to give birth to the Messiah, whose revelation opened the era of humanity, of moral perfection, or, which amounts to the same, to know the everlasting God! In this way, following in the path of the prophets' craving, I came to the Gospels — to the Gospel of John!! Here on the first pages I saw the essence of the entire Gospels — I saw that John the Baptist was charged by God to prepare the people to receive the teaching of the Messiah and, finally, to introduce Him personally to the people! This last moment is what I am choosing as the subject of my painting, i.e. when John, after seeing Christ walking towards him, says to the people: 'Behold the Lamb of God which taketh away the sins of the world! This is He of whom I said: After me cometh a Man which is preferred before me, for he was before me. And I knew him not, but that he should be made manifest to Israel.' This subject has not yet been treated by anybody, consequently it will already be interesting just for its novelty.[21]

This passage is extremely revealing about Ivanov's initial concept of his work. A few points deserve to be underlined. First, his initial focus on the Jewish people, chosen for its spiritual role in the history of humanity. Second, his presentation of himself as the direct heir to the Hebrew prophets ('following in the path of the prophets' craving'). Third, his emphasis on the prophetic figure of John the Baptist (not on the Messiah, as one might have expected) and his relationship with the people ('John the Baptist was charged by God to prepare the *people* to receive the teaching of the Messiah and, finally, to introduce Him personally to the *people*') — this emphasis becomes even more evident in the painting itself. Finally, his choice of text as the source for his painting. The verses cited from the Gospel of John (1:29-31) emphasize the dependence of the projected visual image on a pre-existent verbal tradition of prophecy. They incorporate the characteristic move in biblical accounts of prophecy from the moment of

[20] Overbeck, originally of Protestant German descent, moved to Rome in 1810 and converted to Roman Catholicism in 1813. A member of the Nazarenes, he worked in Rome for fifty-nine years, completing several works on biblical subjects, including episodes from the life of Joseph.

[21] Vinogradov, *Aleksandr Ivanov v pis′makh*, pp. 108–09. Part of Ivanov's report was published in 1835 in A. V. Timofeev, 'Russkie khudozhniki v Rime', *Biblioteka dlia chteniia*, July 1835.

personal visual revelation ('after seeing Christ walking towards him') to the verbal message delivered to the public ('says to the people'). They also embody the fulfilment of prophecy by including phrases that echo the Hebrew prophets (Is. 53:7, 11).

Ivanov rounds off his report by claiming that his work will be interesting because its subject has not been treated before. As he was undoubtedly familiar with the numerous representations of the 'Ecce Agnus Dei' scene in Western European art, this claim can only refer to his choice of what he calls the 'last moment': John the Baptist presenting Christ to the *people*. Most well-known Western European representations of the 'Ecce Agnus Dei' scene depict John the Baptist in two ways: either alone, sometimes pointing towards Christ but without a crowd of people, or preaching to the people but without the figure of Christ.[22] Ivanov's painting is unique in that it combines all three elements — John the Baptist, Christ and a large audience — thereby simultaneously showing the prophet prophesying, the fulfilment of his message in the appearance of the Messiah and its public impact on a mixed crowd of recipients.

It is difficult to imagine what might constitute a more concentrated artistic representation of prophecy. Ivanov has not just chosen to focus on the prophet of greatest importance in Christian tradition ('Amongst those that are born of women, there is not a greater prophet than John the Baptist', Luke 7:28) with a unique role linking the Hebrew prophets to the New Testament. He has also chosen to highlight a particular moment from his life that enables him to depict the three stages of reception, transmission and fulfilment of the prophetic message on a single canvas.

Ivanov's father, a well-known artist and academician, wrote to his son on 14 February 1833, discussing the possible publication of the report and disputing Overbeck's view that the finding of the cup in Benjamin's sack was too episodic a subject. Despite these reservations he expressed an interest in seeing a sketch of the projected work and recommended following the 'perfect' image of John the Baptist created by Raphael in his 'Madonna of Foligno', conveying the prophet's years of isolation and

[22] For examples of John the Baptist shown in isolation, see Rogier van der Weyden, 'John the Baptist' (*c.*1450), Musée du Louvre, Paris; Leonardo da Vinci, 'John the Baptist' (1513–16), Musée du Louvre, Paris. For examples of John the Baptist pointing towards Christ, see Dirk Bouts, 'Ecce Agnus Dei' (*c.*1464), Munich; Raphael, 'Madonna of Foligno' (1511), Vatican Museum, Rome; Philippe de Champaigne, 'Ecce Agnus Dei', Musée de Grenoble. For examples of John the Baptist preaching to a crowd of people, see Raphael, 'Saint John the Baptist Preaching' (1505), National Gallery, London; Pieter Brueghel the Elder, 'Sermon of St John the Baptist' (1566), Museum of Fine Arts, Budapest.

inner nobility.[23] Ivanov evidently listened to his father's advice as there is some similarity between his representation and Raphael's, principally concerning the prophet's facial expression, hair and beard, the shape of the cross and the gesture of the pointing index finger.

The project was such an ambitious one that Ivanov felt impelled to prepare for it by first carrying out a work on a smaller scale. 'The Appearance of Christ to Mary Magdalene' (1834) earned him the reputation of being the top artist in the Russian colony in Rome after the departure of K. P. Briullov. In the meantime he continued to work on several sketches of the future painting, corresponded about his plans, tried to find ways to finance his extended stay in Rome and petitioned the Society for permission to travel to Palestine to collect further materials for his subject.[24]

His belief in the significance of his projected work grew apace alongside his utopian hopes for the future of Russian art. In 1832, even before starting work on the painting, he had already drafted a letter to Briullov, outlining his vision of the dawn of a new 'Golden Age' of Russian art: just as the Levite priests used to conduct their holy service in Solomon's temple, so too Russian artists stationed in Rome would continue to serve their 'mother', the Academy of Arts.[25] In the spring of 1833 he sent V. I. Grigorovich, the Secretary of the Academy of Arts, a practical suggestion to advance the 'Project of the Golden Age of Russian Artists'. Fired by the belief that the new era of historical painters and sculptors would bring 'political glory' to the 'great fatherland', he proposed that a 'temple of the arts' (*khram iskusstv*) should be established in St Petersburg for artistic gatherings, readings of literary works, musical performances and the display of future works of historical painting and sculpture (to the exclusion of all other genres). Visitors would be invited to make donations to finance the construction of a further purpose-built building.[26]

In an undated draft letter from the 1830s he even begged Grigorovich to help raise funds to enable him to begin his 'large painting': 'for the creation of an image embodying the essence of the entire Gospels — in

[23] Vinogradov, *Aleksandr Ivanov v pis′makh*, p. 110. Ivanov could view Raphael's painting in the Vatican Museum.

[24] Ivanov's persistent but unsuccessful attempts to get the Society to support a trip to Palestine reflected his desire to follow in the path of the biblical prophets in order to create a 'historical' representation of the subject of his painting. For references to Ivanov's planned trip in November 1833 and February 1834, see ibid., pp. 129, 135. At the end of December 1847 Ivanov expressed the hope in a letter to Gogol′ that they could travel to Palestine together (ibid., p. 487). In the event Gogol′ went on his own; in a letter to Ivanov of 14/26 April 1848 he mentioned having completed his trip to Jerusalem (ibid., p. 492).

[25] Ibid., p. 97.

[26] Ibid., p. 114.

order to place it opposite the iconostasis in the Church of the Saviour in Moscow, once built.'[27] The money was to be collected from the public or temporarily loaned by the Tsar. The wording of this appeal makes it clear that Ivanov saw his future painting as a sacred work of religious and national significance, a modern counterpart to the traditional iconostasis.

In June 1833 Ivanov asked his father to send him more money and to encourage Grigorovich to carry out his wishes without further delay.[28] His father, clearly anxious about the state of his son's mental health, replied to him at length on 15 June. On the question of a suitable subject, he reminded him of the need to choose a topic that would be possible to execute, given the limitations of visual art ('*the meaning of the entire Gospels* — a rather important subject, but how will you depict this?'). He counselled against attempting anything unusual, new, or large-scale, recommending instead the virtues of simplicity and artistic mastery. He found his son's professed ambition to create an image 'comprising the essence of the whole Gospels' arrogant and redolent of pride and advised him to be more circumspect in his use of language, hinting at the need to overcome the insinuations of the devil by returning to the truth of the Gospels.[29] In a follow-up letter of 19 June he continued to express similar reservations, insisting that his son should not ask for any further financial support from the Society without first submitting a sketch of the proposed work and begging him not to fling himself 'at anything high-flown'.[30]

Some years before Ivanov started work on the large version of his painting, he had therefore already formed a clear idea of its threefold prophetic subject-matter (reception, transmission and fulfilment), sacred nature (to be displayed in a church opposite the iconostasis) and national significance (to be financed by the Tsar and members of Russian society, for the glory of the fatherland). These views were fully established well before he met Gogol′ in the late 1830s and cannot therefore (in their initial form) be attributed to the writer's influence, as has often been alleged. However, Gogol′ undoubtedly did influence the *further* development of Ivanov's painting and understanding of its significance, just as the image itself influenced Gogol′'s own work. Unravelling these lines of mutual influence is no simple matter, not least because Ivanov worked on his painting

[27] Undated draft in ibid., pp. 117–18. The second version of the Cathedral of the Saviour in Moscow (originally planned by Alexander I in 1812 to commemorate the victory over Napoleon) was initiated in 1831, under active construction from 1839 until 1866, and sanctified in 1883.

[28] Ibid., p. 120.

[29] Ibid., pp. 120–21.

[30] Ibid., p. 122.

for nearly a quarter of a century, creating a vast number of preliminary versions and sketches (nearly four hundred in all), most of which cannot be precisely dated.[31] The following account will trace the development of his work on two levels: the evolution of the image itself, from early sketches until the final version completed in 1857, and his understanding of its conception and purpose, pieced together on the basis of his reports to the Society, letters to his father, brother, patrons, friends and writers (including Gogol′, Iazykov, Zhukovskii).

The earliest pencil and chalk drawing of the painting (dated 1833), described by Ivanov as his 'first sketch of the appearance of the Messiah', was later given by him to Zhukovskii for his album (Figure 2). It differs strongly from all later versions. The focal figure is not John the Baptist but Christ, placed in the centre at the front of the sketch, surrounded by penitents falling to their knees and reaching out to him in dramatic poses of entreaty; John the Baptist stands to the left by the water's edge, facing the viewer, stretching out both arms sidewise towards Christ in a somewhat awkward pose, reminiscent of iconographic depictions of the prophet.[32]

The first oil sketch (dated 1834) is quite different from the original pencil drawing and from all subsequent versions (Figure 3).[33] The scene is now pastoral; the figures, enclosed in a lush green landscape, still include women, children and infants. The most significant change lies in the positioning of Christ and John the Baptist. Christ, clothed in light robes, is now placed at some distance from the people and walks from the back right side of the picture towards the central figure of John the Baptist in the foreground (not towards the group on the right as in subsequent versions). Although the prophet's body faces Christ and points towards him with a raised right arm and extended index finger (holding no cross in the other hand), his head is turned round to the right, looking directly out towards the viewers of the painting, who are thereby drawn into the scene as witnesses of its prophetic content.[34]

[31] Over three hundred sketches are held in Moscow in the Tret′iakov Gallery and approximately another eighty in St Petersburg's Russian Museum. See Iovleva, *Aleksandr Andreevich Ivanov*, p. 15.

[32] 'Iavlenie Khrista narodu: Pervonachal′nyi eskiz kompozitsii kartiny', 1833, brown paper, charcoal pencil, chalk, 25,2 x 42,2, GTG, reproduced in ibid., p. 152. In a letter to his father of January–February 1839 Ivanov reported giving this work to Zhukovskii. Vinogradov, *Aleksandr Ivanov v pis′makh*, p. 201.

[33] 'Iavlenie Khrista narodu: "Pervonachal′nyi" eskiz', 1834, canvas, oil, 60,5 x 90,5, GRM, reproduced in Iovleva, *Aleksandr Andreevich Ivanov*, p. 50.

[34] The first oil sketch is quite similar to an early pencil sketch, paper, Italian pencil, 52,6 x 74,8, GRM, reproduced in Goldovskii, *Aleksandr Ivanov*, p. 55. This pencil sketch shows

Fig. 2: 'The Appearance of Christ to the People' (first pencil and chalk sketch, 1833).
From the Collection of the State Tretyakov Gallery, St Petersburg. © State Tretyakov Gallery, 2013

Fig. 3: 'The Appearance of Christ to the People' (first oil sketch, 1834).
© 2013, State Russian Museum, St. Petersburg

The centenary album published by the Tret′iakov Gallery in 2006 reproduces four further preliminary oil sketches of the whole painting, including the large 'small version' of the final work used by Ivanov as a working tool.[35] Although not provided with exact dates, these sketches were clearly completed after Ivanov's first meetings with Gogol′, since they now include a figure resembling the writer. Many of the changes made in these later versions were suggested by the German artists, Overbeck and Peter von Cornelius, whose opinions were carefully recorded by the artist in his notebook.[36] The foliage in the landscape is much reduced and the original fresh green has given way to a predominantly golden brown palette, tinged with darker green. Several figures, including women and infants, have been removed. The positions of Christ and John the Baptist have changed to those of the final painting (Figure 4). Christ now approaches the scene from a greater distance and faces a larger group to the right of the painting in the background. John the Baptist, bearing a cross in his left hand, points as before with the extended index finger of his right hand towards Christ, but his face is now shown in three-quarter view, meaning that his range of vision can take in the viewers of the painting, the people on the right of the canvas and the advancing figure of Christ in the distance.

John the Baptist in the same position, but with a cross in his left hand. The top part of the painting including the figure of Christ is entirely overhung by a tree and surrounding vegetation. Both these sketches follow Raphael's depiction of John the Baptist (suggested to Ivanov by his father as a model for his painting) in that they present the prophet facing the viewer, drawing him in to the picture, unlike all the other sketches and the final version, where the prophet is shown in three-quarter view.

35 'Iavlenie Khrista narodu: "Stroganovskii" eskiz', second half of 1830s, canvas, oil, 47,8 x 66,2, GTG; 'Iavlenie Khrista narodu: Eskiz', 1836–1837 (?), canvas, oil, 53,5 x 74.5, GRM; 'Iavlenie Khrista narodu: "Venetsianskii" eskiz', after 1839 trip to Venice, canvas, oil, 54,8 x 74,5, GTG; 'Iavlenie Khrista narodu: Malyi variant kartiny, odnovremenno sluzhivshii Ivanovu eskizom', 1836 to no later than 1855, canvas, oil, 172 x 247, GTG. All four sketches are reproduced in Iovleva, *Aleksandr Andreevich Ivanov*, pp. 51–54. The final painting, 'Iavlenie Khrista narodu (Iavlenie Messii)', 1837–57, canvas, oil, 540 x 750, GTG, is reproduced in ibid., pp. 48–49.

36 A. A. Ivanov, 'Zametka v al′bome', mid 1830s, cited in Vinogradov, *Aleksandr Ivanov v pis′makh*, p. 147. Peter von Cornelius (1784–1867) advised Ivanov to reduce the landscape and the number of naked figures and to emphasize the features of the people listening to the prophet; he recommended consulting Overbeck's composition of John the Baptist prophesying in the wilderness as a representation of the effect of the prophet's word on his audience. Overbeck suggested turning John the Baptist's head to profile (commenting that having him face the viewer made him look too much like an actor) and accentuating the expressions on the faces of the penitent sinners. Ivanov also notes suggestions from two other artists resident in Rome, the Danish Icelandic sculptor Bertel Thorvaldsen (1770–1844) and the portraitist and historical painter Vincenzo Camuccini (1771–1844), but did not follow these up.

Fig. 4: 'The Appearance of Christ to the People' (final version, 1837–57).
From the Collection of the State Tretyakov Gallery, St Petersburg. © State Tretyakov Gallery, 2013

The inclusion of the viewer in the prophet's field of vision suggests that the painting does not just represent a distant, past event in Christian history, but also carries a message of direct relevance to present-day Russia. The *narod* (people) in the painting represents the contemporary Russian people as well as the original recipients of the prophet's message. In 1841 P. V. Annenkov underlined this particular aspect of the painting's impact. After describing the powerful effect of John the Baptist's prophetic words on his audience as he points towards Jesus, he commented on the way this energy was transmitted to the contemporary viewer: 'the electrical effect of this movement can be seen on all the faces and also spreads to the viewer, who knows that from this time the sermons of Jesus and our religion begin...'[37]

To make this point even clearer, Ivanov introduced two contemporary Russians into all the later versions of the painting: Gogol′ and himself. As we shall see, the positioning of these two figures and the colour of their attire is of great significance. After experimenting with various options (including lending Gogol′'s features to the old man with the staff coming out of the water on the left, or to the slave at the centre of the foreground), Ivanov finally settled on linking the writer with the figure in the painting known as the 'closest to Christ' (*blizhaishii ko Khristu*).[38] Gogol′'s likeness can easily be recognized in this figure's hairstyle and moustache, similar to the features depicted by Ivanov in his portraits of the writer (Figures 5 and 6).[39] His bent body suggests a mixture of conflicting emotions: despair,

[37] P. V. Annenkov, 'Pis′ma iz-za granitsy' (1841), in Vinogradov, *Aleksandr Ivanov v pis′makh*, p. 232.

[38] See 'Rabota Ivanova nad portretom Gogolia' and 'Aleksandr Ivanov i Gogol′', in N. G. Mashkovtsev, *Gogol′ v krugu khudozhnikov: Ocherki*, Moscow, 1955, pp. 63–88, 89–131 (p. 99). Gogol′'s features can be traced in 'Figura obnazhennogo naturshchika dlia raba (s chertami litsa N. V. Gogolia)', 1833–1840-e, paper, Italian pencil, 44,3 x 58,5, GTG, reproduced in Iovleva, *Aleksandr Andreevich Ivanov*, p. 155. In the sketch 'Golovy blizhaishego k Khristu, starika v kapiushone i peshego voina', paper on canvas, oil, 46 x 60, GTG, reproduced in ibid., p. 91, the head of the figure closest to Christ also bears some resemblance to Gogol′. At one stage Gogol′ was also associated with the man holding a draped cloth, standing next to the shivering boy on the right; according to Vinitsky, these two figures represented Gogol′ and his young friend Iosif Viel′gorskii (whose death in 1840 affected Gogol′ deeply), depicted in the style of the father and possessed son from the bottom right of Raphael's 'Transfiguration'. See Ilya Vinitsky, '"Exegi Testamentum": Gogol′'s Posthumous Ode', *Ulbandus: The Slavic Review of Columbia University*, 6, 2002, pp. 85–112 (p. 106).

[39] In 1840–41 Ivanov made two pencil and watercolour sketches of Gogol′'s head on one sheet and two oil portraits of the writer. The sketches on 'List iz zapisnoi knizhki s nabroskami', 1840 (?), paper, watercolour, 27,2 x 38,8, NIOR RGB, are reproduced in Iovleva, *Aleksandr Andreevich Ivanov*, pp. 217–18. The first oil portrait, 'Portret Nikolaia Vasil′evicha Gogolia', 1841, wood, oil, 14 x 12,5 (oval), GRM, is reproduced in ibid., p. 23 and in

Fig. 5: The 'closest to Christ' (Gogol′). Detail from 'The Appearance of Christ to the People'. From the Collection of the State Tretyakov Gallery, St Petersburg. © State Tretyakov Gallery, 2013

Fig. 6: 'Portrait of Nikolai Gogol′' (1841). © 2013, State Russian Museum, St. Petersburg

shame, repentance, hope. In some versions his head hangs forward and down, but in the final painting it is raised and turned round towards the figure of the approaching Christ. The russet colour of his full-length tunic matches the colour of the under-robe worn by the Messiah and that of the garment worn by the writer in Ivanov's 1841 portraits of him.

Ivanov has accordingly linked Gogol′ to Christ in three ways: through his position (standing closest to him), his gaze (turned towards him) and the colour of his robe. In symmetrical fashion, he has linked himself to John the Baptist through a variety of similar devices. Just as he introduced Gogol′ into the painting as the man closest to Christ, he put himself into the painting by adding a small figure, known as the 'wanderer' (*puteshestvennik*), seated immediately below the outstretched arms of the prophet. This person can easily be recognized as a self-portrait by his angular features, pointed beard, wide-brimmed floppy hat and staff (the last item, symbolic of the artist's path, significantly leads up to and intersects with the prophet's cross extended above him).[40] Ivanov has taken his association with John the Baptist one step further. As well as positioning himself as the 'wanderer' next to the prophet, he has also modelled John the Baptist's head in the final painting and in various preparatory oil and pencil sketches on his own appearance: both share similar features, including a pointed beard and moustache on the upper lip (Figures 7 and 8).[41]

Goldovskii, *Aleksandr Ivanov*, p. 109 (illustration) and p. 149 (note). Ivanov painted the first portrait for Zhukovskii, who received it from Gogol′ in September 1841; it subsequently passed into the collection of Alexander III. Ivanov's second portrait, a copy of the first, held in IRLI, Pushkinskii dom, was given by Gogol′ to M. P. Pogodin. After Gogol″s death Ivanov wrote to Zhukovskii about the two portraits of the writer he had completed 'in great secrecy', now to be reproduced; see his letter of 21 April 1852, in Vinogradov, *Aleksandr Ivanov v pis′makh*, p. 535.

[40] The 'wanderer' resembling Ivanov appears in all the preliminary versions of the painting listed in note 34 (but not in the earlier sketches described in notes 31–33) and can be identified by the hat and beard; the staff only appears later in the final painting and the 'small version' of the large painting. See also the separate oil self-portrait of the same figure, 'Puteshestvennik: Predpolagaemyi avtoportret', paper on pasteboard, oil, 57,2 x 43,7, GTG, reproduced in Iovleva, *Aleksandr Andreevich Ivanov*, p. 83.

[41] Compare the head of the 'wanderer', 'Puteshestvennik: Predpolagaemyi avtoportret', paper on pasteboard, oil, 57,2 x 43,7, GTG, reproduced in ibid., p. 83, with the three different versions in oil of 'Golova Ioanna Krestitelia', paper on canvas, two from GTG, one from GRM, reproduced in ibid., pp. 62–63 and the preparatory sketch in pencil, reproduced in ibid., p. 153. The upper half of John the Baptist and the head of the 'wanderer' with hat and staff appear alongside each other on the sketch 'Ioann Krestitel′: Podmalevok srednei chasti kartiny, sdelannyi poverkh neokonchennogo etiuda kamnei', paper on canvas, oil, 45,3 x 62, GTG, reproduced in ibid., p. 61. For contemporary portraits of Ivanov, see V. I. Shternberg, 'A. A. Ivanov za obedom: List iz al′boma M. I. Skotti', 1842, paper, watercolour,

Fig. 7: 'The Head of John the Baptist'. From the Collection of the State Tretyakov Gallery, St Petersburg. © State Tretyakov Gallery, 2013

Fig. 8: 'The Wanderer' (self-portrait). From the Collection of the State Tretyakov Gallery, St Petersburg. © State Tretyakov Gallery, 2013

Ivanov is also linked to Gogol′ and Christ through the composition and the interaction of the three figures in the painting. The face of Ivanov the 'wanderer', shown in profile, looks upwards and across towards the figure of 'Gogol′' with an expression of keen visual interest. 'Gogol′' in turn looks towards Christ, whose forward gaze encompasses both artists. All three figures are thus inscribed in a triangle, linked by their gazes and the colours of their attire (Ivanov and Gogol′ share between themselves the colours of Jesus's upper and lower robes, royal blue and russet brown).

By including himself and Gogol′ in the painting, Ivanov suggests that they are both recipients of the prophetic message spread by John the Baptist and witnesses of its fulfilment in the arrival of Christ; as such, they become part of a chain of prophets, chosen to receive and to transmit the divine message to contemporary Russia — Ivanov through visual means (in painting) and Gogol′ through verbal means (in writing). The closer association of Ivanov as the 'wanderer' with John the Baptist (through their proximity and shared features) may be understood as reflecting his primary role in the preliminary stage of prophecy, whereas Gogol′'s greater proximity to Christ reflects a more intimate association with its fulfilment. Their paths are different, but connected: Ivanov sits under the protective arms of John the Baptist, but looks for clarification towards Gogol′, who is closer to Christ.

The final image created by Ivanov may therefore be interpreted on several different levels. Most obviously, its subject is the one described by the artist in his initial thoughts about the work: the appearance of the Messiah to the people, at the precise moment when John the Baptist is foretelling the coming of a Saviour who will remove the sins of the world. The emphasis is placed on the moment of prophecy to the people and its fulfilment, as well as on the promise of redemption from sin and the varying degrees of faith exhibited by the recipients of the prophetic message. Although this message belongs to a specific point in time at the beginning of Christian history, it can also be read as a universal one, transcending historical, spatial and national boundaries, and within this broader context as one with particular relevance to contemporary Russia. This last reading, supported by the inclusion of figures resembling Ivanov and Gogol′, raises potentially provocative questions about the extent

charcoal pencil, 23,7 x 21,3, GTG, reproduced in ibid., p. 236 (Ivanov is shown seated at a table wearing a white brimmed rounded hat), and M. I. Skotti, 'A. A. Ivanov, idushchii po Ripetta: List iz al′boma "Risunki russkikh khudozhnikov v Rime"', 1843–44, paper, watercolour, charcoal pencil, ink, 34,7 x 28,5, GTG, reproduced in ibid., p. 237 (Ivanov is shown wearing a white brimmed cylinder hat, draped in a royal blue cape, striding along the road, staff in hand).

to which the Christian message of redemption from sin and salvation through faith had been successfully 'heard' in tsarist Russia (this may perhaps explain why Alexander II took a particular interest in the central figure of the slave when Ivanov showed him the completed painting in the Winter Palace in May 1858).[42]

These combined readings of the painting, taken in conjunction with the similarity noted above between the features of John the Baptist and Ivanov, lead to an interesting parallel: just as the original prophet offered a message of salvation to the people, so too the artist (Ivanov) now presents the same message to the Russian people. By advancing the same message in visual form, the artist fulfils a role akin to that played by the original prophet — an idea that found support in Gogol′'s essay on the painting (1846) and in Ivanov's own 'Mysli, prikhodiashchie pri chtenii Biblii' ('Thoughts Arising upon Reading the Bible', 1846–47), as we shall see below. Ivanov is present in his painting both visibly — as a recipient of the prophetic message, and invisibly — as the prophetic author of its transmission to a modern audience. Through the creation of this image he has in effect established his credentials as a fully-fledged artist-prophet.

3. Ivanov and Gogol′: The Dialogue of Image and Word

How, then, did Gogol′ respond to Ivanov's creation of a powerful image linking the role of the artist to that of the prophet? Did it affect his own, previously established view of the writer's prophetic mission? How did he seek to influence the image or its understanding by the public? Did he use it to promote his own agenda and reputation? Did his active involvement foster mutual support or generate tension between the two friends? How did Ivanov react to the writer's reading of his work? These questions will be addressed, drawing on Gogol′'s correspondence, his short story, 'The Portrait', and his essay on Ivanov's painting.[43]

Early encounters (1838–40)

When Gogol′ left Russia in June 1836, disappointed by the reception of *Revizor* (*The Government Inspector*, 1836), he had already cast himself in the role of unrecognized prophet, rejected by his fellow countrymen. As

[42] See Ivanov's account in his letter to his brother S. A. Ivanov of 31 May 1858, in Vinogradov, *Aleksandr Ivanov v pis′makh*, p. 606.

[43] On aspects of the relationship, see Igor′ Vinogradov, 'N. V. Gogol′ i A. A. Ivanov: K istorii sozdaniia kartiny "Iavlenie Messii"', in Vinogradov, *Aleksandr Ivanov v pis′makh*, pp. 670–708, and his earlier article, 'Iavlenie kartiny — Gogol′ i Aleksandr Ivanov', *Nashe nasledie*, 54, 2000 <http://www.nasledie-rus.ru/podshivka/5410.php> [accessed 15 May 2012].

he wrote to the writer and historian M. P. Pogodin on 15 May before his departure:

> I'm going abroad, there I will shake off the misery that my compatriots inflict on me every day. The up-to-date writer, the comic writer, the writer of social customs must be far from his native land. No prophet is accepted in his own country.[44]

By the time he arrived in Rome in March 1837, he faced a turning-point in his literary life. Upset by the news of Pushkin's recent death, he was determined to honour the poet's directive to write *Dead Souls*, yet felt that he had lost confidence in his ability to carry out the task without the guidance of his revered mentor.[45] If he was to succeed Pushkin as literary prophet for his generation, he needed a receptive audience, both in Rome and back in Russia. As we shall see, his encounter with Ivanov provided him with just what he required: a malleable disciple and striking example of dedication to the creation of 'prophetic' art (demonstrated by the artist's life-style and the subject of his projected painting), an image that could be presented to Russian readers as the living proof and validation of his own ideal.

After four years of prevarication, planning and preliminary sketches Ivanov finally took the plunge in May 1837, ordering a large canvas for his painting and moving to a new studio in the following autumn, big enough to accommodate his projected work.[46] Over the next year he worked intensively on his painting, sending sketches and progress reports to the Society and his father at regular intervals. His project acquired a new level of recognition when Zhukovskii brought his former pupil, Aleksandr Nikolaevich (Nicholas I's eldest son and heir to the throne) to the painter's studio in December 1838. After the young crown prince (only twenty years old at the time) expressed his approval of the work in progress, Ivanov was emboldened to ask for another three years' financial support, promising

[44] A. A. Karpov and M. N. Virolainen (eds), *Perepiska N. V. Gogolia v dvukh tomakh*, 2 vols, Moscow, 1988, 1, pp. 362–63.

[45] See Gogol′'s letters to P. A. Pletnev of 16 March 1837, M. P. Pogodin of 30 March 1837 and V. A. Zhukovskii of 18/6 April 1837, in V. Veresaev, *Gogol′ v zhizni: Sistematicheskii svod podlinnykh svidetel′stv sovremennikov*, Moscow, 1990, pp. 206–09.

[46] On 10 May 1837 Ivanov informed the Society for the Encouragement of Artists that he had ordered the canvas and planned to start work on it in September, after spending the summer travelling and collecting further materials in Italy. Vinogradov, *Aleksandr Ivanov v pis′makh*, pp. 185–86. The new studio was located at Via del Vantaggio, 7, off Via di Ripetta.

his painting as a gift in exchange (another twenty years would pass before he delivered the completed painting to Alexander II in St Petersburg). Gogol′ was in Rome at the time and excitedly described the visit of the heir and Zhukovskii in his correspondence.[47]

Gogol′ therefore encountered Ivanov just at the point when the artist's grand idea was beginning to acquire a tangible shape and a degree of public recognition and official support. As this was the very outcome that Gogol′ craved for his own work, it is not difficult to understand why he latched on to Ivanov as a figure who embodied many of his own ideals and demonstrated that they could be fulfilled. He was adept at formulating the purpose of the painting and found in the much less articulate Ivanov an eager recipient of his views. In his memoirs the artist and engraver F. I. Iordan (1800–83) described Gogol′'s role at the heart of a circle of artists in Rome including himself, Ivanov and Moller. He emphasized the exceptional 'reverence' (*pochtenie*) that Ivanov displayed towards Gogol′ and noted that he was a good listener but a very poor speaker; together, the two friends formed an 'inseparable pair' (*nerazluchnaia parochka*).[48] Later he added an even more candid comment, underlining Gogol′'s status as a prophet in Ivanov's eyes:

> A. A. Ivanov was a strange individual; he was always smiling and saw in Gogol′ some kind of prophet. Gogol′ gave him directives, which Ivanov listened to slavishly. Moller and I, Gogol′'s evening visitors, were nonentities in his eyes compared to Gogol′, and I laughed heartily at his infatuation.[49]

The hierarchical nature of the relationship was manifest from the beginning of their correspondence, in which Gogol′ assumed the leading role, despite the fact that he was three years younger than Ivanov. Significantly, in Gogol′'s first known letter to Ivanov of 8/20 September 1839 written from Vienna, he adopted the tone of a benevolent mentor, enquiring after the sketch of the 'large painting' completed by Ivanov

[47] Gogol′, Letter to A. S. Danilevskii of 31 December 1838, in Veresaev, *Gogol′ v zhizni*, p. 226. After this visit Ivanov gave his first sketch of the painting to Zhukovskii for his album. See note 32 above. In a letter to Zhukovskii of 18/6 April 1837 Gogol′ expressed his envy of the generous financial aid received by Russian artists in Rome and asked Zhukovskii to intercede on his behalf with the Tsar. Ibid., p. 208.

[48] 'Vospominaniia F. I. Iordana' (1879), in Vinogradov, *Aleksandr Ivanov v pis′makh*, pp. 197, 238.

[49] F. I. Iordan, 'Zapiski rektora i professora Akademii Khudozhestv Fedora Ivanovicha Iordan[a]' (1918), cited in ibid., p. 198.

over the summer in Venice and wishing him God's assistance with his work. He then gave details of various items, clearly charged with symbolic value, that he had despatched to Ivanov in Rome. The first was a silver watch, purchased by Gogol′ at Ivanov's request in Geneva. By sending this time-keeping gift to the artist, Gogol′ symbolically established his right to set the pace of Ivanov's work (a major theme of his essay of 1846 on the painting was its slow composition, defended by him as essential for spiritual reasons). The second item was Gogol′'s stick, used by him in Rome, which Ivanov was firmly instructed to put in the corner of his room and to keep there until Gogol′'s return to Rome. Elsewhere, in letters to his close friend from childhood A. S. Danilevskii and to the poet N. M. Iazykov, Gogol′ frequently referred to his stick or staff (*posokh*) as a symbol of his true spiritual home or of the spiritual legacy that he hoped to pass on to his chosen disciple or successor[50] (possibly represented by the staff held by Ivanov, portrayed in his painting as the artist-wanderer, sitting under the cross extended by John the Baptist). The third item consisted of three dozen Viennese pencils — a dozen for Ivanov, a dozen for Moller and a dozen to be put aside for Gogol′. The gift of this craftsman's tool, shared alike by artists and writers, reflected the unity and common goal of word and image that Gogol′ sought to promote.[51]

In the following summer of 1840 Gogol′ wrote once more to Ivanov from Vienna, enquiring after the progress of Ivanov's 'celebrated' (*famosa*) painting, asking whether it was approaching completion or would still need another 'fatal three years', and expressing his longing to 'behold it' (*uzret′ ee*), to embrace the 'maestro' and to resume their 'paradisical life' together in Rome in September.[52]

Ivanov responded in July with a detailed account of his trips to Perugia, Assisi, Florence and the mountains around Rome in search of materials for his painting (faces, landscapes, vegetation). Using the period of their separation as a yardstick by which to measure progress on his painting (rather slow, by his own admission), he expressed his recurrent worry that he had undertaken a task beyond his strength. He rounded off, however, by noting an important event of the current year: in Overbeck's studio he had seen his mentor's monumental canvas, 'The Triumph of Religion in the Arts' (1840), finally completed after more than a decade's work.[53] Clearly

[50] See Gogol′'s letters to A. S. Danilevskii of 11 April 1838 (Veresaev, *Gogol′ v zhizni*, p. 218) and to N. M. Iazykov of 27 September 1841 (*Perepiska*, 2, p. 372).

[51] *Perepiska*, 2, pp. 441–43.

[52] Ibid., 2, p. 443.

[53] Ibid., 2, pp. 444–45. On 1 July 1835 Ivanov wrote to his father about 'The Triumph

this example gave him encouragement. Like Ivanov, Overbeck was a foreign artist who had settled in Rome and turned to early Renaissance artists such as Raphael and Perugino as models of pure Christian art, untainted by the excesses of the later Renaissance. His painting gave allegorical expression to an idea cherished by Ivanov and Gogol′ alike: the link between all forms of art (writing, painting, sculpture) and the Christian faith. Although Ivanov greatly revered Overbeck, referring to him as his 'prophet' and 'only mentor', he was also driven by the desire to demonstrate through his own work that Russian artists were more capable of creating an ideal form of Christian art than their Western counterparts.[54] Overbeck's conversion to Catholicism may have fuelled this patriotic aim, which was echoed by Gogol′ and the Slavophile thinker A. S. Khomiakov in their comments on Ivanov's painting and its superiority to the German artist's work.[55]

Visual and verbal portraits (1841–42)

As well as conversations conducted in person or by correspondence, Gogol′ also turned to the creation and commissioning of portraits as a method for drawing others closer to his ideas and influence. He attached great significance to the power of portraiture, both verbal and visual, and used this medium to build stronger links with Ivanov.

of Religion in the Arts', commenting 'Overbeck the hermit prays, prays in his paintings' (Vinogradov, *Aleksandr Ivanov v pis′makh*, p. 155). In the symmetrical style of compositions by Raphael, this painting presents the 'upper' world, centred on the enthroned Madonna surrounded by prophets, evangelists and saints, above the 'lower' world of artists, sculptors, painters, architects and writers. The fountain in the centre symbolizes the upward dedication of art to Christian ideals.

[54] Ivanov, Letter to his father of November–December 1840, in Vinogradov, *Aleksandr Ivanov v pis′makh*, p. 225. Overbeck's work was often censured by Russian artists and critics for being too cold and allegorical. This criticism echoed Friedrich Vischer's harsh condemnation of Overbeck's painting in 1841 'for being an allegory in which there is no clear demarcation between linguistic and pictorial signs' (following Goethe and Schelling, allegory was commonly regarded as completed and dead, as opposed to the symbol, seen as living and dynamic). Overbeck composed a written explanation of the significance of his allegorical work (as Gogol′ did for Ivanov's painting). See Mitchell B. Frank, '"Castrated Raphael": Friedrich Overbeck and Allegory', *Word & Image: A Journal of Verbal/Visual Enquiry*, 18, 2002, 4, pp. 87–98 (p. 87).

[55] In early October 1841, when Gogol′ asked Zhukovskii to request the Tsar to provide further support for Ivanov's painting, he suggested pointing out that Overbeck's painting was half the size of Ivanov's but had taken over ten years. *Perepiska*, 1, p. 172. Khomiakov acknowledged Ivanov's debt to Overbeck but insisted that German painters were not able to rise to the ideal Christian art to which they aspired (due to the inadequacies of Protestantism and Catholicism). 'Kartina Ivanova: Pis′mo k redaktoru Russkoi Besedy' (1858), in *Polnoe sobranie sochinenii Alekseia Stepanovicha Khomiakova* (hereafter, *PSS*), 3rd edn, 8 vols, Moscow, 1900, 3, p. 354.

In 1841 Ivanov painted two oil portraits of Gogol′ in Rome, evidently at the writer's request and 'in great secrecy from everyone', as he later informed Zhukovskii after Gogol′'s death. The first portrait was made for Zhukovskii and given to him by Gogol′ in September 1841 when they met up in Frankfurt. The second portrait, a copy made for Pogodin, was also given to its recipient by Gogol′.[56] However, when Pogodin published an engraving of this portrait in *Moskvitianin* in 1843, Gogol′ felt betrayed. He was upset at the thought that people would be ripping out of the journal a portrait showing him in his dressing-gown, with tousled hair and a moustache, looking like a dissolute rake.[57] In the final section of his 'Zaveshchanie' ('Testament', 1845), he laid down three conditions for the publication of his portrait: it should only be reproduced if God granted him the power to finish his great work (*Dead Souls*), if his fellow-country men, recognizing the novel's worth, wished to see the features of its publicity-shy author, and only in an engraving made by Iordan, to recompense this artist for all the years he had dedicated to engraving Raphael's 'Transfiguration'.[58] A few months after Gogol′'s death, even though *Dead Souls* had not been completed, Ivanov therefore asked Zhukovskii to send the portrait in his possession to Iordan in order to carry out the wishes of the deceased.[59]

The art historian N. G. Mashkovtsev has argued quite convincingly that the original drawings and portraits were done in private to prepare for the inclusion of Gogol′'s likeness in 'The Appearance of Christ to the People'; complete secrecy was necessary because Gogol′ did not want Ivanov's portrait of him in his domestic appearance to be revealed to the public before the unveiling of his more elevated likeness as the figure 'closest to Christ' in Ivanov's master work.[60] It is also likely that Gogol′

[56] For details of the portraits, see note 39 above. On Gogol′'s gift of the first portrait to Zhukovskii in September 1841, see P. A. Efremov, 'Portrety Gogolia i risunki k ego sochineniiam' (1878), in Vinogradov, *Aleksandr Ivanov v pis′makh*, p. 240.

[57] Gogol′, Letter to S. P. Shevyrev of 2/14 December 1844, in *Perepiska*, 2, p. 308.

[58] 'Zaveshchanie', in N. V. Gogol′, *Vybrannye mesta iz perepiski s druz′iami*, comp. V. A. Voropaev, Moscow, 1993, pp. 28–29. Gogol′ added that he would prefer the public to buy Iordan's engraving of the transfigured Saviour, rather than his own portrait. As noted by Vasari (whose *Life of Raphael* was known to Gogol′), the 'Transfiguration' was Raphael's last work, displayed above his dead body after he died on Good Friday on his thirty-seventh birthday (Gogol′'s age in 1846); Gogol′ deliberately associates the publication of his portrait with this visual image testifying to the transfiguration of the Saviour's and artist's life after death. See Vinitsky, '"Exegi Testamentum"', p. 104 (Vinitsky mistakenly writes of Iordan's engraving of a portrait painted by *Iordan*, rather than Iordan's engraving of the portrait painted by *Ivanov*).

[59] Ivanov, Letter to V. A. Zhukovskii of 21 April 1852, in Vinogradov, *Aleksandr Ivanov v pis′makh*, p. 535.

[60] N. G. Mashkovtsev, 'Rabota Ivanova nad portretom Gogolia', in *Gogol′ v krugu*

only wanted Ivanov's portrait of him to be published after they had both completed their master works and gained public recognition; the resulting image would then serve as a fitting symbol of the link between the writer and the artist, crowning their joint achievement as national prophets to the Russian nation.

Gogol′'s belief in the power of an image was already clear from the arresting opening line of his story, 'The Portrait', describing the magnetic attraction exerted on the public by the pictures on display at a Petersburg stall: 'Nowhere did so many people stop as in front of the picture stall in Shchukin dvor.'[61] After purchasing a portrait of a merchant from this stall, the artist Chartkov (*Chert*kov in the first version, from *chert* [devil]) gradually falls victim to its demonic power and begins to peddle a cheapened version of his own art. When he is invited to the Academy of Arts to assess the work of a former comrade, a Russian artist who had spent many years in Rome studying Raphael and refining his art, he is so overcome by the purity and innocence of this artist's work that he is unable to pronounce a critical opinion and runs away like a madman, overcome with tears. When Gogol′ revised the story in 1841–42 (around the time Ivanov painted his portrait), he added many details that clearly evoked Ivanov (his life in Rome as a hermit [*otshel′nik*], his total dedication to art, affinity with Raphael, indifference to public opinion, inability to socialize, unfashionable attire) and emphasized the way his art exuded an 'inner force' that emanated directly from his soul.[62]

It is clear from the two versions of 'The Portrait' that Gogol′ had already formed his ideal of the dedicated, spiritual artist in 1831–32 well before his arrival in Rome, but then chose to associate his ideal with Ivanov after their meeting. In Gogol′'s view, a work of art, in particular a portrait, could exert a demonic or a spiritually uplifting influence on its owner or viewer. His controlling approach to Ivanov's portraits of him (keeping them secret, giving them to Zhukovskii and Pogodin — two highly influential figures in the literary world, determining the time and the manner of their reproduction) has to be understood in this context. He was evidently trying to facilitate the creation and publication of a 'spiritual' image of the artist-prophet, a visual image of the writer to mirror the verbal portrait of the artist that he had created in his story.

khudozhnikov, Moscow, 1955, pp. 63–88 (pp. 72–78).

[61] N. V. Gogol′, *Peterburgskie povesti*, ed. O. G. Dilaktorskaia, St Petersburg, 1995, p. 49 (cited from the second version, where this line differs only slightly from the first version).

[62] Compare in ibid., pp. 70–71 (revised version of 1842), 178–79 (first version of 1832), 258–59 (on dates of composition), 282–83 (on Ivanov's presence in the revised version).

Around the same time, in December 1841, Gogol′ asked Ivanov to commission on his behalf the artist I. S. Shapovalov (1817–90) to paint copies of the heads of the Saviour from Raphael's 'Transfiguration' and 'Entombment'. Gogol′ planned to distribute these as gifts to select friends and, significantly, asked that the copies of the 'Saviour' should be just 'a little bigger' than the size of his head on Ivanov's portrait of him. After further instructing Ivanov to make a copy for him of the head of the Saviour from his own painting, Gogol′ rounded off his letter by reiterating his role as Ivanov's source of spiritual strength:

> Now for the main thing: be strong! Walk cheerfully and on no account let your spirits fall, or else this will mean that you do not remember me and do not love me: whoever remembers me carries fortitude and strength in his soul. Do not be anxious about the future, everything will be fine. You will have funds.[63]

In all these examples Gogol′ is constantly associating his role as Ivanov's personal saviour with portraits — either of himself or of the Saviour. The juxtaposition is a telling one, reflecting Gogol′'s faith in the power of the image.

Tensions and crisis (1844–47)

We can see from this last letter of 1841 that Gogol′ not only identified himself as Ivanov's saviour but could also be rather firm, even downright bossy, in carrying out his self-appointed role as the artist's spiritual mentor. To some extent Ivanov invited and encouraged this attitude. Plagued by doubts and lacking confidence in his own opinions, he relied on Gogol′'s support to resolve his dilemmas and buttress his beliefs.[64] However, when pushed too far, he could put up some resistance — either retreating into silence, or attempting a countermove of his own. The pressure from Gogol′ built up over the next few years, resulting in a crisis in the two friends' relationship that reached a peak in 1847 and was never fully resolved. Significantly, the main point of tension revolved around who would take on the role of principal prophet — the painter or the writer.

[63] Gogol′, Letter to Ivanov of 25 December 1841, in *Perepiska*, 2, pp. 449–50. Gogol′ offered to pay Shapovalov one hundred roubles per Saviour's head. See note 58 above for Gogol′'s suggestion that Raphael's portrait of the Saviour in the 'Transfiguration' could be substituted for his portrait.

[64] P. V. Annenkov, 'Zamechatel′noe desiatiletie. 1838–1848', in Vinogradov, *Aleksandr Ivanov v pis′makh*, p. 234.

Some early warning signals can be detected in their correspondence. In March 1844, for example, Gogol′ advised Ivanov to strengthen his Christian faith so as to be able to continue what he now referred to as 'our work':

> You have not yet acquired that which alone could move your work forward and impart to you that force which cannot be attained through any amount of effort or knowledge. In a word, you are still far from being a Christian, even though you have planned a painting for the glorification of Christ and Christianity. You have not felt the close involvement of God in our lives or the full loftiness of the intimate union into which he has entered with us. This is what I thought necessary to say to you in addition, so that you could think this over at an appropriate spiritual moment.[65]

By chiding Ivanov for his inadequate level of spiritual wisdom, even accusing him of not being a true Christian, Gogol′ is probing uncomfortably far into the recesses of his friend's soul. In effect he is shifting his role from *artistic* adviser to *religious* mentor, thereby assuming a superior didactic position. Later, as we shall see below, in his 1846 essay on Ivanov's painting, he repeated this approach in a public forum, suggesting that the artist's work could not and would not be finished until he had successfully completed his 'spiritual task'.

Ivanov replied to Gogol′'s letter with a mixture of respect and defensiveness, side-stepping the most hurtful accusation: 'One bit of your letter, [saying] that I am far from being a Christian and so on, obliges me to stop and think. Right now I am not able to find an answer to this.'[66] Gogol′ was not satisfied with this evasive response and returned to his original point more forcibly at the end of the year, this time drawing an explicit parallel between the conversion (*obrashchenie*) that Ivanov first had to undergo himself and his ability to represent this same process in his painting:

> your painting is going slowly because there is no driving force that could spur you on to produce it confidently and firmly. Entreat God for this force. And remember *this word of mine*: until the inner event that you are striving to represent on your painting in the faces of those moved and converted by the *word* of John the Baptist happens with you, or rather within yourself, believe me that your picture will not be finished until

[65] Gogol′, Letter to Ivanov of 6/18 March 1844, in *Perepiska*, 2, pp. 451–52.
[66] Ivanov, Letter to Gogol′ of April 1844, in ibid., 2, p. 453.

> that time. Your work is bound up with your spiritual task. And until this picture is drawn in your soul by the brush of the supreme artist, it will not be painted by your brush on canvas. When it is painted on your soul, then your brush will fly faster than thought itself.[67]

For Gogol′, Ivanov's work on his painting clearly both depicted and depended on the acquisition of true faith; it represented a public enactment or performance of a process of inner spiritual conversion that the true artist-prophet first had to undergo himself. The artist's success in reaching this goal would depend on his ability to follow the 'word' of his spiritual mentor. In the passage cited above Gogol′ clearly links his 'word' (*sie moe slovo*) to the 'word' of John the Baptist, thus associating himself directly with the prophet and casting Ivanov as a disciple still on the path to faith.

Although Ivanov continued in the role of willing disciple, assiduously reading Gogol′'s copy of *The Imitation of Christ* by Thomas à Kempis and duly associating his mentor with the Saviour ('I kissed your little book, thought about you and bowed down to God'),[68] relations between the two friends became strained by the end of 1846 as Gogol′ began to demand a higher level of absolute obedience to his word. After accusing Ivanov of expecting everyone to run around like 'singed cats' attending to his needs, he voiced his exasperation over his disciple's failure to trust and follow his advice. A mounting note of hysteria can be detected in his obsessive references to the importance of his prophetic 'word', repeated five times in the following passage:

> I told you plainly: 'Sit quietly, don't think about anything, don't worry about anything, work — and nothing else, everything will be sorted out just fine. This much I guarantee you.' But you consider me a nonentity; you have no trust whatsoever in my *words*. You are more likely to believe [...] in the eloquent promises of the first blabbermouth than in the *words* of a person who has not yet been found guilty of lying, who did not entice any person with flattering assurances and who kept his *word*. Allow me, finally, to tell you that I have a certain right to demand Respect for my *words* and that it is far too thoughtless and rude on your part to show me so plainly that you don't give a damn about my *words*.[69]

[67] My italics (PD). Gogol′, Letter to Ivanov of 28 December 1844/9 January 1845, in ibid., 2, pp. 455–56.

[68] Ivanov, Letter to Gogol′ of autumn 1846, in ibid., p. 462.

[69] My italics (PD). Gogol′, Letter to Ivanov of 30 November/12 December 1846, in ibid., 2, pp. 464–65.

Gogol′ rounded off by telling Ivanov to remain silent, hinting darkly that he had already taken steps to ensure his well-being. He could perfectly well have told his friend directly about the 'letter' he had written in support of his work. He chose not to, however, preferring the controlling power of mysterious allusion to the as yet unrevealed word (more consonant with the mask of prophet). A month later, in order to make his disciple truly live by his word, he sent him the text of a prayer that he had composed and recited every day — a prayer for spiritual peace, protection from Satan and divine inspiration — clearly wishing his word to become quite literally the artist's daily word.[70]

Gogol′'s insistence that his disciple should fully submit to his 'word' finally provoked an oblique form of rebellion: Ivanov attempted to turn the tables on his mentor by demanding that the writer's 'word' should be put into the service of his art. In January 1847 he somewhat tactlessly instructed Gogol′ to take up the position of 'Secretary of the Russian artists' in Rome; his duties would include writing 'four to five reports' about the best of these artists in order to prepare the Tsar for a 'correct evaluation' of their work in progress. All this was to be done while Ivanov devoted himself to completing his master painting.[71]

The casual assumption that the writer's 'brilliant pen' would be deployed to serve the needs of the artist clearly nettled Gogol′. After pointing out somewhat testily that his 'main task' (*Dead Souls,* 'hardly a trifle') might well require rather more time than Ivanov's project, he raised an objection to being told his exact duties — would Ivanov ever put up with being told to produce five watercolours a year to order? The core issue here is one of power: 'And indeed, whose will is being declared here?' In a tone of heavy irony, he commented that if Ivanov were a boss, he would be very good at allocating jobs to people. Whilst from a Christian point of view there may be nothing wrong with a lackey's job, one must know who to offer it to and, crucially, not seek to divert a person from his chosen path. Moving over to a personal attack, he accused Ivanov of acting like a child and deceiving his mentor by pretending to be working on his painting and praying — if this were the case he would have clarity of mind and no time to dream up such hair-brained schemes. Finally, he returned to his original position: the artist's lack of faith in his mentor's 'words' has led him to fall prey to the spirit of temptation. If only he would have patience, he would see the fruits of Gogol′'s efforts on his behalf.[72]

[70] Gogol′, Letter to Ivanov of 31 December 1846/12 January 1847, in ibid., 2, pp. 465–66.

[71] Ivanov, Letter to Gogol′ of 10/22 January 1847, in ibid., 2, p. 467. Gogol′ was to work for Prince P. M. Volkonskii, who was responsible for the affairs of the Academy of Arts.

[72] Gogol, Letter to Ivanov of 23 January/4 February 1847, in ibid., 2, pp. 469–71.

Gogol′'s essay, 'Ivanov, the Historical Painter' (1846)

These much heralded 'fruits' took the form of a 'letter', entitled 'Istoricheskii zhivopisets Ivanov' ('Ivanov, the Historical Painter', 1846) and addressed to Count Matvei Viel′gorskii, the Vice-President of the Society for the Encouragement of Artists. The 'letter' was never actually sent to its addressee and did not appear until January 1847 in *Selected Passages*.[73] The choice of the open letter as the vehicle for Gogol′'s appeal on behalf of the artist allowed him to combine a personal, at times confessional tone with a message of national import, thereby authenticating and adding pathos to his argument.

The essay builds on the image of the artist as a pure, dedicated being already elaborated in the second version of 'The Portrait' and now explicitly identified with Ivanov as the creator of 'The Appearance of Christ to the People'. The main goal of the painting as defined by Gogol′ is 'to represent in faces the entire course of humankind's conversion to Christ', illustrated through the varying degrees of faith exhibited on the faces of individuals ranging from Christ's contemporaries and future disciples to later recipients and carriers of the same message (such as Gogol′ and Ivanov). This phrase encapsulates the two levels of reading of the painting: the original appearance of Christ to the people and the continuing process of revelation.

Gogol′ makes two main points. First, the general principle that the value of any artist's work depends on the successful accomplishment of a 'spiritual task' (*dushevnoe delo*), defined as the acquisition of faith, to be achieved by 'conversion to Christ' (*obrashchenie ko Khristu*). The second point derives from this general principle: the subject of the painting — the turning to Christ of the people — cannot be understood or depicted by an artist who has not undergone this process himself. This accounts for the number of years Ivanov has been working on his painting, since the task of spiritual self-development is governed by transcendent laws regulated by a timetable independent of mundane affairs.

According to Gogol′'s reading of the image, Ivanov is representing the process of conversion not only as it applied to Christ's contemporaries at a specific historical moment and not only as it might apply to Russia in his time, but also as it applied to himself and by extension to Gogol′ — hence the inclusion of both figures in the painting. The image is therefore at

[73] For the text of the letter and background on its composition, see Gogol′, *Vybrannye mesta*, pp. 136–46 (text), 371–73 (notes).

once universal and personal, eternal and historical, prescriptive as well as descriptive in the message that it conveys. In creating his work, Ivanov is acting out its subject, the acquisition of faith — the performative dimension of the painting in progress becomes the key criterion for determining its status upon completion.

A substantial part of the essay (about a fifth) is devoted by Gogol′ to a recent period in his own life lasting over six years (roughly contemporaneous with his time in Rome and initial closeness to Ivanov), when he was too engrossed in his own 'transitional spiritual state' to be able to write.[74] The artist's delayed completion of his work thus provides a lofty explanation and justification for Gogol′'s own period of silence as a writer. The application of this idea both to Ivanov and to himself builds a bridge between the original prophet (John the Baptist) — who revealed the path for the acquisition of faith to the people — and the contemporary artist-prophets (Gogol′, Ivanov) — who follow the same path, turning to Christ in order first to receive and then to communicate the prophetic message to the people in artistic form. In this process Gogol′ is clearly in the lead: after accomplishing his spiritual task, he had already been able to finish the first part of his major work.

As well as mirroring both artists' anxieties over completing the great works with which they identified the purpose of their lives, this essay and the earlier exchange of letters reflect a crucial underlying issue: the balance of power between image and word as tools in the hands of aspiring prophets. Ivanov clearly placed the image above the word; he saw his painting as the primary source, to which Gogol′'s word would play second fiddle through a series of commissioned 'reports'. This option naturally did not attract Gogol′, who chose a different route: the writing of a 'letter' about Ivanov's painting was a strategy to promote his own agenda. Although ostensibly seeking support for the artist, he was in fact using the genre of the appeal for two purposes: first, to explain his own creative and spiritual path in a favourable light, and second, to establish his controlling position as the arbiter of Ivanov's spiritual level, defining the ultimate criterion by which the 'success' or value of his painting could be judged. The ekphrastic act of writing about an image effectively shifted the balance of power from the original image to its verbal explanation. While Ivanov might have been content to let the image speak for itself, Gogol′ had in a sense hijacked his project, interposing himself as its verbal interpreter and judge of its true

[74] Ibid., p. 142.

value, thus reaffirming the supremacy of word over image. As a result his 'letter' about the artist, as his earlier fictional 'Portrait', served to enhance his own status as a prophetic writer.

Gogol′ clearly expected Ivanov to read his essay and to experience a surge of gratitude towards his mentor and patron. Matters turned out somewhat differently, however. Ivanov did not hear about the essay until Gogol′ drew his attention to it explicitly some months later. Even then, he made no effort to get hold of it, leading Gogol′ in desperation to tear the letter out of his own copy of the book and despatch it to the artist.[75] Ivanov did not immediately read the piece and only responded briefly in December 1847, almost a whole year after the essay had appeared. Somewhat tactlessly he even mentioned that he had not made any effort to get hold of a copy of Gogol′'s book, despite knowing that it was circulating in Rome. Although he commented that reading the essay had caused him to return to his previous state of 'deepest reverence' (faith in Gogol′ and submission to his authority in all matters), he delivered a rather backhanded compliment by describing his friend as the only person capable of interceding with higher management on behalf of artists, thereby confirming the notion of the writer's word serving the artist's agenda.[76]

Ivanov evidently entertained serious reservations about the essay. His notebook includes the observation that Gogol′, by placing him on the highroad of fame, had made it hard for him to walk and impossible to think peacefully.[77] A similar view is recorded in the memoirs of P. M. Kovalevskii. Recalling his visit to Rome in 1856 (on a mission to retrieve the deceased writer's letters to the artist), he noted that Ivanov cited the harmful effect of the essay as the reason for his disinclination to allow members of the public to view his painting: 'Nikolai Vasil′evich [Gogol′] did me much harm with his praises: after his words I have no right to

[75] On 13/25 March 1847 Gogol′ told Ivanov about the essay. In November or December 1847 Ivanov informed Gogol′ that he had not yet seen or read the book. On 2/14 December 1847 Gogol′ expressed his surprise that Ivanov had not read the whole book while in Naples with Sof′ia Petrovna Apraksina and promised to send him the letter, torn out of the book. On 16/28 December 1847 Gogol′ noted that he was pleased that Ivanov had found his letter about him 'satisfactory' and revealed that he had torn the letter out of his own copy. See *Perepiska*, 2, pp. 473, 475, 477. According to V. M. Zummer, 'O vere i khrame A. Ivanova', cited in Vinogradov, *Aleksandr Ivanov v pis′makh*, p. 734, Ivanov only read the full text of Gogol′'s *Selected Passages* in 1848.

[76] Ivanov, Letter to Gogol′ between 2/14 and 16/28 December 1847, in Vinogradov, *Aleksandr Ivanov v pis′makh*, pp. 484–85.

[77] Cited in *Perepiska*, 2, pp. 479–80 (note 1).

exhibit my painting… Too much will be asked of me.'[78] Gogol′'s 'word' had created an inflated alternative version of his painting that — paradoxically — undermined the value of the original image.

Ivanov's 'Thoughts Arising upon Reading the Bible' (1846–47)

At the same time as Gogol′ was composing his essay, Ivanov was engaged on a new writing project of his own, which could perhaps best be described as an extended experiment in developing his own mastery of the art of verbal prophecy. From the second half of 1846 through to the end of 1847 he regularly jotted down his 'Thoughts Arising upon Reading the Bible', a patchwork miscellany of reflections gleaned from reading the Bible in Church Slavonic, Russian and French translations, interspersed with private prayers, diary notes, work plans and draft letters to friends and patrons.[79] The most useful sections for our subject are those that concern his vision of Russian artists as prophets for the contemporary age, modelled on biblical precursors. In these passages, with numerous repetitions and almost identical formulations, he delineates his view of the prophetic mission of the artist in relation to the tsar and the Russian people, all in the context of a strong eschatological expectation of the dawn of a new era of peace for humanity.

The essence of the 'argument' involves four stages, relating to the tsar, the artist-prophet, their ideal interaction and its envisaged outcome:

1. Ivanov starts from the premise that the Russian tsar is a divine figure, identified with the future Messiah, whose absolute power makes him

[78] P. M. Kovalevskii, 'Ob Ivanove i ego kartine'(1859), in Vinogradov, *Aleksandr Ivanov v pis′makh*, p. 547.

[79] Ivanov's 'Thoughts' were first published (surprisingly) in Soviet Russia in the late 1920s in V. M. Zummer, 'Eskhatologiia A. Ivanova', *Uchenye zapiski. Nauchno-issledovatel′skoi kafedry istorii evropeiskoi kul′tury Kharkovskogo universiteta*, 1929, 3, pp. 393–408. All citations are taken from the text reprinted with minor corrections based on the manuscript in Vinogradov, *Aleksandr Ivanov v pis'makh*, pp. 648–69, 732–33 (notes). For the dating of the 'Thoughts', see ibid., p. 732. Many ideas in the 'Thoughts' echo Ivanov's letters to Gogol′, including draft passages not included in editions of his correspondence, but published in V. M. Zummer, 'Neizdannye pis′ma Al. Ivanova k Gogoliu', *Izvestiia Azerbaidzhanskogo gosudarstvennogo universiteta imeni V. I. Lenina*, 4–5, *Obshchestvennye nauki*, 1925, pp. 38–53. On Ivanov's careful reading of different translations of the Bible, see his letter to F. V. Chizhov of 1844. He seized every opportunity to read his neighbour's copy of a rare Russian version of the Old Testament translated by G. P. Pavskii (published in a limited lithograph edition of over 700 copies in 1828, but collected and burnt in 1844 by decision of the Holy Synod). He complained that the Church Slavonic translation was not always comprehensible, differed from the Russian version, and asked Chizhov to get hold of a French translation done by a 'scholarly rabbi', published in Paris. See Vinogradov, *Aleksandr Ivanov v pis′makh*, pp. 314, 720 (note 155).

the 'most divine' of temporal rulers. However, the tsar is also human and may not be entirely flawless. He therefore needs a mentor to guide him along the path to spiritual perfection.[80]

2. This mentor will be the artist, whose role is modelled on various biblical antecedents: the Levite priests who provided spiritual guidance to the nation and the prophets who offered advice to the kings of Israel (as Samuel to King Saul, or Nathan to King David). The surprising shift from priest or prophet to the figure of the artist as spiritual mentor is justified by invoking a pseudo-historical argument. After the Israelites fell into idol worship, they were allegedly unable to sustain their faith despite the efforts of their prophets. Following the advent of Christianity, the task of redeeming the world therefore passed to the Russian nation, whose artists (not writers) were chosen to carry out this holy mission.[81]
3. The interaction of the artist-prophet and the tsar was to follow a particular pattern. First the artist had to abstain from wine and women so as to embrace the path of isolation and suffering. He was then required to immerse himself in reading the Bible and in preparing visual 'representations' (*izobrazheniia*) of select episodes. In order to prepare the tsar's mind for the contemplation of these sacred images, he had to engage him in edifying conversation about the biblical narratives illustrated. At the appropriate moment the artistic image would then be revealed, first to the tsar, then to the public. The creation and correct reception of these images thus depended on a constant cycle leading from the initial narrative through its expression in an image and on to its explication in words — with the artist remaining in control of both the visual and the verbal dimensions.[82]
4. Following this process of spiritual education and refinement through exposure to artistic images and verbal explanations, the Russian tsar, now truly Christ-like, would be able to adopt the role of Messiah and lead the last nation (Russia) and other Slav peoples to teach all humanity through their example; in this way Russia would fulfil its final mission of establishing eternal peace and harmony in this world, as prophesied by Isaiah.[83]

[80] Ibid., pp. 657, 659, 661.

[81] Ibid., pp. 652–53, 655, 661, 663–64, 666–67. Ivanov's painting, with its inclusion of the 'wanderer' artist, can be read as an illustration of this idea.

[82] Ibid., pp. 653–55, 657, 662, 665, 667.

[83] Ibid., pp. 640, 651, 659, 661, 663.

In putting forward this model, Ivanov was building on well-known literary precedents. Zhukovskii's poetic address of 1814 to Alexander I had already presented the poet as a prophetic figure, mediating between God, the Tsar and the people.[84] In one of the letters of *Selected Passages*, 'Predmety dlia liricheskogo poeta v nyneshnee vremia' ('Subjects for the Lyric Poet at the Present Time', 1844), Gogol′ issued an explicit call for Russian poets to model their verse on the Hebrew prophets, following the example of Iazykov.[85] Ivanov regularly met and corresponded with all three of these writers and was undoubtedly affected by their ideas. However, by shifting the role of the prophet from the writer and his text to the artist and his image, he added an entirely new dimension to the existing literary tradition of prophecy.

Ivanov experimented with the relation between text and image in an innovative way. He not only created a sacred image based on a biblical narrative, but also accompanied its creation with a text of his own making, thereby setting up a framework for understanding and promoting the prophetic dimension of art. This constant interaction between text and image was also reflected in his working methods. He frequently wrote out biblical passages next to his art work. For example, on the back of a sketch of the legs and clothing of John the Baptist and two apostles, he copied out texts from Jeremiah and Chronicles in French translation.[86]

Despite the prolonged time invested in compiling his 'Thoughts Arising upon Reading the Bible', Ivanov evidently remained dissatisfied with his attempt at articulating his prophetic mission in words. The 'Thoughts' were chaotic, repetitive and unclear and did not amount to a coherent manifesto. In the summer of 1848 he drafted a letter to Gogol′, trying to set out his views in a more organized fashion and asking him once more to serve as his mouthpiece. Writing from Naples, at a distance from his painting, he was anxious to resolve previous differences of opinion and to establish once and for all 'what services can be rendered by the man of letters to the artist and by the artist to the man of letters'.[87]

[84] For a discussion of Zhukovskii's 'Imperatoru Aleksandru: Poslanie' (1814), see Davidson, 'Between Derzhavin and Pushkin', pp. 187–91. By giving his early sketch of the painting to Zhukovskii for his album, Ivanov was building a bridge between the literary tradition of prophecy established by the poet and his own visual image of prophecy. See note 32 above.

[85] Gogol′, *Vybrannye mesta*, pp. 87, 90.

[86] 'Zemlia; nogi, odezhda: Etiud dlia figur Ioanna Krestitelia, Ioanna Bogoslova i apostola Andreia', paper, oil, 45 x 35, GTG, reproduced in Goldovskii, *Aleksandr Ivanov*, pp. 54, 152 (illustration, note with biblical texts).

[87] Vinogradov, *Aleksandr Ivanov v pis′makh*, pp. 497–500 (p. 498).

Citing the biblical promise that Japheth 'shall dwell in the tents of Shem' (Gen. 9:27), Ivanov suggested that the Russian nation (according to tradition descended from Japheth) is called upon to fulfil this prophecy.[88] In enabling Japheth to reach the last heights of its potential, Russia will be led by its historical painters, whose unique moral vision builds on the achievements of European artists. However, Ivanov adds, these talented but self-taught artists cannot achieve their goal without their message being made plain to society in a clearly comprehensible form. Hence the need for the writer, who will take from the artist his truth and the essential laws of his existence and render them accessible through verbal explanation. This task must be carried out by Gogol′, an 'imposing man of letters' (*predstavitel′noi literator*); the success of both writer and artist depends on this joint undertaking.

Ivanov is returning in a more determined and extended fashion to the proposal he had already made a year and a half earlier in his letter to Gogol′ of January 1847.[89] As noted above, this request upset Gogol′ at the time and he did not respond any more favourably to the painter's repeated attempt to enlist his literary skills in support of his visual art. While Ivanov took pains to flatter Gogol′ by emphasizing how crucial his role as verbal commentator would be, he left no room for doubt that the artist remained the primary agent of prophecy, communicated through the images that he created and the example of his life.

The final revelation of Ivanov's image of prophecy (1858)

Although the two friends' relations were restored on a superficial level, the underlying tension over who was to assume the leading prophetic role and whether this was to be expressed through images or words was never resolved during their lifetimes. After Gogol′'s death in 1852, Ivanov continued to work on his painting obsessively, rarely allowing visitors into his studio. In the spring of 1857 he finally consented to show it to Aleksandra Fedorovna, the widow of Nicholas I, and then to select artists. When the influential patron of the arts, Grand Duchess Elena Pavlovna

[88] Noah had three sons, Shem, Ham and Japheth. After Noah became drunk, Ham saw his nakedness (for which his son Canaan was cursed), while Shem and Japheth covered up his nakedness (for which they were rewarded). Shem is the ancestor of the Semitic races, while Japheth is commonly regarded as the father of the Europeans (according to a traditional reading of Gen. 10:5). Based on a link between the name *Iafet* and the adjective *iafe* (beautiful), Japheth has also been associated with the Greeks and their cult of beauty in art.

[89] *Perepiska*, 2, p. 467.

(married to Mikhail Pavlovich, the uncle of Alexander II) saw the painting in February 1858, she offered to pay for its transportation back to Russia.[90] Some twenty-eight years after his original departure for Rome, filled with trepidation at the prospect of returning home, Ivanov embarked on the lengthy journey through France and Germany, arriving in St Petersburg on 20 May 1858. Public excitement was stirred by numerous press reports announcing the long-awaited return of the artist and his celebrated work, soon to be unveiled.

The painting was first put on display in the White Hall, a grand room forming part of the Tsar's own suite of rooms in the Winter Palace, decorated with Corinthian columns surmounted by statues of the arts. On 28 May 1858 Ivanov was granted a personal audience to show his work to Alexander II. The Tsar recalled having seen it in Rome (twenty years earlier, in December 1838), asked about the significance of the slave (no doubt related in his mind to the problematic issue of the serfs' emancipation) and thanked him at length.[91] The painting was then transferred to the Academy of Arts on 9 June and exhibited to the public in a room chosen by Ivanov, alongside a large body of related studies and sketches, offered for sale together with photographs of the painting taken in Rome. One of these photographs was officially presented by Ivanov to the Petersburg Public Library, others were bought by members of the royal family.[92] In this way the original image of prophecy was reproduced and disseminated to a wider audience.

Events appeared to be unfolding according to the utopian scenario mapped out by Ivanov in his 'Thoughts Arising upon Reading the Bible': the artist had completed a sacred image based upon his reading of a biblical text, presented it to the Tsar with an explanation of its significance, received the ruler's blessing and finally revealed it to the public. In actual fact, however, the situation was far from ideal. Ivanov's anxiety over how much he would be paid for his painting was exacerbated by endless rumours (the decision was delayed during the Tsar's absence from the

[90] Iovleva, *Aleksandr Andreevich Ivanov*, pp. 16–17.

[91] Ivanov's letter to his brother S. A. Ivanov of 27–31 May 1858, in Vinogradov, *Aleksandr Ivanov v pis′makh*, p. 606.

[92] Iovleva, *Aleksandr Andreevich Ivanov*, pp. 16–17. On Ivanov's choice of a room at the Academy, see his letter to his brother S. A. Ivanov of 6 June 1858, in Vinogradov, *Aleksandr Ivanov v pis′makh*, p. 613. On the move of the painting to the Academy, see his letter to his brother S. A. Ivanov of 8–12 June 1858, in ibid., pp. 618–19. On his gift of a photograph to the library, see 'Vospominaniia V. V. Stasova' (1879), in ibid., p. 613. On sales of photographs to Grand Duke Mikhail Pavlovich and Empress Aleksandra Fedorovna, see ibid., pp. 619, 622.

capital).[93] Although the pomp surrounding the final return of the painting from Rome to the imperial capital and its unveiling to the Tsar bolstered the image's importance, Ivanov could no longer call upon Gogol′ to act as his mouthpiece and provide an appropriate verbal explication of his art. He was upset by a harsh review of his painting signed by V. V. Tolbin but evidently partly authored by his fellow artist F. A. Bruni.[94] When attending viewings at the Academy, alone and often unrecognized, he overheard visitors' comments and was confused by the public's failure to grasp the significance of his work.[95]

On 30 June Ivanov set off for the country estate of Sergievka near Peterhof to clarify the terms for the acquisition of the painting with the current President of the Academy of Arts, Grand Duchess Maria Nikolaevna (the sister of Alexander II and former pupil of Zhukovskii). He waited for three hours but was not received. He returned to the city upset and agitated, fell into a fever and died three days later, just before his fifty-second birthday. When a messenger finally arrived the next morning with an official letter informing the artist that the Tsar would purchase his painting for 15,000 roubles and had awarded him the order of St Vladimir, it was already too late.[96]

Although Ivanov's death was clearly due to the cholera epidemic, widespread in Petersburg at the time, many of his contemporaries ascribed it to quite different causes, such as his failure to emerge victorious from the moral struggle that Gogol′ had written about, his return to the suffocating atmosphere of Russia, or the lack of recognition received by his work.[97] His sudden demise after the final unveiling of his painting was a potent factor sealing the myth of the holy artist, sacrificing his life on the altar of

[93] Ivanov's letters to his brother S. A. Ivanov of 8–12 and 27 June 1858, in ibid., pp. 619, 633.

[94] V. V. Tolbin, 'O kartine g. Ivanova', *Syn Otechestva*, 25, 22 June 1858, pp. 710–13, in Vinogradov, *Aleksandr Ivanov v pis′makh*, pp. 624–25. Tolbin attacked the colours, figure of the slave, 'unchristian' nakedness, perspective and composition of the painting, as well as the detrimental influence of Overbeck. For Ivanov's reactions, see his letter to his brother S. A. Ivanov of 27 June 1858, in ibid., pp. 633–34.

[95] See 'Vospominaniia V. V. Stasova' (1879), M. P. Botkin's account (1880) and the satirical description of visitors' comments by M. Z<aguliaev> (1858), in ibid., pp. 620, 634, 636–37.

[96] See the detailed account in M. P. Botkin's letter to S. A. Ivanov of 27 July 1858, in Iovleva, *Aleksandr Andreevich Ivanov*, pp. 17–18, and the descriptions of Ivanov's last days by D. A. Obolenskii, A. I. Herzen (1858) and M. P. Botkin (1880), in Vinogradov, *Aleksandr Ivanov v pis′makh*, pp. 637–39. Ivanov had originally hoped to receive 30,000 roubles for his painting.

[97] See the views of D. A. Obolenskii, V. A. Cherkasskii and A. F. Tiutcheva, in ibid., pp. 640, 642, 645.

art dedicated to the Tsar and his people. If death is read in the Bakhtinian sense as the final creative act, retrospectively determining the meaning of an artist's life, then Ivanov's premature passing effectively established the myth of the *artist*-prophet in Russia, just as Pushkin's early death by duel in the same city some twenty years earlier had laid the ground for the myth of his redemption and status as national *poet*-prophet.[98]

The importance of the visual image and its legacy to the tradition of art as prophecy

We have seen that Ivanov's image of prophecy, supplemented by Gogol′'s verbal comments, played a crucial, even pivotal role in establishing the Russian tradition of art as prophecy on a national level. We are now in a position to draw some more general conclusions about the importance of the visual image in this tradition and its long-term legacy.

Why did the image play such a significant role? Part of the answer to this question takes us back to our initial starting-point, to the prioritizing of vision over word in biblical accounts of prophecy. Prophetic *vision* precedes *verbal* expression and is therefore on a higher level. The prophet is defined as one who *sees*, his vision is complete and equated with fullness of understanding. As the modern equivalent of the original prophetic seer, the artist-prophet carries forward this unique ability to see with full vision. A natural consequence of the prioritizing of the act of seeing over hearing in the reception of prophecy is the ranking of image over word in its transmission. The static image, which can embrace and convey the entire vision, is superior to the fragmented, sequential nature of verbal communication. It enables the viewer to take in the picture in one go, as a whole, in the same way as the prophet receives his initial vision. Images, once completed, create their own model of reality; they appear to 'exist' in the real world and can command a greater degree of authority than made-up texts, open to dispute.

These general differences were magnified in the case of Gogol′ and Ivanov by their different styles. Both artists had similar aspirations: to convey to contemporary Russians in artistic form the path by which a vision of harmony and spiritual wholeness could be attained. Gogol′ succeeded in providing a picture of the antithesis of this ideal in the first part of *Dead Souls*, but never managed to complete the ensuing parts showing the route to redemption. Although he was driven by the desire for wholeness, his

[98] See the section 'Martyrdom and Death as Moral Categories', in Davidson, 'The Moral Dimension of the Prophetic Ideal', pp. 510–14.

works were marked by the very opposite — by fragmentation of structure and literary technique. As Gary Cox has shown in his study of montage in Gogol′, the writer's frequent use of visual blocks and tangential perspective led to a pervasive sense of disjointedness and division.[99] Even his last work, *Selected Passages*, designed to promote unity through its architecture and claims for the redemptive power of the divinely inspired prophetic word, was severely criticized by contemporaries for its fragmented structure and arrogant tone.[100]

Ivanov, by contrast, created a vision of harmony; his painting exudes a static quality of serenity and calm, both in its composition and in the manner of its execution. It provides the viewer with the perfect illusion of being able to embrace the whole picture without sacrificing any of the details, and even manages to combine different temporal planes (past, present and future) on a single canvas. It is easy to understand why Gogol′ found his image so compelling; it was so utterly different from anything that he could produce in writing. Ivanov projected in visual art what Gogol′ was unable to convey in verbal form: a vision of redeemed Russia and humanity. He created a modern icon in the style of Leonardo da Vinci and Raphael, testifying to his own prophetic vision and enabling the contemporary viewer to take part in this vision.

Another reason for the perceived superiority of image over word lay in its public dimension of performance. The artist could be observed in his studio, creating the work of art, often over a period of many years, as was the case with Ivanov's magnum opus (twenty-four years from 1833 to 1857) or later in the century with Viktor Vasnetsov's 'Bogatyrs' (eighteen years from 1881 to 1898). The highly visible example of Ivanov, dedicating his whole life to art, provided Gogol′ with the model and disciple that he needed to validate his own status as literary prophet. The public dimension also made possible the involvement of high-profile patrons, including the Tsar and members of the imperial family; all the stages from initial viewings through monetary support to final purchase effectively transformed the private work of art into an object of national significance. Gogol′ had good reason to envy Ivanov, whose painting was personally viewed and funded by one heir to the throne and two subsequent tsars.[101]

[99] Gary Cox, '"Montage" in Gogol′'s *Dead Souls*: The View from the Bachelor's Carriage', in Anderson, *Russian Narrative & Visual Art*, pp. 63–77.

[100] See Lina Bernstein, *Gogol's Last Book: The Architechtonics of Selected Passages from Correspondence with Friends*, Birmingham Slavonic Monographs, 24, Birmingham, 1994, pp. 38, 101–03.

[101] At the end of 1845 Nicholas I visited Ivanov's studio to see his work in progress. In a

The writer could not possibly compete with this level of impact; the public readings he gave of his works were not well attended and often fell flat.

The high status of the image would not have been possible, however, without the element of verbal explanation that invariably accompanied its creation. Ivanov needed Gogol′, just as in a later generation, Mikhail Vrubel′ would need Blok and Lev Bakst would need Viacheslav Ivanov to provide readings that aligned their work with prophetic tradition. The success of the image promoted the standing of the literary prophet, called upon to explain its sacred significance. The artist and the writer therefore often tended to work together in a partnership of mutual benefit.

What was the legacy of the relationship between Ivanov's image and Gogol′'s word? In the ensuing development of the tradition of art as prophecy, which would carry more weight — the image or the word? Who would achieve greater prominence — the artist-prophet or the writer-prophet? Would they collaborate or compete with each other?

To a considerable extent, the answer to these questions depended on the fashioning of Ivanov's posthumous reputation, a task largely determined by writers. After his death his reputation as a national prophet steadily grew.[102] A key role in this process was played by Khomiakov, who embarked on a study of the artist's work after meeting him a few times in 1858.[103] In what turned out to be an extensive obituary article, he attributed Ivanov's death to his desire to live not for himself but for *all* Russians through his work. He overcame the latent tension between the competing myths of the artist and writer as prophets by skilfully combining them into a harmonious

letter of 15/27 January 1846 to A. O. Smirnova Gogol′ described how he had glimpsed the Tsar from afar during his visit to Rome, but had not dared to introduce himself, as he had not yet achieved anything worthy of attracting the ruler's attention. He then commented on the Tsar's particularly favourable disposition to the Russian artists in Rome and on his high praise of Ivanov's painting (*Perepiska*, 2, pp. 178–79).

[102] See the eulogistic memoirs and writings by F. I. Iordan (1879), P. M. Kovalevskii (1859), V. P. Gaevskii (1879), I. S. Turgenev (1861), K. D. Kavelin (1879), V. V. Stasov (1879), S. A. Ivanov (1862) and the extensive list of posthumous articles that appeared from 1858 to 1879 about the artist and his painting, compiled by N. P. Sobko, in Botkin, *Aleksandr Andreevich Ivanov*, pp. 397–429, 472–77.

[103] Ivanov and Khomiakov met at the home of Iordan. On 6 June 1858 Ivanov wrote to his brother that Khomiakov wished to write an article about his painting. After his death, Khomiakov commented on how dear Ivanov had become to him over the course of their two or three meetings: 'He was a holy artist because of the humble attitude to religious art that constituted his whole life.' Vinogradov, *Aleksandr Ivanov v pis′makh*, pp. 613–14. Khomiakov owned several works by Ivanov, including the 'Venetian' oil sketch of the painting and the oil sketch of the full-size Christ, purchased for him from M. P. Botkin by I. S. Samarin (reproduced in Iovleva, *Aleksandr Andreevich Ivanov*, pp. 53, 55); see the lists of works and their owners in Botkin, *Aleksandr Andreevich Ivanov*, pp. 445–46, 461.

vision of joint architects building a unified national prophetic tradition: '[Ivanov] was the same in painting as Gogol′ was in writing and Kireevskii in philosophical thought.'[104]

The view of Ivanov as a national prophet has subsequently become so well entrenched in Russia that it is reiterated unquestioningly. In 2006, for example, Grigorii Goldovskii rounded off his introduction to the Russian Museum's two-hundred year anniversary album on Ivanov with the hope that the 'Master's' utopian project of a golden age of Russian art would be realized by the time of his three-hundred year anniversary when Russia will have finished building the 'temple of humanity' envisaged by 'one of its greatest prophets'.[105]

Khomiakov's vision of supportive cooperation was very much in tune with the unity of word and image in the biblical and iconographic traditions absorbed by Gogol′ and Ivanov into their literary and artistic representations of prophecy. Other contemporaries, however, emphasized differences and tension rather than unity and collaboration. Soon after Ivanov's death, his brother, the architect Sergei Ivanov, took pains to expose the deep rift that had existed between the artist's views and Gogol′'s ideas. In a frank letter to the art critic V. V. Stasov he attempted to correct a frequent misconception:

> Do you really think that Gogol′ ever did anything important to determine the direction of A. A. Ivanov? [...] My brother never shared the same thoughts with Gogol′, he never agreed with him internally, but at the same time he also never argued with him, avoiding whenever possible Gogol′'s unpleasant and, let's speak frankly, even insolent replies, which Gogol′ with his pride did not skimp on.[106]

Not surprisingly, the balance between the collaborative and the competitive approaches to the relations between word and image continued to fluctuate throughout the nineteenth century. The increase in the number of prophetic writers towards the end of the century was matched in visual terms by a corresponding rise in the number of portraits of literary figures depicted with prophetic or Christ-like features. At the

[104] Khomiakov, *PSS*, 3, p. 347.

[105] Goldovskii, *Aleksandr Ivanov*, p. 25.

[106] S. A. Ivanov, Letter to V. V. Stasov of 15/3 May 1862, in Botkin, *Aleksandr Andreevich Ivanov*, p. 429. On Sergei Ivanov, see Liudmila Markina, 'Sergei Ivanov: v teni velikogo brata', *Tret′iakovskaia galereia*, 2007, 2, pp. 38–47 <http://www.tg-m.ru/img/mag/2007/2/038-047.pdf> [accessed 26 August 2012].

turn of the century the ethereal, visionary quality of Ivanov's late biblical works was given a new lease of life by Mikhail Vrubel′ (1856–1910). His remarkable series of prophets, starting with an illustration of Pushkin's 'Prophet' (1898) and culminating in 'The Vision of the Prophet Ezekiel' (1906), included his 'Head of a Prophet' (1904–05), closely modelled on his own 'Self-portrait' (1904–05).[107] These works not only captured the Silver Age resurgence of the cult of the artist as a prophet, they also reinforced the power of the visual image over the written word. As the poet Aleksandr Blok commented in his obituary essay on Vrubel′ of 1910: 'The worlds which he *saw*, we have not yet *seen in full*.'[108]

A significant shift in the centre of gravity of this cult is reflected in the work of Mikhail Nesterov (1862–1942). 'The Soul of the People' (1914–16) can be seen as an early twentieth-century response to Ivanov's 'Appearance of Christ to the People', indicating a new stage in the path of 'turning towards Christ' followed by the Russian people (Figure 9). Like its predecessor, it blends historical figures (the tsar) with contemporary prophetic thinkers (Dostoevskii, Tolstoi, Vladimir Solov′ev). Christ is now replaced by an icon of the Saviour, held up at the centre of a mixed crowd including priests, monks, nuns, writers and a soldier. The role of the prophet John the Baptist has passed to that of a dancing holy fool, leading the people not towards the Messiah, but towards a young blond boy (modelled on Nesterov's son), who walks towards the water. This representation of the soul of the people evokes the biblical verses 'a little child shall lead them' (Isa. 11:6) and 'unless you turn and become like children, you will never enter the kingdom of heaven' (Mat. 18:3). If Ivanov's painting depicted the prophet revealing the path of faith to the *narod*, Nesterov's response suggests that the people itself, led by its writers and empowered by the artist, has now become the carrier of this prophetic force. This compelling image of the national prophetic mission in Russian culture would not have been possible without the pioneering contribution of Ivanov's visual representation of prophecy. Neither, however, would it have been possible without the verbal contribution of writers, as Nesterov signalled in a later painting, daringly executed during the Soviet period. 'Holy Week' (1933) presents Gogol′ in a vast Russian landscape kneeling at the foot of the crucified Christ, while Dostoevskii stands behind him. Once more, following Ivanov, Gogol′ is cast as the one 'closest to Christ'.

[107] I. Shumanova, 'Obrazy Proroka i Serafima v tvorchestve Mikhaila Vrubelia' <http://www.liveinternet.ru/users/julia_zubareva/post125201431/> [accessed 27 August 2012].

[108] My italics. 'Pamiati Vrubelia', in Aleksandr Blok, *Sobranie sochinenii*, ed. V. N. Orlov, 8 vols, Moscow and Leningrad, 1962, 5, p. 422.

Fig. 9: Mikhail Nesterov, 'The Soul of the People' (1916).
From the Collection of the State Tretyakov Gallery, St Petersburg.

The interactive dialogue between image and word in the construction of the Russian tradition of art as prophecy continues to develop. In 2009 a new film about Gogol′ directed by Natal′ia Bondarchuk was released, billed as the first cinematic attempt to lift the Soviet taboo on representing Gogol′ as a spiritual seeker. Significantly, its title, 'Gogol′. Blizhaishii' ('Gogol′: The Closest'), and opening episode were taken from Ivanov's painting. Yet again, this time through the mixed visual and verbal medium of film, the artist's image of prophecy was used to validate the myth of the writer as a national prophet.

Londoners and Outlanders: Polish Labour Migration through the European Lens

KRIS VAN HEUCKELOM

Introduction

Following the collapse of the Iron Curtain and the subsequent enlargement of the European Union, immigrants from former Communist countries have increasingly received cinematic representations across the European continent.[1] Compared to the overall body of research on European migration film and diasporic cinema, however, the on-screen appearance of these newcomers from the former Eastern Bloc has been given relatively little scholarly attention.[2] In order to correct this imbalance, the present article sets out to cover a series of prominent tropes and shifts that characterize the cinematic portrayal of immigrant workers from Poland in contemporary European film, with a special focus on the on-screen treatment of Polish jobseekers moving to the United Kingdom after the

Kris Van Heuckelom is Professor of Polish Studies at KU Leuven (Belgium).

[1] An extensive bibliography on the topic of European migrant and migration cinema is available on the website of the research network, *Migrant and Diasporic Cinema in Contemporary Europe* <http://www.migrantcinema.net/bibliography> [accessed 9 August 2011].

[2] So far, most attention has been paid to cinematic responses to earlier migration waves, for instance in French 'beur cinéma' and German-Turkish film. As far as migration from the former Eastern Bloc is concerned, a couple of articles have been devoted to the changed status of Russian protagonists in European and American cinema after 1991. See Birgit Beumers, 'Through the Other Lens? Russians on the Global Screen', in Stephen Hutchings (ed.), *Russia and its Other(s) on Film: Screening Intercultural Dialogue*, Basingstoke, 2008, pp. 166–83, and Dina Iordanova, 'The New Russians in Film: Nostalgia for the Occupier, Commiseration for the Immigrant', *Canadian Slavonic Papers*, 17, 2000, 1–2, pp. 113–31. Single films that deal with migration from post-Communist states, such as Damjan Kozole's *Rezervni deli* (*Spare Parts*, 2003) and Paweł Pawlikowski's *Last Resort* (2000), have been discussed by, among others, Yosepha Loshitzky in *Screening Strangers: Migration and Diaspora in Contemporary European Cinema*, Bloomington and Indianapolis, IN, 2010.

country's accession to the European Union in 2004. As I will argue, recent films set in London, such as Ken Loach's *It's a Free World* (2007) and Dominic Lees's *Outlanders* (2007), add a particular twist to the narrative function of Polish labour migration in post-1989 European cinema. Moreover, in order to juxtapose these foreign cinematic representations with their Polish counterparts, this article also provides a discussion of the high-budget Polish drama series, *Londyńczycy* (*Londoners*, 2008–09), that ran shortly after the aforementioned films.

The case of Polish labour migration and its cinematic representations deserves detailed examination for a number of reasons. First of all, it should be noted that Poland has a long-standing tradition of emigration reaching back more than two centuries. While a substantial part of these migration flows have been triggered by political circumstances (the partitions of Poland at the end of the eighteenth century, the Polish uprisings in the nineteenth century and the Sovietization of the country in the aftermath of the Second World War), economic factors have increasingly played a decisive role in motivating Polish citizens to emigrate. Not surprisingly, the question as to whether to leave the fatherland or not has become one of the cornerstones of Polish cultural and artistic discourses, most notably within the realm of literature.[3] Although the fall of Communism has inevitably led to the gradual decline of Polish exilic and émigré culture, new waves of (mainly employment-driven) resettlement have perpetuated the typical character of emigration in Polish cultural and political debates after 1989. What is more, the significant proliferation of recent European films that feature Polish immigrant characters seems to indicate that the issue of Polish migration has gained relevance and prominence on a transnational level as well. In fact, although post-Cold War European film tends to portray the incoming workforce from a wide range of former Communist countries, Polish jobseekers, more than any other European ethnicity, seem to have become Europe's most prototypical labour migrants, both in the public arena and on the silver screen.[4] Therefore, a closer look into

[3] As Halina Filipowicz notes, 'the emigration provided Poland's culture with much of its alphabet of referential immediacy, not only in the life of the literary imagination and the realm of aesthetic valuation, but in the spheres of political thought and social institutions as well'. Halina Filipowicz, 'Fission and Fusion: Polish Emigré Literature', *The Slavic and East European Journal*, 33, 1989, 2, p. 158.

[4] Over the past three decades, migrant protagonists from Poland have made their appearance in more than forty European films. In the 1980s and the first half of the 1990s, they were brought to the screen predominantly in major European countries such as France, the UK and Germany. Soon after, the cinematic interest in Polish labour migrants also spread to Austria, the Netherlands, Denmark, Sweden, Norway and Switzerland,

these cinematic portrayals allows one to go beyond the framework of national cinemas and to discuss representational practices in post-1989 European migration film on a cross-cultural basis. As I shall argue, the method of 'watching across borders'[5] is instrumental in uncovering an array of common tropes and narrative devices that characterize European screenings of migrants from the former Eastern Bloc. Also, combined with the cross-cultural reach of these representational practices, the enduring visibility of Polish protagonists in European migration film makes their case highly suitable for diachronic analysis and helps to acknowledge the fact that not only the patterns of migration themselves have changed after the fall of the Iron Curtain, but also the way in which these migrants from East Central Europe are brought to the screen.

Screening Cold War Migration

Whereas American filmmaking has a long-standing tradition of depicting migrants of Polish (and Slavic) descent,[6] the emergence of immigrants from East Central Europe in European cinema is relatively recent. Moreover, European films rarely bring into view second- and third-generation East European characters ('ethnics'), but tend to focus on 'fresh' migrants from the region.[7] Also, whereas American film-makers fall back on marks of Slavic or East European descent, mainly to envision class differences (casting these characters in the prototypical role of the poor and dumb white working-class American), most European directors make use of such ethnic labels to bring into view the impact of the Cold War and its aftermath on the continent's changing sociocultural space.

which indicates the almost continent-wide nature of the phenomenon. Moreover, most of these productions have been authored by non-Polish directors, which indicates that their portrayal of Polish labour migrants involves foreign constructions of Polishness rather than Polish self-images.

[5] Dina Iordanova, 'Migration and Cinematic Process in Post-Cold War Europe', in Daniela Berghahn and Claudia Sternberg (eds), *European Cinema in Motion: Migrant and Diasporic Film in Contemporary Europe*, Basingstoke, 2010, p. 61.

[6] See Caroline Golab, 'Stellaaaaaa...... !!!!!!: The Slavic Stereotype in American Film', in Randall M. Miller (ed.), *The Kaleidoscopic Lens: How Hollywood Views Ethnic Groups*, Englewood Cliffs, NJ, 1980, pp. 135–55; John J. Bukowczyk, 'The Big Lebowski Goes to the Polish Wedding: Polish Americans – Hollywood Style', *Polish Review*, 47, 2002, 2, pp. 211–29, and Danuta V. Goshka, 'The Bohunk in American Cinema', *Journal of Popular Culture*, 2006, 3, pp. 407–29.

[7] In the case of European cinema featuring Polish protagonists, only a limited number of films, such as the French drama, *Une minute de silence* (*A Minute of Silence*, 1998), and the English film, *Small Time Obsession* (2000), focus on the ethnic world rather than on the immigrant world.

It appears that the first notable examples of Polish immigrant protagonists in European film emerged only in the late 1970s. Significantly, these early cinematic portrayals of Polish characters refrain from foregrounding the protagonist's East European provenance. An interesting case is Roman Polański's *The Tenant* (1976). Based on the novel, *Le locataire chimérique* (*The Chimerical Tenant*, 1964), by Roland Topor, it offers the story of a Parisian clerk of Polish descent (Trelkovsky) who gradually turns mad after moving into an apartment that is be haunted by the unfortunate fate of its previous female tenant (a lesbian Egyptologist who has made a suicidal leap from her window). Significantly, Polański barely exposes the Polish background of the main character (played by the director himself), but rather focuses on Trelkovsky's gradual transformation from an insider into an outsider (which culminates in his attempt to commit suicide by throwing himself through the same window).[8] Another case in point is the Belgian movie, *Exit 7* (1978), which brings into focus a successful and wealthy architect (Marc Dumont) who suffers from a severe mid-life crisis. After falling in love with a Polish antique shop assistant (Jadwiga) he abandons his Belgian wife and children and flees to Greece with his new beloved. Not unlike Polański's Trelkovsky, the Polish origin of the female antagonist seems to be incidental rather than essential to the storyline (which remains devoid of any references or allusions to the socio-political and ideological fault lines dividing post-war Europe).

The early 1980s, when Communist Poland became embroiled in a severe political and economic crisis and received increasing media coverage in the international press, heralded a new stage in the on-screen treatment of Polish immigrants. The sudden enactment of martial law in 1981 turned out to be a rewarding source of inspiration for film-makers on the other side of the Iron Curtain, particularly in France and the United Kingdom. Typical of most of these films is that they highlight the political underpinnings of migration from Poland and feature Polish intellectuals, artists and political activists who — while living in exile — try to come to terms with the dramatic situation in their home country. The political turmoil in Poland

[8] The only scene that foregrounds the main character's East European roots takes place when Trelkovsky is interrogated by a police officer. Asked if he has a Russian name, Trelkovsky immediately replies, 'Polish, Polish'. As such, the filmscript diverges from the book version of *The Tenant* (in which Trelkovsky is said to be Russian). Katarzyna Marciniak interprets the main character's non-French descent as a mark of Otherness that is not accepted by French society (just like the lesbian tenant's sexual Otherness leads to her eventual expulsion from the local community). See Katarzyna Marciniak, 'Cinematic Exile: Performing the Foreign Body on Screen in Roman Polański's *The Tenant*', *Camera Obscura: A Journal of Feminism, Culture, and Media Studies*, 15, 2000, 1_43, pp. 1–43.

gained particular attention in the artistic output of Jerzy Skolimowski who, like Polański, was born in Poland and devoted two feature films to the impact of martial law on the lives of Polish immigrants in the UK (*Moonlighting* from 1982 and *Success Is the Best Revenge* from 1984). French cinematic responses to the crisis in Poland were offered by Jean-Luc Godard's *Passion* (1982) and Charles Nemes's *La fiancée qui venait du froid* (*The Fiancee Who Came From the Cold*, 1983). Notwithstanding the fact that each of these films has its aesthetic and generic particularities, they share a set of common concerns and narrative threads. Most similarities can be drawn between Godard's *Passion* and Skolimowski's *Success Is the Best Revenge*, each of which features as its main protagonist a Polish artist who works in exile and experiences difficulties in bringing to an end his artistic endeavours.[9] The French romantic comedy, *La fiancée qui venait du froid*, in turn focuses on a group of young Polish political activists who ended up in exile in Paris. Set between March 1980 and December 1981, *La fiancée* covers the period preceding the imposition of martial law and revolves around the attempts of Polish exiles to get one of their colleagues out of the country to prevent her from being arrested.[10]

The only production that stands apart from these politically-oriented films is Jerzy Skolimowski's *Moonlighting*.[11] Through its narrative focus

[9] Godard's *Passion* is set in Switzerland in January 1982 and focuses on a Polish film director (Jerzy) who is working on a film consisting of 'tableaux vivants'. While most critics have ignored the various (more or less implied) links between the film and the context of martial law in Poland, Ewa Mazierska has drawn particular attention to the fact that the director's inability to complete his artistic project partly has to do with lingering concerns about the dramatic events in Poland. Ewa Mazierska, 'Polish Martial Law of 1981 Seen from Abroad', *New Cinemas*, 7, 2009, 3, pp. 197–209. Quite similar to the artistic and existential dilemmas of Jerzy is the position of Alex Rodak, the main character in Skolimowski's *Success is the Best Revenge*. Emotionally attached to his home country, he tries to set up a spectacle that focuses on the deplorable fate of Poland as a result of the political and ideological divide of Europe after the Second World War. The film also envisions a conflict between Rodak and his older son Adam who is critical of his father's artistic endeavours and eventually decides to go back to Poland.

[10] The film focuses on Zosia, a Polish dissident and member of the opposition movement who enters into a paper marriage with a French director of commercials (Paul), in order to obtain French citizenship and escape from being imprisoned by the Polish Communist regime. Not unlike other romantic comedies in the paper marriage genre, the story ends with the paper bride and groom falling in love with each other.

[11] *Moonlighting* focuses on a crew of Polish workers remodelling the London residence of a high-placed Polish Communist ('the Boss'). Their trip to the UK is set in December 1981, a week before the introduction of martial law in Poland. When the crew leader (Nowak, played by Jeremy Irons) hears about the events in Poland he decides not to inform his fellow workers. Gradually, the boss turns into a totalitarian character, exploiting his fellow workers in order to increase labour.

on employment-driven migration from Poland, Skolimowski's film marks the beginning of a new paradigm in representing protagonists from the Eastern Bloc on the European screen. Instead of portraying Eastern Bloc characters the West European audience needs to be afraid of — clever secret agents from Cold War Russia — or can sympathize with — political activists who oppose the Communist regime — the films from this new paradigm fix attention on the fortunes of ordinary men and women who seek material well-being on the other side of the Iron Curtain. Other feature films that offer a similar approach toward pre-1989 westbound migration from Poland include Michael Klier's *Überall ist es besser wo wir nicht sind* (*The Grass is Greener Everywhere Else*, 1989) and Peter Del Monte's *La ballata dei lavavetri* (*The Ballad of the Windscreen Washers*, 1998).

As the available corpus of European migration films indicates, the socio-political context of the Cold War constitutes a decisive fault line in the representations of Central and East European labour migrants before and after 1989. In most of the Poland-related productions that are set during the Cold War, the action focuses on the troublesome life of Polish expatriates and their interaction with fellow immigrants (rather than with local characters). As is usually the case, these Polish protagonists hardly if ever enter into contact with locals. A second thread that links these films is the extreme hostility of the Western host society towards newcomers, which forces them to commit criminal acts (such as robbery and murder). A final characteristic shared by the films involved is the fact that their plot lines bear obvious marks of tragedy and fatality. One of the most dramatic stories is offered by the Italian film, *La ballata dei lavavetri*, which brings into view a Polish family moving from Poland to Rome. Set in the late 1980s, the film shows the gradual disintegration of a Polish family in a hostile and alien environment.[12] Similarly dramatic is the fate of the Polish immigrant workers featured in Skolimowski's *Moonlighting*. At the very end of the film, we see the crew members walking all the way to Heathrow Airport, flat broke and exhausted. Another interesting case, finally, is

[12] While awaiting permission to travel on to Canada, each member of the family attempts to make a living in Rome. Whereas the male protagonists (the father figure, Janusz, his son Rafał and his mentally unstable brother Zygmunt) try to earn some money by cleaning windscreens at traffic lights, the women (Janusz's partner Helena and his daughter Justyna) perform cleaning services for the Italian upper class. Gradually, however, the entire family falls apart: Janusz disappears without a trace and is presumed to have committed suicide, his brother descends into alcoholism and suffers from hallucinations, Justyna is killed as a result of a rape attempt by two young Italians, while her brother Rafał commits murder.

provided by Klier's *Überall ist es besser wo wir nicht sind*. Although its two Polish lead characters (Jerzy and Ewa) manage to leave Warsaw for Berlin in the late 1980s and finally make it to America, neither of them manages to move upward or onward in socio-economic terms.[13]

Significantly, although these feature films partly draw on non-realist aesthetics and are not devoid of symbolic and allegorical elements, they usually come with a strong dose of social realism. As such, these films link up with the strong socio-political imperative that is shared by many migration narratives in European cinema.[14] In the meantime, however, they strongly focus on what Yosepha Loshitzky has called the migration fantasy.[15] While the immigrant characters are driven by the dream of a better life for themselves and their relatives in the West (preferably North America), they often fail to recognize the futility and contingency of this fantasy. The collapse of their dreams in the encounter with reality ensues not only from the immigrants' inability to adapt to the host society, but also from the inability (and unwillingness) of the host society to adopt them (an attitude that is usually embodied by restrictive immigration legislation and discriminating employment procedures). In other words, the individual project of the immigrant is incompatible with the policies of the nation state and eventually culminates in misery, if not catastrophe.

On the one hand, through their social realist strain, these films might be said to condemn the inhumane treatment of foreign jobseekers in Western Europe and call for a change in attitudes and policies. On the other hand, however, while focusing on the migrants' 'naive' fantasies about living in the West, they seem to suggest that these immigrants would be better off staying in their own country and building a dignified existence for themselves in their place of origin. As David Clarke has convincingly argued, by centring on the immigrants' illusions rather than on the issues of local protagonists, films like these fail to confront Western audiences with their own fantasies, in particular when it comes to grasping the deficiencies of the capitalist system.[16]

[13] The film ends in a New York bar where Ewa and Jerzy accidentally meet each other. In the final scene, Ewa remarks that one cannot get 'much further to the West', after which Jerzy ironically responds 'Mal sehen' ('We'll see').

[14] See Daniela Berghahn and Claudia Sternberg, 'Locating Migrant and Diasporic Cinema in Contemporary Europe', in Berghahn & Sternberg (eds), *European Cinema in Motion*, pp. 12–49.

[15] See Loshitzky, *Screening Strangers*, p. 32.

[16] David Clarke, 'Going West: Migration and the Post-Communist World in Recent European Film', *Cultural Politics*, 2005, 1, pp. 279–94.

Turning Troublemakers into Problem Solvers

Whereas pre-1989 films tend to underline the fatality of the migration project (resulting in failure, misery or even death), the fall of Communism and the dissolution of the Eastern Bloc seem to have provoked a series of significant shifts in the on-screen image of westbound labour migration, at least as far as Polish migrant characters are concerned.[17] The storyline of Krzysztof Kieślowski's *Blanc* (*White*, 1994) can serve as an interesting frame of reference here, although the film does not deal directly with Polish labour migration. Not unlike pre-1989 films such as *Moonlighting* and *La ballata dei lavavetri*, the introductory (French) part of *Blanc* brings into view the harsh and dramatic fate of a Polish expatriate (Karol Karol) in a hostile and strange environment. Driven into divorce by his French spouse Dominique, the Polish anti-hero falls victim to a series of humiliations which destroy his life and career. Significantly, as we hear Karol Karol explain during the divorce trial in a Parisian courtroom, the break-up with his wife has been provoked by his long-lasting 'impotence'. As such, his divorce with Dominique seems to epitomize the mental and civilizational distance separating West European societies from the 'impotent' immigrants from the East (which eventually forces these newcomers to return home).[18] Significantly, however, upon his return to Poland Karol takes a crash course in capitalism and becomes a wealthy and powerful businessman, which eventually enables him to take revenge on his former French spouse.

As the ending of *Blanc* indicates, the alleged 'impotence' of Polish immigrants would soon turn out to be nothing but temporary. Highly indicative of this shift in the depiction of Polish jobseekers is the Austrian film, *Die Ameisenstrasse* (*Ant Street*, 1995), the action of which takes place in Vienna in a huge apartment building that houses a cross-section of Austrian society. Set in the first years after the fall of the Iron Curtain, the film envisions the dissolution of the old order in favour of something as yet unknown. When the owner of the building dies, the house falls

[17] See Kris Van Heuckelom, 'Polish (Im)Potence: Shifting Representations of Polish Labour Migration in Contemporary European Cinema', in Joanna Rostek and Dirk Uffelmann (eds), *Contemporary Polish Migrant Culture in Germany, Ireland, and the UK*, Frankfurt am Main, 2011, pp. 277–98.

[18] It goes without saying that the manifold symbolic layers of *Blanc* defy easy analysis and need to be discussed in their close engagement with Polish national mythology in general and the country's historically conditioned relationship with France in particular. For a detailed discussion of these elements, see Elżbieta Ostrowska and Joanna Rydzewska, 'Gendered Discourses of Nation(hood) and the West in Polish Cinema', *Studies in European Cinema*, 4, 2007, 3, pp. 187–98.

into the hands of his nephew who decides to renovate it in order to make more money out of it. Along with the arrival of an enterprising team of Polish construction workers, however, the house turns into complete chaos and anarchy. On the one hand, the cinematic portrayal of these jobseeking Poles bears obvious marks of orientalization, in the sense that they are represented as intruders from the uncivilized outskirts of Europe threatening the Old Continent's social and economic order.[19] Afraid of losing their welfare and benefits, the Austrian locals look for scapegoats and project their fears onto a group of 'thieves', the East European Other. On the other hand, however, the director of *Die Ameisenstrasse* puts much effort into showing that the ultimate decline of the Viennese house results from its immanent internal weaknesses rather than from the sudden intrusion of external forces. Most of the 'indigenous' Austrian protagonists find themselves viewed in an unfavourable light, troubled as they are by illness, solitude, strange habits, addictions and obsessions. Whereas many of the male Austrian characters descend into alcoholism or die, the Polish protagonists display a remarkable physical strength and youth. Characteristically, they eventually run off with some of the female Austrian residents, not without setting the degenerating Viennese house on fire. In short, while the old Europe is sick and dying, floods of potent young 'thieves' coming in from the former Eastern Bloc literally and symbolically precipitate its inevitable decline.

Whereas *Die Ameisenstrasse* spells out a doomed scenario for Europe after the fall of Communism, other European films that draw on the widespread 1990s trend of Polish immigrants entering Western Europe display a more optimistic and progressive view of the encounters between locals and immigrant characters. In opposition to most of the pre-1989 films, these post-Cold War films usually feature both Polish and local protagonists as lead characters and tend to envision a growing interaction between the local community and the newcomers. This manifests itself most obviously through the introduction of an inter-ethnic romance emerging between the main characters. In many cases, these labour migrants start to use their body not only in terms of physical labour, but also for the purpose of love and reproduction.[20] A second narrative thread

[19] The appearance of the work crew is followed by a plague of insects that slowly invade the tenement building and the individual apartments. Significantly, by the middle of the film, ants and other insects become the most prominent leitmotiv in the film, reappearing in various — realistic and less realistic — configurations. Both the mise-en-scène and the title of the film suggest a close link between the invading insects and the human intruders.

[20] The motif of an inter-ethnic romance is deployed, for instance, in the French films *Les*

that sets the newer films apart from the older ones is the fact that the foreign jobseekers usually act as catalysts for emotional healing and moral change within the host community. Instead of being depicted as bad guys from the periphery of Europe, these 'saving angels' from the East turn out to possess regenerative and redemptive potential with regard to the ailing host society. This is most aptly illustrated in the French TV production *Le clandestin* (*The Illegal*, 1994) which casts Zbigniew Zamachowski (the very same actor who played the impotent Karol Karol in Kieślowski's *Blanc*) in the role of a Polish construction worker. The story focuses on the friendship between this Jacek and a lonely old French lady whose husband has died and whose children and grandchildren refuse to look after her.[21] The opening scenes set the tone for the narrative function that is ascribed to the Polish character: when there is a gas leak in the old woman's apartment, she is ultimately saved from death by the freshly arrived Polish construction worker.[22]

Contrary to the pre-1989 representations, films like *Le clandestin* display a high degree of critical self-examination and focus on the personal issues of the local characters rather than on the problems of the immigrant characters. As such, the post-1989 portrayal of Polish labour migrants combines a negative (West European) self-image with a far-reaching revalorization of the (East European) Other. As it appears, this significant shift in paradigm first came to the fore in French cinema of the 1990s — in feature films such as *Les amoureux* and *Comme des rois* — and was then followed by similar developments in other European cinemas. After the turn of the millennium the device has become particularly widespread in German cinema, where 'Polish characters are introduced into German space as agents of personal rescue. After these films introduce German protagonists trapped in calcified, self-destructive behaviour patterns, Polish characters arrive on the scene to offer them a new set of options,

amoureux (*Lovers*, 1994) and *Comme des rois* (*King for a Day*, 1997), the Dutch productions *De Poolse bruid* (*The Polish Bride*, 1998) and *Polonaise* (2002) and the Scandinavian films *Fyra veckor i juni* (*Four Weeks in June*, 2004) and *Upperdog* (2009).

[21] Given the considerable difference in age, this particular film refrains from developing a love story between both protagonists. In the meantime, however, Jacek partially comes to replace the old woman's late husband (which is clearly exemplified by the fact that he starts to wear his clothes).

[22] Significantly, *Le clandestin* came out in the very same year as Krzysztof Kieslowski's *Blanc*. While both films feature Zbigniew Zamachowski in the role of a Polish immigrant, the narrative function performed by the Polish protagonist is completely different. Contrary to the impotent Karol Karol in *Blanc*, Zamachowski's character in *Le clandestin* plays the role of a diligent problem-solver with the potential to vitalize and rejuvenate the Old Continent.

usually by providing themselves as libidinal objects'.[23] Remarkably, although most of the films under discussion target specific national audiences and address domestic concerns (for instance in post-unification Germany), the available corpus displays a striking similarity as far as the narrative function of Polish migratory characters is concerned. Of course, while some productions focus on the personal problems of individual heroes or tackle the issue of disintegrating social and family structures, other films extrapolate these problems into the domain of politics and economics.[24] In most cases, however, the narrative space occupied by the Polish protagonists is demarcated in a very similar way: their fictional mission is to rejuvenate and cure the European continent.

One could ask to what extent these findings could be generalized to other East Central European ethnicities. Although research on the subject

[23] Kristin Kopp, 'Christoph Hochhäusler's *This Very Moment*: The Berlin School and the Politics of Spatial Aesthetics in the German-Polish Borderlands', in Brad Prager and Jaimey Fisher (eds), *The Collapse of the Conventional: The German Film and its Politics at the Turn of the New Century*, Detroit, MI, 2010, p. 301. German films that belong to this paradigm include *Engelchen* (*Little Angel*, 1996), *Herz im Kopf* (*Heart over Head*, 2001) and *Nachbarinnen* (*Neighbours*, 2004).

[24] The French drama, *Les amoureux*, focuses on the relationship between a French adolescent (Marc) and his half-sister Viviane who leads a loose life, hanging out with various men, until she finds stability in the arms of a Polish immigrant worker. The comedy, *Comme des rois*, offers the story of a Polish immigrant worker who poses as an Islandic film director at a French film festival and enters into a romance with a famous filmstar who is fed up with the film industry. Thanks to his disarming humour and uprightness, the actress eventually retrieves her interest in film-making and decides to pick up acting again. In the Dutch feature film, *De Poolse bruid*, the local lead character is a grumpy and antisocial single man who faces serious financial problems. Typically, through his relationship with the Polish cleaning lady Anna he learns how to put things into perspective and how to deal with his emotions. Quite similar is the case of Sandra, the female protagonist in the Swedish production, *Fyra veckor i juni*. Traumatized by a series of violent relationships with men, she develops an emotionally unstable personality with strong self-destructive tendencies. Yet, as a result of her romance with the Polish construction worker Marek (and her Jewish neighbour Lily) Sandra manages to get rid of her distrust of other people, especially men. In the German production, *Nachbarinnen*, the local protagonist is a lonely and taciturn German who has been deserted by her husband. Her Polish guest (a female bartender) helps her to regain her confidence and love for life. Another German film, *Herz im Kopf*, centres on the romance between an erratic German teenager who has just lost his mother and a Polish au pair who works in Germany. The Swedish comedy, *Blåbärskriget* (*The Blueberry War*, 2007) starts out as an underdog story about two Polish blueberry pickers who are exploited by their Swedish employer. While the film offers a very unfavourable picture of Swedish and EU politics (plagued by corruption, nepotism and power abuse), the Swedish locals eventually manage to transform a run-down holiday resort into a profitable liquor factory, mainly thanks to the inventive and creative spirit of the Polish blueberry pickers. In the Norwegian film, *Upperdog*, a labour migrant from Poland succeeds in reuniting two troubled Norwegian half-siblings who had been adopted to different families in their childhood.

is scant, individual cases seem to suggest that representatives of other — albeit less visible — migrant groups from the former Eastern Bloc have been cast in similar cinematic roles.[25] An exceptional case, however, is that of Russian characters represented in post-Cold War cinema. As Birgit Beumers has indicated, Russians rarely if ever appear as agents of change in migration narratives and are usually represented as victims.[26] As such, their narrative role seems to be quite similar to the pre-'89 cinematic portrayals of Polish immigrant workers, for whom emigration usually ends in tragedy.

'Inlanders' in a 'Free World'

As the available body of work indicates, recent British cinema adds a particular twist to the narrative threads that reappear in post-1989 cinematic portrayals of Polish immigrant workers. Particular attention should be paid to two migration-related films that came out in 2007, Ken Loach's social drama, *It's a Free World*, and Dominic Lees's migration thriller, *Outlanders*.[27] Significantly, both films begin with grey images of urban Poland — the gloomy cityscape of Katowice in *It's a Free World* and the industrial seaport landscape of the Tri-city in *Outlanders* — and bring into view male Polish immigrant characters who seek their fortune in the UK after Poland's accession to the European Union. What is more, the post-emigration part of both films is set in the very same industrial environment of East London.

To a certain extent, Loach's *It's a Free World* seems to be in line with the typical representation of Polish immigrants in other post-Cold War films, in the sense that it focuses on the personal issues of a local protagonist and the problem solving capacities of a Polish jobseeker. The film offers

[25] Some notable examples that support such a hypothesis are Barbara Albert's *Nordrand* (*Northern Skirts*) and Jasmin Dizdar's *Beautiful People* — which feature migrants from the Balkans in, respectively, Austria and the UK (see Loshitzky, *Screening Strangers*, for a discussion of both films) — and the Belgian feature film *Man zkt vrouw* (*A Perfect Match*) which focuses on the romance between a young Romanian cleaning lady and a lonely Belgian widower.

[26] Beumers, 'Through the Other Lens', pp. 173–82.

[27] Both films came into existence in more or less the same time frame and received their first public screenings in September 2007 (*Outlanders* at the Polish Film Festival in Gdynia, *It's a Free World* at the Venice Film Festival). More recent cinematic accounts of Polish labour migration to the UK are offered by *Somers Town* (2008), *Mum and Dad* (2008) and *Tortoise in Love* (2010). For a comparative analysis of *Somers Town* and *Mum and Dad*, see Joanna Rydzewska, 'Ambiguity and Change: Post-2004 Polish Migration to the UK in Contemporary British Cinema', *Journal of Contemporary European Studies*, 20, 2012, 2, pp. 215–27.

the story of a young British woman (Angie) and her friend (Rose) who establish a recruitment agency for foreign jobseekers. A single mother born and raised in a working class family, Angie stakes everything to attain a better life for herself and her son. In spite of her seemingly good intentions and her sense of justice, she eventually ends up exploiting the foreign jobseekers she initially wanted to help. One of the immigrants she employs is Karol, a kind-hearted young Pole who occasionally acts as Angie's lover. Apart from helping her in all kinds of practical matters, the Pole also serves as a problem solver on a more psychological level, in particular when he warns Angie not to put profit above people. Quite typically, the appearance of an East European protagonist who can tell right from wrong serves here to criticize the deplorable moral condition of the host society as well as to undermine the verification of the free market as a superior economic model. Dirk Uffelmann and Joanna Rostek are undoubtedly right in their claim that

> Karol is not as much voicing a Polish position, but that of his English creator: by criticising the capitalist system and urging a return to human solidarity, he turns into Ken Loach's mouthpiece (one could, in fact, speculate as to whether Karol is just coincidentally Marx's namesake). In this manner, he is functionalised as a clichéd bearer of morality and idealistic values.[28]

In a similar vein, the prominent focus on the socio-economic situation of the host society sets Loach's film apart from a pre-1989 London-set film such as *Moonlighting*, which hardly touches upon local issues and strongly privileges a Polish perspective.[29]

There is, however, an essential difference in comparison with most of the previously discussed films. In the approach adopted by Loach, the deployment of an inter-ethnic romance does not hold the promise of

[28] Joanna Rostek and Dirk Uffelman, 'Can the Polish Migrant Speak? The Representation of "Subaltern" Polish Migrants in Film, Literature and Music from Britain and Poland', in Barbara Korte, Eva Ulrike Pirker and Sissy Helff (eds), *Facing the East in the West: Images of Eastern Europe in British Literature, Film and Culture*, Amsterdam and New York, 2010, pp. 318–19.

[29] Like many other films directed by Ken Loach, *It's a Free World* might be said to bring into view the enormous impact of the Thatcherite years on the political and socio-economic landscape of Great Britain. As John Hill rightly asserts, Angie can be seen as 'an exemplary "Thatcherite" entrepreneur', counterposed to her father who represents 'an older tradition of stable employment, regulated working conditions and union representation'. John Hill, *Ken Loach: The Politics of Film and Television*, London, 2011, pp. 194–95.

transnational redemption nor does it allow for a happy ending. Unlike the local characters in, for instance, the Dutch film, *De Poolse bruid* (*The Polish Bride*), and the Swedish production, *Fyra veckor i juni* (*Four Weeks in June*) — who finally unite with their Polish partners — Angie rejects Karol's advice to drop out of the capitalist rat-race for money and eventually proceeds with her own project. Characteristically, the film ends with images of Angie looking for a cheap labour force in the capital of Ukraine, while her former lover Karol is determined to return to Poland.

From several perspectives, Dominic Lees's *Outlanders* can be seen as a remarkable complement to Loach's film. One of its lead characters is Jan Jasiński, a former Polish soccer player whose promising career is cut short by a serious injury, after which he moves to London in search of employment. Contrary to the almost angelic virtues of Karol in *It's a Free World*, Jan Jasiński is represented as a ruthless character who radically adapts to the demands and principles of a deregulated economy. As a fixer of the illegal labour force in London, he does not flinch from using violence and from taking criminal action. Involved in the trafficking of illegal immigrants into the UK, he strips these undocumented jobseekers of their passports, accommodates them in overcrowded and run-down houses and sends them to work without any documents. Reluctant to pay his employees, he reports them to the police when payday is drawing near, after which he takes on a new load of undocumented jobseekers. The spirit of lawlessness that permeates his professional activities ensues not only from the fact that he operates outside the official job market and refrains from following any kind of legal procedures (such as paying taxes, preparing contracts, taking safety measures), but also from the fact that he wears a gun and opts for violence without any hesitation (for instance when he tries to secure the money one of the building contractors owes him). Moreover, Jan Jasiński gives the impression of being untouchable, even when the police come after him and confront him with the crimes he has committed.

At first sight, the depiction of Jasiński as a ruthless criminal and exploiter may be linked to the far-reaching criminalization that often crops up around the portrayal of East European (especially Russian) 'outlanders' in contemporary Western film. However, if we juxtapose *Outlanders* with Ken Loach's *It's a Free World*, a completely different picture arises. From this perspective, Jasiński's character does not operate as an unambiguous representation of the criminal (East European) Other, but rather as a more radicalized masculine version of the British female protagonist in *It's a Free*

World. In striking accord with Jan Jasiński's fortunes, Angie's life has been marked by a series of personal and professional setbacks. A single mother who has often been deceived by her (mostly male) employers, she decides to take control and set up her own business. Not unlike Jasiński, she starts to work as a supplier of cheap (foreign) labour to the local job market. Significantly, whereas the transient pool of casual day labourers depicted in *Outlanders* and *It's a Free World* has to cope without any proper means of transportation, both Jan and Angie occupy the other end of the mobility spectrum, easily traversing London and its surroundings in motorized vehicles. While Jasiński drives a Jaguar and an SUV, Angie initially makes use of a motorbike (which she finally — when her business takes off — replaces with an expensive SUV).

Whereas Jasiński solely works with illegal labour migrants (whose trafficking he organizes), Angie initially refuses to employ undocumented jobseekers. However, determined to escape poverty and build a better life for herself and her son, she develops a feeling of being untouchable and starts to operate in a moral grey zone, gradually moving in the direction of Jasiński's cynical and selfish behaviour. At first trying to benefit from not paying taxes (although she claims otherwise in front of her employees) and from violating rental laws, she soon ventures into other realms of illegal activity (providing undocumented immigrants with false passports, recruiting Ukrainian jobseekers on a tourist visa). Just like Jasiński, she is at pains to move upward in life and shudders at the thought of returning to the deplorable situation from which she departed. Not unlike Jasiński (who reports his own workers to the police when payday is near), Angie cynically appeals to the letter of the law whenever it suits her own plans. This is most notably the case when she calls the immigration service (on behalf of 'a concerned group of citizens from a local church') and warns about the presence of undocumented immigrants at a London campsite (which would allow her to use the caravan park for her own workers). Significantly, when close friends or relatives call into question the far-reaching cynicism that underlies the behaviour of both protagonists, they react in harsh language that reveals a highly similar attitude towards the society they live in. Whereas Jan assures his younger brother Adam that 'I found out how the fucking world worked. And made it work for me', Angie turns away from her friend Rose by saying: 'It's a free world. Cos I don't give a shit. OK? Just do what you fucking want.' These striking convergences do not alter the fact, however, that Angie's attitude remains much more ambiguous (while Jasiński is depicted rather one-dimensionally as a reckless and brutal character).

As might be expected, the gender difference seems to have a considerable impact on the way both protagonists make their way in the perilous world of illegal labour. Whereas Jasiński easily and unscrupulously resorts to violence, Angie refrains from violent behaviour and eventually becomes a victim of physical maltreatment herself. These variations come to the fore most notably in a couple of additional narrative threads that both films have in common, most notably the problem of industrial accidents and the issue of payment delays on the black labour market. In terms of plotline, *Outlanders* strongly revolves around the absence of security measures on building sites: when an undocumented Belarusian immigrant worker falls from an unsecured scaffold, Jasiński decides not to call an ambulance and quickly finishes him off. *It's a Free World* in contrast does not directly show the problem of industrial accidents, but brings it up in passing when a couple of immigrant workers threaten to kidnap Angie's son and tell her about the terrible accidents that happened to some of their friends. However, the immediate reason for them to intimidate their former boss is the fact that she still owes them their wages. Significantly, Jasiński and Angie deal with such pay-related issues in different ways. At a certain point in the story, both of them try to lay hands on a considerable amount of money (in both cases £40,000) in recompense for the sub-contractor jobs their employees carried out. Whereas Jasiński uses violence to obtain his cash from the general contractor he worked for, Angie is not able to oppose her criminal debtors and does not succeed in retrieving the money, which prompts some of her immigrant workers to violent actions.

The most important difference between both films, however, is the angle from which the issue of labour migration is addressed. Whereas *It's a Free World* focuses on Angie as a recruiter of foreign labour, *Outlanders* focuses not so much on the story of labour fixer Jasiński as on the fate of his younger brother Adam. After the death of his father, Adam Jasiński leaves his Polish hometown in search of his sibling and manages to track him down in London. Significantly, while restoring the ties with the older brother he used to hero-worship, Adam almost immediately succumbs to his influence and quickly adopts some aspects of his behaviour and lifestyle. Adam's swift transformation from a freshly arrived foreign jobseeker into an 'inlander' finds expression in a series of narrative details. Not only is he urged by his brother to talk English from the very start, he soon makes his appearance in more tidy clothes (a shirt and a leather jacket, just like his brother usually wears). Moreover, while being initiated in the peculiarities of his brother's profession and lifestyle, Adam quickly changes his transportation habits and starts using his brother's cars. In the meantime, he unwittingly becomes an accomplice to his brother's dubious professional occupations, most notably when Adam agrees to dump his brother's Jaguar (in the boot of which Jasiński has hidden the corpse of the deceased Belarusian immigrant worker). Disagreements between both siblings rise to the surface when Adam begins to entertain serious doubts about his brother's immoral and reckless behaviour.

As such, the function of Adam in the storyline of *Outlanders* is quite similar to the position of Angie's friend Rose in the narrative space of *It's a Free World*. Both of them are taken in by their energetic companions and get involved in the hazardous business of foreign labour force recruitment. At a certain point, each one of them is faced with the choice of either following their moral sense and dropping out of business or sticking to their respective partners. Significantly, in both cases, the resolution of this dilemma is linked to the appearance of a third protagonist, from the 'outside', who puts the moral sense of the local characters to the test. If Angie's lover Karol performs this narrative role in *It's a Free World*, then Dominic Lees casts an undocumented female Russian (Anna) in the role of such a 'moral' agent. What is more, the British-Polish romance that unfolds in *It's a Free World* (Angie and Karol) is mirrored by the emergence of a similar Polish-Russian romance (between Adam Jasiński and Anna) in *Outlanders*.

In more general terms, the underlying narrative structure of both films displays striking similarities. Whereas *It's a Free World* features two British leading characters (Angie and Rose) and one Polish protagonist (Karol), *Outlanders* features two Polish protagonists (Jan and Adam) and a female immigrant character from Russia (Anna). Although there are significant shifts in gender and ethnicity, the narrative roles these protagonists perform neatly correspond. The main difference between both films is the fact that *Outlanders* — with its narrative focus on two London-based Poles — strongly engages with the shifted position of Polish migrants within the European Union's sociocultural space: the Poles now occupy the position of locals, whereas the role of 'outlander' is assigned to an illegal immigrant from outside Fortress Europe. Significantly, it is the 'outlander' who calls into question the ruthless and immoral behaviour of the Polish locals and forces them to make a choice between right and wrong, just as Karol does in Ken Loach's *It's a Free World*.

From 'Outlander' to 'Inlander'

As *Outlanders* seems to suggest, the post-enlargement period has filtered out a new set of 'outlanders': those who are excluded from the process of European integration and lack the means and permission to 'migrate' legally, such as Russians, Belarusians and Ukrainians. What is more, the film reflects this shifting geopolitical reality in the way it depicts the interaction between British, Polish and Russian characters and reveals the symbolic hierarchy of different ethnic groups in London. Poles are now identified as equal partners within Europe's new political and economic space, at least in strictly legal terms. For Ukrainians, Russians and Belarusians, on the contrary, the borders of 'Fortress Europe' still stand. Jan Jasiński's position as an 'inlander' is underlined by a series of narrative threads: he speaks English fluently and refuses to speak Polish with his brother, he collaborates on a daily basis with two British companions and has quickly adapted to the British way of life. Also, whereas many migration films focus on the difficulties involved in human trafficking and border crossing, the opening scenes of *Outlanders* emphasize the non-problematic character of Adam Jasiński's travel to the UK. Characteristically, the depiction of his arrival in London abounds in touristic snapshots and postcard images of the British capital. Adam's status as a 'scopophilic' touristic spectator (rather than an undocumented jobseeker) stands in sharp contrast with the migratory trajectory of a Belarusian immigrant he meets on his first day in London (the very same immigrant who will later die in the scaffold accident). Similar divergences arise in the relationship between Adam and Anna and the way they experience urban space. Afraid of being caught by the Immigration Office, the Russian woman puts much effort into concealing her position as a non-Schengen resident (for instance by wearing a T-shirt with the inscription, 'LITHUANIA'). This also explains why she is reluctant to consume and enjoy the touristic landmarks that surround her and why she prefers to focus on her job in a late-night burger van. Her perilous status as an 'outlander' comes to the fore most explicitly when the Immigration Office organizes a raid on one of the building sites and Adam rescues her from being arrested. Moreover, whereas Adam and his brother occupy a luxurious apartment with a view of the City and traverse the wide London area in motorized vehicles, Anna lives in a run-down caravan on the street and always moves on foot. Finally, the Schengen border also leaves its symbolic marks on the space these immigrants occupy in their private time. Whereas Jan and Adam frequent a trendy bar popular among locals, the Russian immigrants (Anna and her uncle, among others) attend a cheap joint frequented by immigrant workers. In short, the touristy glamour of London with its desirable downtown locations is completely absent from the daily life of these characters.

Ken Loach's *It's a Free World*, in contrast to Lees's *Outlanders*, far less explicitly engages with the shifted position of Poles in the post-accession period. Over the course of the film, there are but a few allusions to the fact that the status of Polish immigrant workers has changed in recent years.[30] Undoubtedly, Karol's relation to space, housing and mobility in *It's a Free World* strongly differs from the 'inlander' behaviour of the Jasiński brothers and rather reminds the viewer of the unprivileged socio-economic position taken up by Anna in *Outlanders*. Remarkably, there is one particular scene that highlights the equal position of Karol and Anna in an absolutely literal way. In both films, the inter-ethnic romance reaches its climax in a love scene that is set in the immigrant's caravan. In each case, crossing the caravan's threshold functions not solely as an entry into the space of physical and sexual intimacy, but also as an ingression into the domestic realm of the ethnic outsider. Significantly, whereas Karol lures Angie inside by offering her a 'typical Polish speciality', Anna asks Adam to undress on the threshold of the caravan because this is a 'tradition at home'.

The particular triangular relationships that unfold in both *It's a Free World* and *Outlanders* allow for further comparative analysis. In both cases, the central moral dilemma revolves around the question as to whether personal well-being and attachment to family bonds can take precedence over the well-being of others (in this case foreign jobseekers). In *It's a Free World*, this applies in particular to Angie's inclination to subordinate the fate of other people to her personal interests and to the material comfort of herself and her son. In *Outlanders*, similar ideas come to the fore when Jan Jasiński voices his concerns about Adam's well-being ('I won't have my own brother work as a lumb') and expresses his desire to pursue a better destiny for his younger brother, just as Angie tries to secure a better life for her son. In both cases, the emerging inter-ethnic romance confronts the local protagonists with the ultimate choice between

[30] This is exemplified, for instance, in a conversation between Angie and one of her business partners who complains about the Polish jobseekers he hired from her. Now that they have official papers and are allowed to work legally, he contends, they are becoming more assertive and refuse to keep their heads down instead of just working: 'Yeah, these fucking new Poles. They are doing my nut, man. I swear, bring me back to the old days. No complaints. They kept their heads down and kept that fucking quiet. Now they have got a bit of paper, they think they own the joint.'

love and blood. Angie's rejection of Karol's proposals (both as a lover and as an emotional adviser) epitomizes her — albeit halfhearted — choice for the second option ('I honestly really wish I met you another time', are the final words she shares with Karol). Angie's friend Rose, on the other hand, turns out to be more susceptible to Karol's critique and finally breaks with her ambitious business partner. In *Outlanders*, not Jan — whose return to the right path is represented as a lost cause — but Adam Jasiński is the person who is put in a moral dilemma. If he refuses to help the police in finding and arresting his brother, the Immigration Office will send his Russian partner back to Russia. Influenced by Anna's attempts to foster his ethical awareness ('Your brother is a man. He can decide what he does'), his decision to side with her and not with his brother bears remarkable resemblance to Rose's rupture with Angie in *It's a Free World*. Just like Adam in *Outlanders*, Rose voices her deep concern about the fact that Angie keeps pushing things further and further. In both films, the protagonist's reckless behaviour leads to a feeling of estrangement from their immediate relatives and friends. During a police interrogation at the very end of *Outlanders*, Adam voices his feelings about his brother in the following way: 'I don't know much about him. I don't know him anymore. Don't know if I ever did.' Significantly, Rose uses very similar phrasings in her final conversation with Angie (right after she reported on the illegal campsite). Asked by Rose if there is 'anything you won't do', Angie frankly responds, 'I don't know. Probably not, no', after which Rose concludes: 'I don't know you anymore.'

In view of the recurring representation of Polish immigrants as catalysts for emotional and moral change in post-1989 European cinema, a comparative analysis of *It's a Free World* and *Outlanders* points in the direction of a model of ethnic succession: Polish characters are gradually climbing up the social ladder within Fortress Europe, getting rid of their label of prototypical labour immigrants, whereas the empty space is taken up by immigrants from outside the Schengen zone.[31] As both films attest, non-EU countries such as Ukraine or Russia may very well become the new suppliers of labour migrants on film screens across Europe. Significantly, *It's a Free World* begins with images of a job market in Katowice, Poland, and closes with a quite similar scene of labour force recruitment in Kiev, Ukraine. In a somewhat similar vein, the 2003 German film, *Lichter* (*Distant Lights*, 2003), focuses on the desperate attempts of Ukrainian

[31] Compare Golab, 'Stellaaaaaa', and Bukowczyk, 'The Big Lebowski', on the issue of 'ethnic succession' in cinematic portrayals of Polish Americans.

jobseekers to cross the German-Polish border. *Outlanders* in turn presents an interesting shift in the post-Cold War representation of Russian immigrants. On the one hand, the film literally confirms the clichéd image of Russian protagonists in post-1989 foreign film ('Russians are trouble', Jan Jasiński exclaims at one point). On the other hand, however, through the very fact that the catalyst function previously fulfilled by Polish immigrant workers is now taken over by a Russian character, *Outlanders* breaks with the tradition of criminalizing or victimizing Russian immigrant protagonists and casts them in a more active and positive cinematic role.

New Londoners through the Polish Lens

If we were to attribute a moral judgement to the behaviour of the Polish protagonists in *Outlanders* and *It's a Free World*, Jan Jasiński and Karol would occupy the opposite ends of the spectrum. Whereas Jan Jasiński is portrayed as corrupted by the materialist West, Karol, in contrast, comes to the conclusion that the emperor is wearing no clothes. Bereft of his dreams, he abandons the West as an object of desire in favour of a moderate, but honest existence in his home country. The opposite fate of these two protagonists gains additional relevance and significance if we compare their cinematic treatment with on-screen representations of Polish immigrants aimed at Polish audiences and authored by Polish directors, in particular the series, *Londyńczycy* (*Londoners*), aired on Polish public television in 2008 and 2009. This high-budget serial follows the fates of a group of Polish immigrants working and living in London in the post-accession period.[32]

Remarkably, there is a significant overlap in the on-screen talent involved in the production of *Londyńczycy* and the two British films under discussion. In fact, two of the major male parts in the serial were performed by Przemysław Sadowski (Jan Jasiński from *Outlanders*) and Lesław Żurek (Karol from *It's a Free World*). At first sight, the first episodes of *Londyńczycy* might be said to cast both actors in a role quite similar to the role they performed in the aforementioned UK productions. Darek Michalski (Przemysław Sadowski) runs a London building company,

[32] See Joanna Rostek, 'Living the British Dream: Polish Migration to the UK as Depicted in the TV Series *Londyńczycy* (2008–2010)', in Joanna Rostek and Dirk Uffelmann (eds), *Contemporary Polish Migrant Culture in Germany, Ireland, and the UK*, Frankfurt am Main, 2011, pp. 245–75, and Joanna Rydzewska, '"Great Britain, Great Expectations": The Representation of Polish Migration to Great Britain in Londynczycy/Londoners', *Critical Studies in Television*, 6, 2011, 2, pp. 127–40.

whereas Andrzej Koryn (Lesław Żurek) is one of his crew members.[33] In a variety of ways, however, both actors' appearance in *Londyńczycy* adds a particular twist to the roles they performed in the British films under discussion and — more particularly — to the function of inter-ethnic romances in many European films that feature Polish immigrant characters.

Interestingly, whereas many of the aforementioned European films construct a fantasy of transnational unity and community formation through heterosexual coupling, the picture that arises from *Londyńczycy* is quite different. Although some of the Polish lead characters have short love affairs with representatives of the host community they all seem to be destined to end up in a relationship with a Polish partner. Characteristically, the final episode of the first season ends with the announcement of the engagement between two of the Polish protagonists (Darek Michalski and his girlfriend Mariola). This device becomes even clearer in the second season, which closes with a double Polish wedding in a London church: both Darek (Jan Jasiński from *Outlanders*) and Andrzej (Karol from *It's a Free World*) get married to their respective Polish fiancées. Remarkably, if we take into account all the lead characters featured in the final season of *Londyńczycy*, at least four Polish couples make their appearance (and not a single Polish-British couple). This narrative approach seems to be in line with recurring elements of Polish patriotism and community formation that are woven into the storyline of both seasons of *Londyńczycy*.

[33] To a certain extent, one could claim that the Polish TV serial resumes and develops a couple of narrative threads that have been introduced by the screenplay writers of *It's a Free World* and *Outlanders*. An interesting case in point is offered by the acting career of Lesław Żurek. He made his first screen appearance in the 2005 Polish film, *Oda do radości* (*Ode to Joy*), which focuses on the fate of three young Poles who eventually decide to move to the UK. While suggesting that Ken Loach must have seen this film before casting Żurek in the role of Karol, Ewa Mazierska has justly remarked that *Oda do wolności* can be seen as a prefiguration of the part Lesław Zurek came to play in *It's a Free World*. See Ewa Mazierska, 'In Search of Freedom, Bread and Self-fulfilment: A Short History of Polish Emigrants in Fictional Film', in Kathy Burrell (ed.), *Polish Migration to the UK in the 'New' European Union*, Farnham and Burlington, VT, 2009, pp. 107–25. In a similar vein, *Londyńczycy* can be seen as a narrative follow-up to *It's a Free World*. Just like Karol in *It's a Free World*, Andrzej decides to quit his London job and return to Poland. His remigration, however, turns out to be only temporary. After discovering that his former girlfriend ran off with all the money he earned in the UK he goes back to London and starts again from scratch. The very fact that he sets up his own business in London, a successful Polish catering service that distributes food among the many Polish immigrant workers in the UK, can be seen as a subtle allusion to the role of Karol in *It's a Free World*. In his final conversation with Angie, Karol refers to two of his friends who have decided to start a business in London, but instead of joining them, he prefers to go back to Poland (one of the elements he seems to miss in England being Polish food).

Whenever conflicts occur within the Polish community in London, the makers of the serial put much effort in showing that these conflicts and problems need to be resolved and that cooperation between emigrants is much more effective than competition. A key role is granted here to the lead character played by Lesław Żurek (Andrzej Koryn) who repeatedly fulfils the function of a problem solver within the Polish community and gradually becomes the local Polish hero. Therefore, with its strong focus on the protective community spirit that pervades the Polish migrant circles in post-accession London, the serial differs from 'tragic' pre-1989 films such as *Moonlighting* which bring into view the marginalization and degradation of Poles living in a foreign and hostile environment. In the meanwhile, contrary to the post-'89 cinematic exposure of romances between locals and Poles and the desired problem-solving capacities of the latter, one might say that in *Londyńczycy* the problem-solving potency of the Polish characters is expected to have a redemptive impact on the Polish migrant community itself rather than on the host community. As such, the particular role these immigrant characters come to play in the Polish migration narrative seems to be a compromise between the extremes that have been played out in recent British cinema. Jan Jasiński from *Outlanders* — an immigrant who easily defies his Polish roots and cynically adjusts to the British way of life — and the angel-like Karol from *It's a Free World* — who refuses to become part of this immoral system and eventually returns to Poland — are replaced in *Londyńczycy* by two positive immigrant heroes who succeed in realizing their dreams outside of their home country, in the meantime remaining attached to their fatherland and their countrymen.

Finally, the remarkable differences separating foreign cinematic responses to Polish labour migration from domestic ones also come to the fore in the particular Polish reception of UK productions such as *It's a Free World* and *Outlanders*. Its most significant manifestation are the titles both films have been given in Poland. Ken Loach's film, to begin with, received screenings in Poland under the title *Polak potrzebny od zaraz* (*Pole Needed Immediately*). If the original title aptly reflects the central position of the British character Angie in the storyline (the phrase 'It's a free world' being a quote taken from one of her conversations with her associate and friend Rose), then the Polish equivalent explicitly shifts focus to the role performed by immigrant workers in the film, especially the Polish protagonist Karol. Dominic Lees's *Outlanders* in turn has been released in Poland under the title *Londyńczyk* (*Londoner*), which is an obvious allusion to the Polish TV serial, *Londyńczycy*.[34] If the English title foregrounds the marginalized position of undocumented 'outlanders' in British society, then the Polish title clearly shifts focus to the migrant fate of 'Londoner' Jan Jasiński. In both cases, these significant changes neatly reflect the different narrative function contemporary Polish labour migration performs within Poland and abroad. Foreign film-makers tend to deploy Polish immigrant characters in films that envision the changes in Europe's socio-political space in the aftermath of the fall of Communism, while perceiving these newcomers from Poland as bearers of qualities and virtues the Old Europe seems to have lost. The makers of *Londyńczycy* in turn serve a domestic Polish agenda: while presenting Polish labour migration to the UK as a story of success, they refrain from developing a successful transnational love story and smuggle subtle elements of patriotism and nationalism into the storyline of the serial.

Conclusion

A diachronic survey of the on-screen treatment of Polish immigrant workers across Europe allows the discovery of trends which would remain invisible if we focus on a single film or films from one national cinema. If the pre-1989 narratives mostly deal with migrants who are not able to adapt to the new environment of a foreign country, then the portrayal of migrants has significantly changed after the fall of Communism. Over the past two decades, film-makers from a variety of European countries have increasingly engaged with the changing hierarchies on Europe's mental and geopolitical map in the aftermath of the Cold War, not the least by projecting onto the screen images of transnational conciliation. More often than not, the image of a troubled host society receives a counterbalance in the depiction of dynamic and vigorous newcomers from the East who possess the potential to rejuvenate the Old Continent and restore its disintegrating social and moral frameworks (which often goes hand in hand with the deployment of an inter-ethnic love story). This trend interestingly deviates from the aura of victimization and criminalization that tends to surround migrant characters from Russia in post-Cold War European cinema.

As the available body of films attests, the recent on-screen treatment of Polish jobseekers to the UK is indicative of another significant geopolitical

[34] Although *Outlanders* was made earlier than *Londyńczycy*, the Polish DVD edition of the film was released almost a year after the TV screening of the final episode of the serial's second season.

shift in European cinema, setting undocumented jobseekers apart from those with an EU passport. A detailed comparative analysis of Ken Loach's *It's a Free World* and Dominic Lees's *Outlanders* points to the existence of specific ethnic hierarchies in the cinematic portrayal of immigrants from the former Soviet sphere of influence. Whereas Loach employs a Polish immigrant as an agent of potential redemption and moral healing, the storyline of *Outlanders* grants moral authority to a Russian immigrant character, while casting Polish immigrant workers in the role of locals. By contrast, the Polish TV serial, *Londyńczycy*, adds a particular twist to the problems that are at stake in foreign cinematic responses to Polish labour migration (not the least because of the significant overlap in cast with British productions such as *It's a Free World* and *Outlanders*). Instead of creating fantasies of transnational redemption and conciliation through heterosexual coupling, the Polish narrative envisions the beneficial potency of immigrant characters who succeed in becoming successful entrepreneurs on British soil but remain attached — at least in matrimonial terms — to their Polish roots and their fellow migrants.

In more general terms, the research presented in this article exemplifies the need for comparative and diachronic approaches in the study of European migration cinema (and migration cinema at large). As Yosefa Loshitzky has convincingly shown, going beyond the confines of national cinemas allows us to uncover a series of common tropes, motifs and metaphors characterizing the cinematic treatment of much debated issues such as displacement, exile and migration.[35] Notwithstanding the fact that such a transnational perspective should not exclude in-depth interpretations of individual films, future research into European migration film is likely to benefit from a more geographically diversified and diachronic approach to cinematic representations of Europe's changing sociocultural space in the aftermath of the Cold War. Undoubtedly, as the particular case of Polish labour migration indicates, such a historicized and contextualized perspective will allow us to expose in more detail the fluid fault-lines and changing hierarchies on the continent's mental map in the post-1989 era.

[35] See Loshitzky, *Screening Strangers*.

The Intertwining of Religion and Nationhood in Interwar Yugoslavia: The School Celebrations of St Sava's Day

PIETER TROCH

THE relation between nation and religion has been understood in seemingly antithetical ways by nationalist and religious thinkers alike. Explicitly secular national ideologies relegate religion to a marginal aspect of national identity, although they rarely discard and remove religion completely. On the other side of the nationalist spectrum, religion often serves to sacralize the nation, either through the opportunistic use of religious figures or rituals in national ideologies, or in confessional definitions of the nation in which a dominant confessional identity becomes nearly identical with the nation itself.[1] Religious thinkers have repudiated nationhood as incompatible with the universalistic claims of religion, but the organizational and discursive aspects of religion too have been nationalized.[2] Such varying degrees of intertwining of nation and religion indicate the overlap of both phenomena as analogous categories of social, cultural and political identification and organization. However, with Rogers Brubaker I maintain that overlap implies intertwining but not identity: 'Even when the languages [of nationalism and religion] are intertwined, the fundamental ontologies and structures of justification

Pieter Troch recently obtained a PhD in East-European Languages and Cultures at Ghent University. Research for this article was carried out with the support of the Research Foundation – Flanders.

[1] James C. Kennedy, 'Religion, Nation and European Representation of the Past', in Stefan Berger and Chris Lorenz (eds), *The Contested Nation: Ethnicity, Class, Religion and Gender in National Histories*, Basingstoke and New York, 2008, pp. 104–34 (pp. 109–27).

[2] Rogers Brubaker, 'Religion and Nationalism: Four Approaches', *Nations and Nationalism*, 18, 2012, 1, pp. 2–20 (pp. 11–12).

differ.'[3] These fundamentally different lines of reasoning in nationalist and religious thinking explain the diverging understandings of the relation between the two.

The close intertwining of religion and nationhood is a prominent feature of modernity in Eastern Europe. The fragmentation in autocephalous churches in Orthodox Christianity became a crucial storage of symbolic material for nation-building in the modern period and promoted a strong symbiosis of religious and national traditions. This has come to expression in the sacralization of the nation, that is, the use of religious symbols in nationalist ideologies, and in the nationalization of religion, that is, the adoption of nationalist discourse in adaptations of religious thinking to modernity.[4] This bidirectional symbiosis also applies for many non-Orthodox communities in Central and Eastern Europe, regardless of the more international organization of the religious institutions in question.[5] This article seeks to transcend a mere descriptive account by examining how the intertwining of various religious and national categories of social identification and organization is continuously shaped and reshaped within the context of the nationalizing state. I shall look specifically at interwar Yugoslavia and argue that the appropriation of religious categories of identification by the nationalizing state had a fundamental impact on the relations between religion and nationhood.

The availability of alternative categories of collective identification alongside that of the aspired nation-state, amongst which region, nation and religion stand out, was a common feature of all nationalizing states after the First World War in Central and Eastern Europe. In that regard the following study of the intertwining between religion and nationhood within the context of the Yugoslav nationalizing state is of broader comparative relevance for the entire region. The case of the Kingdom of Serbs, Croats

[3] Ibid., pp. 16–17.

[4] For the sacralization of the nation in the nationalizing policy of the Bulgarian nation-state, see Claudia Weber, *Auf der Suche nach der Nation. Erinneringskultur in Bulgarien von 1878–1944*, Berlin, 2006. For the adoption of elements of contemporary secular Serbian nationalism by Serbian clergy in South Hungary during the late nineteenth century, see Bojan Aleksov, *Religious Dissent between the Modern and the National*, Wiesbaden, 2006, pp. 165–79. For a comparison of national saints in Serbian, Macedonian and Bulgarian nationalist programmes, see Stefan Rohdewald, 'Sava, Ivan von Rila und Kliment von Ohrid. Heilige in nationalen Diensten Serbiens, Bulgariens und Makedoniens', in Stefan Samerski (ed.), *Die Renaissance der Nationalpatrone in Ostmitteleuropa im 20./21. Jahrhundert*, Cologne, Weimar and Vienna, 2007, pp. 182–217.

[5] See the various case-studies in Martin Schulze Wessel (ed.), *Nationalisierung der Religion und Sakralisierung der Nation im östlichen Europa*, Stuttgart, 2006.

and Slovenes (from 1929 the Kingdom of Yugoslavia) is particularly instructive because it involves the intertwining of different religions with various categories of national identity. With regard to the national question, the idea of Yugoslav national unity was the central ideology that underpinned the interwar Yugoslav state, but it was understood in varying ways by different political and cultural actors. Especially controversial was the relation between the Yugoslav and Serbian, Croatian and Slovenian categories of national identification. In the Yugoslav national discourse of the period Serbs, Croats and Slovenes were called the three 'tribes' (*pleme*) of the Yugoslav nation. This term indicates an intermediary level of collective identity between the national (Yugoslav) — to which political claims are attached — and the regional — to which no claims for the political organization of the state are attached. The specific relevance of these intermediary 'tribal' identities for the organization of politics and culture was disputed throughout the period under scrutiny.[6]

As a result of the instability and polarization of political rule during the 1920s the specific understanding of the Yugoslav idea remained vague and its institutionalization limited. This changed with the Royal Dictatorship established by King Alexander on 6 January 1929 and the pseudo-parliamentary and authoritarian successor system installed in September 1931. During this period the idea of integral Yugoslavism served as the central principle behind the organization of politics and culture. Essentially, this idea recognized sub-national Serbian, Croatian and Slovenian categories within the Yugoslav nation, but argued that the corresponding sub-national identities could no longer play a role in the political and cultural life of Yugoslavia.[7] After the assassination of King Alexander in October 1934 and the formation of a new government under Milan Stojadinović in June 1935, the authoritarian character of government was relaxed and the Serbian, Croatian and Slovenian categories of social and cultural identification were gradually re-introduced into the state's nationalities policy. The agreement on Croatian autonomy of August 1939, finally, marked a turn towards a more civic and supranational understanding of Yugoslav unity, in the sense of the state unity of clearly

[6] When paraphrasing the national ideology of the period I use the term 'tribe' to indicate the specific position of Serbs, Croats and Slovenes within the framework of Yugoslavism.

[7] Ljubodrag Dimić, *Kulturna politika u Kraljevini Jugoslavije*, 3 vols, Belgrade, 1996–97, 1, pp. 274–328; Dejan Djokić, '(Dis)integrating Yugoslavia: King Alexander and Interwar Yugoslavism', in idem (ed.), *Yugoslavism: Histories of a Failed Idea, 1918–1992*, London, 2003, pp. 135–56.

different constituent nations. It was accompanied by sub-Yugoslav national delineations that signalled the failure of the integral Yugoslav policy of the Royal Dictatorship.

* * *

An additional complicating factor for proponents of Yugoslav national unity in the period, beside the relation between the Serbian, Croatian and Slovenian 'tribes' and the Yugoslav nation, was the question of how the religious diversity of Muslim, Catholic and Orthodox South Slavs could be reconciled with Yugoslav national unity. Schematically, there were three possible routes to answer this question. First, national unity could be safeguarded by the religious unification of the Yugoslavs. In an article in the Zagreb-based, pro-Yugoslav and liberally orientated *Nova Evropa*, the publicist Milutin Jakšić argued that it was natural for a nation to belong to one state and one religion. For Jakšić the Yugoslav nation was given, the religious division among them was external and superficial and had to be brought in line with Yugoslav national unity. Whereas the Serbian Orthodox Church had managed to obtain national autonomy, the Yugoslav Catholics were still subjected to the Pope in Rome, which was counterproductive for the Yugoslav national case. The solution, according to Jakšić, would be the establishment of an autonomous Yugoslav Catholic Church, which could then bring about the unification of the Yugoslav Christian Church.[8]

Another possible way to reconcile religious diversity with Yugoslav national unity was to detach modern and secular national unity from religious affiliation. This line of thinking was evident in some schematic Yugoslav programmes published in *Nova Evropa* in the immediate post-war period. These argued that 'tribal' and religious identities were remnants of past times which should immediately be replaced by a modern Yugoslav national culture with no place for religious fanaticism or traditionalism. In a 1924 article the publicist Jovo Zubović explicitly interpreted every form of clericalism as a problem for Yugoslav national unity. In his opinion, the unification of the Yugoslav churches was a naive solution for this problem, much more realistic was the rationalization of religion: 'We have to get rid of the idea of miracles, the supernatural or fate and we have to push people to life and earth, where they live by their free will within the boundaries

8 Milutin Jakšić, 'Uloga crkve u ujedinjenoj državi', *Nova Evropa*, 7, 1923, 1, pp. 1–6.

of natural and human laws.'[9] For Zubović religious diversity was not a real problem because religion in general would become irrelevant in the fundamentally modern and secular Yugoslav nation he had in mind. In his monumental *Karakterologija Jugoslovena* (*Characterology of the Yugoslavs*, 1939), one of the most prominent products of interwar Yugoslav national thinking, the philosopher Vladimir Dvorniković refuted claims that religious diversity was the most important hindrance for Yugoslav national unification:

> The faith of the Yugoslavs too will become more and more a case and problem of the personal spiritual life, and less and less a Balkan-oriental external characteristic of tribal totemism.[10]

Unlike Zubović, Dvorniković explicitly recognized the constituent place of religiosity in Yugoslav national identity but refuted its institutional diversification. In other words, for Dvorniković the problem was not religion as such, but the specific institutionalization of religion among the Yugoslavs.

A third possible approach installed religious tolerance as a crucial aspect of Yugoslav national identity. In fact, this was a compromise between the two lines of reasoning outlined above, as it preserved religious identity and institutions as crucial components of the Yugoslav nation and society, but at the same time avoided religious exclusiveness by highlighting the parallel national character of Yugoslav Catholicism, Orthodoxy and Islam, and their corresponding institutions. It was this reasoning that was systematically promoted by the Yugoslav state authorities after the establishment of the dictatorship. On 14 March 1929 Minister of Religious Affairs Dragiša Cvetković argued that the separation of church and state was 'not yet taken into consideration' and that

> it was the patriotic duty of all religions in the Kingdom to unite all their spiritual and wise strengths towards the quick consolidation of the State, to assist the unification process of soul and heart, to spread peace and love between citizens and to make even and fill all gaps which centuries have created between brethren of the same blood and language.[11]

9 Jovo Zubović, 'Jugoslovenski čovek', *Nova Evropa*, 10, 1924, 6, pp. 145–56 (p. 153).

10 Vladimir Dvorniković, *Karakterologija Jugoslovena*, Belgrade, 2000, p. 973.

11 Quoted in Ljubodrag Dimić, Nikola Žutić and Blagoje Isailović (eds), *Zapisnici sa sednica Ministarskog saveta Kraljevine Jugoslavije 1929–1931*, Belgrade, 2002, p. 50.

In other words, instead of the typical East-European model of one national church per nation, all Yugoslav religions were conceived as parallel national churches.

Crucially, the Yugoslav state authorities focused on nation and state, religion being only a means toward national and state unity. In order to guarantee that religious institutions would carry out their patriotic duty the government established a strict legal framework which regulated the relation between religious institutions and the nation-state, as well as inter-confessional relations. In the course of 1929–31 the Royal Dictatorship adopted a number of laws and regulations for the Serbian Orthodox Church, the Islamic Religious Community, the Jewish Community, Reformed Churches and Evangelical Churches. The Concordat with the Roman Catholic Church, for which negotiations had started in 1925 but which was finally only signed in 1935 and submitted to parliament for ratification in 1937, was the last step in this process. However, the ratification of the Concordat provoked fierce protests from leaders and supporters of the Serbian Orthodox Church, and Stojadinović's government was finally forced to withdraw the question from parliamentary procedure.[12]

* * *

The Concordat crisis not only revolved around disputes between religious institutions and the state, but also around inter-religious, especially Orthodox-Catholic, polarizations and indicates the eventual failure of the state's policy on religious diversity. The crisis also illustrates a broader complication of the intertwining between Yugoslavism and religious thinking in Yugoslavia. During the 1920s Catholic, Orthodox and Muslim religious thinkers had adopted a rather ambiguous position toward the Yugoslav state and national idea. Although the religious diversity and cultural, institutional and political novelties associated with the new state generated defensive fears and anxieties, many religious thinkers in fact deployed the language of Yugoslav nationhood in support of their religious agendas. The Croatian Catholic Movement strove for Catholic activism and rallied clergy and laypersons behind the rechristianization of society. A relatively strong wing in this movement, represented by the Seniory, an association of Croatian Catholic lay intellectuals that served as the executive branch of the Croatian Catholic Movement, and the

[12] Klaus Buchenau, *Auf russischen Spuren. Orthodoxe Antiwestler in Serbien, 1850–1945*, Wiesbaden, 2011, pp. 409–36.

Croatian Popular Party, the political party which spearheaded Catholic activism, made use of Yugoslav national discourse to pursue this agenda.[13] The Yugoslav idea allowed Bosnian Muslim elites to demand the equal position in culture, religious affairs and politics of Bosnian/South Slav Muslims as a constituent group within the Yugoslav nation, and to circumvent the thorny and internally divisive question of the Serbian or Croatian affiliation of South Slav Muslims. As Xavier Bougarel has aptly put it, 'in the 1920s, "Yugoslavism" represented a framework within which the Bosnian Muslim elites could reproduce their "neo-*millet*" strategy, while remaining ambiguous about their national affiliation'.[14] In other words, the Yugoslav national idea was deployed to pursue the religious and political togetherness of South Slav Muslims and to guarantee their rights within the Yugoslav nation-state. Serbian Orthodox thinkers, finally, enthusiastically embraced the Yugoslav national discourse of the 1920s, but at the same time retained a Serbian Orthodox ontology. They considered the Yugoslav nation-state as the framework within which the church's internal organization could be consolidated and as an expansion of their working terrain.[15]

During the Royal Dictatorship Yugoslav religious thinkers and institutions increasingly turned away from Yugoslavism. The Yugoslav strand in the Croatian Catholic Movement was completely outshone by the Croatian political nationalism of the Croatian Peasant Party, the undisputed political representative of the Croats in interwar Yugoslavia, which developed into a Croatian national mass movement. After the ban on political parties during King Alexander's Royal Dictatorship the Catholic Church became a Croatian national *Ersatz* medium, and

[13] Mark Biondich, 'Radical Catholicism and Fascism in Croatia', *Totalitarian Movements and Political Religions*, 8, 2007, 2, pp. 383–99 (pp. 384–85); Klaus Buchenau, 'Katholizismus und Jugoslawismus. Zur Nationalisierung der Religion bei der Kroaten', in Hartmutt Lehmann and Michael Geyer (eds), *Religion und Nation, Nation und Religion. Beiträge zu einer unbewältigten Geschichte*, Göttingen, 2006, pp. 225–54 (pp. 229–33); Jure Krišto, 'Katoličko priklanjanje ideologiji jugoslavenstva', *Časopis za suvremenu povijest*, 24, 1992, 2, pp. 25–45; Zlatko Matijević, 'Politika katoličkog jugoslavenstva', in Hans-Georg Fleck and Igor Graovac (eds), *Dijalog povijesničara-istoričara*, 11 vols, 1998–present, 1, pp. 155–70.

[14] Xavier Bougarel, 'Farewell to Ottoman Legacy? Islamic Reformism and Revivalism in Bosnia-Herzegovina', in Nathalie Clayer and Eric Germain (eds), *Islam in Inter-War Europe*, London, 2008, pp. 313–43 (p. 340). In the Ottoman Empire the *millet* system provided religious, educational and judicial autonomy to non-Muslim confessional communities.

[15] Maria Falina, 'Pyrrhic Victory: East Orthodox Christianity, Politics and Serbian Nationalism in the Interwar Period', unpublished PhD dissertation, Central European University, 2011, pp. 89–100.

Catholic opposition against the state authorities increasingly concurred with political and cultural Croatian opposition against the Yugoslav state authorities.[16] Serbian Orthodoxy was firmly linked to Serbian nationhood through the ideas of *Svetosavlje*, named after St Sava, a prominent saint of the Orthodox Church in Serb-populated lands, whom I shall discuss in more detail below. Although the diverse cluster of ideas grouped under the term *Svetosavlje* included anti-Western, anti-secular, anti-modernist as well as modernist elements, the interpretation of St Sava as the fundament and embodiment of the Serbian national Church and sacred nation signals a turn to a one church-one nation model, away from the coexistence of the Yugoslav and Serbian categories of national identity in the thinking on Serbian Orthodoxy.[17] In the second half of the 1930s Mehmed Handžić, the leading figure of Islamic revivalism — which called for a strict implementation of Shari'a rules in Bosnia-Herzegovina — formulated a nascent contemporary Bosniak nationalism which concurred with similar forms of nationalization of religion among representatives of the Catholic and Orthodox Church in Yugoslavia. Handžić argued that Islam was compatible with nationalism, an idea which in fact fitted in with the ideological framework of the interwar Yugoslav state. However, instead of inscribing this nationalized Islam within a Yugoslav national framework, Handžić adopted a notion of Bosnian Muslim religious and national identity (*bošnjaštvo*) and thus separated Bosnian Muslims from Croatian Catholics and Serbian Orthodox, not only religiously but also nationally.[18]

* * *

These evolutions should not be understood as evidential of the inherent and long-term incompatibility of religious diversity and nationhood, or nationalized rivalry between different religious institutions. In what follows I shall relate the reshuffling of alliances between religious and national categories of identification to the institutionalization of nationhood

[16] Buchenau, 'Katholizismus und Jugoslawismus', pp. 233–38.

[17] Klaus Buchenau, 'Svetosavlje und Pravoslavlje. Nationales und Universales in der serbischen Orthodoxie', in Martin Schulze Wessel (ed.), *Nationalisierung der Religion und Sakralisierung der Nation im östlichen Europa*, Stuttgart, 2006, pp. 204–32 (pp. 215–24); Buchenau, *Auf russischen Spuren*, pp. 391–407; Maria Falina, 'Svetosavlje: A Case-Study in the Nationalization of Religion', *Zweitserische Zeitschrift für Religion- und Kulturgeschichte*, 101, 2007, pp. 505–27 (pp. 520–25); Falina, 'Pyrrhic Victory', pp. 191–204; Zoran Milutinović, *Getting over Europe: The Construction of Europe in Serbian Culture*, Amsterdam and New York, 2011, pp. 147–67.

[18] Bougarel, 'Farewell to Ottoman Legacy', pp. 341–42.

and religion in the Yugoslav nation-state. I shall do so more specifically within the domain of education, and in particular by focusing on the celebration of religious holidays in school. Article 16 in the constitutions of 1921 and 1931 stated that 'schools should provide moral education and develop civic consciousness in the spirit of national unity and religious tolerance'.[19] In other words, national unity and religious tolerance were very closely intertwined and in fact formed the foundations of the state's educational policy. This line of reasoning was clearly manifested in the celebration of school holidays. Yugoslav schools were closed on state holidays: 1 December (the day the Kingdom of Serbs, Croats and Slovenes had been officially formed in 1918), 17 December (the anniversary of King Alexander), as well as 24 May, the Orthodox holiday of Saints Cyril and Methodius (11 May OS).[20] The commemoration of SS Cyril and Methodius relied on a concurring pre-First World War tradition in Catholic Croatia and Orthodox Serbia. In Croatia-Slavonia Bishop Josip Juraj Strossmayer, in cooperation with Franjo Rački, had established a cult of Cyril and Methodius as Slavonic Apostles, who could serve as the foundation for the religious, political and cultural unity of Orthodox and Catholic (South) Slavs.[21] In pre-First World War Serbia SS Cyril and Methodius were commemorated within a broader Slav Orthodox dimension, certainly in contrast with the narrow Serbian national commemoration of St Sava or the national commemoration of SS Cyril and Methodius in Bulgaria.[22]

An additional important school holiday was 28 June — *Vidovdan* — when the school year ended festively with popular lectures, concerts, gymnastics performances and festivities organized by the school in cooperation with cultural-educational associations.[23] *Vidovdan* occupied a central position in the historical narrative of the Serbian Orthodox Church and the Serbian nation. In essence, it commemorated the defeat of the army of the Serbian Prince Lazar by the advancing Ottomans at Kosovo in 1389. However,

[19] Quoted in Dušan Mrđenović (ed.), *Ustavi i vlade Kneževine Srbije, Kraljevine Srbije, Kraljevine SHS i Kraljevine Jugoslavije 1835–1941*, Belgrade, 1988, pp. 21, 251.

[20] 'Pravilnik o praznovanju praznika u osnovnim, srednjim i stručnim školama u Kraljevini Srba, Hrvata i Slovenaca', *Prosvetni glasnik*, 44, 1928, pp. 796–98 (p. 796).

[21] Buchenau, 'Katholizismus und Jugoslawismus', pp. 228–29; Geert van Dartel, *Ćirilometodska ideja i Svetosavlje*, Zagreb, 1984, pp. 33–66.

[22] Stefan Rohdewald, 'Figures of (Trans-)National Religious Memory of the Orthodox Southern Slavs before 1945: An Outline on the Examples of SS. Cyril and Methodius', *Trames*, 12, 2008, 3, pp. 287–98 (pp. 290–93). For the commemoration of SS Cyril and Methodius in independent Bulgaria before the Second World War, see Weber, *Auf der Suche nach der Nation*, pp. 113–17, 190–202, 219–24, 342–49.

[23] 'Pravilnik o praznovanju praznika', p. 796; 'Vidov-dan, praznik narodnog prosvećivanja', *Prosvetni glasnik*, 43, 1927, p. 158.

this historical event carried multiple meanings. In the popular-folk oral literature the battle was the setting for heroic folk songs, especially around the figure of Miloš Obilić, the alleged assassin of the Ottoman sultan Murad. The event was an important symbol in the religious narrative of the Orthodox Church, centred around the martyrdom of the canonized Prince Lazar, whose self-sacrificing choice of the heavenly kingdom in the battle against the advancing Muslims lay the foundation for the spiritual victory of Orthodox Christianity.[24] In the second half of the nineteenth century the Serbian state authorities established a national commemoration of *Vidovdan* and the Battle of Kosovo, which appropriated religious and folk-popular motives. The festive ending of the school year on *Vidovdan* was part of this national commemoration.[25] Finally, from the beginning of the twentieth century folk-popular and religious motives related to *Vidovdan* and the Battle of Kosovo were used in what Andrew Wachtel has termed multicultural synthetic articulations of Yugoslav national identity, which combined elements from existing 'tribal' cultures.[26]

In interwar Yugoslavia the Ministry of Education continued the Serbian tradition of the festive ending of the school year on *Vidovdan*. Although the authorities and Yugoslav ideologists attempted to detach *Vidovdan* from a narrow Serbian Orthodox meaning and pointed to the relevance of the Battle of Kosovo for the entire Yugoslav people and its abstract meaning as a sign of the heroic vitality and messianic role of the Yugoslav people, the date remained closely associated with the Serbian 'tribe' and as such was extremely controversial in interwar Yugoslavia. An element which certainly added to the controversy was the fact that 28 June was the date when the first centralized constitution of the Kingdom of Serbs, Croats and Slovenes had been legalized in 1921. This constitution had been forced through with votes of the Serb-dominated Radical and Democratic Parties, and was vehemently opposed by the Croatian Peasant Party. As such, the date symbolized growing Serb-Croat political polarization and Serbian political hegemony.

St Sava's Day (27 January), finally, was intended as 'a day of general cultural-national school celebration'.[27] St Sava occupied a central position in the history, the religious thinking and practices of the Orthodox Church

[24] Milica Bakić-Hayden, 'National Memory as Narrative Memory: The Case of Kosovo', in Maria Todorova (ed.), *Balkan Identities: Nation and Memory*, London, 2004, pp. 25–40.

[25] Wolfgang Höpken, 'Zwischen nationaler Sinnstiftung, Jugoslawismus und "Erinnerungschaos"', *Österreichische Osthefte*, 47, 2006, pp. 345–91 (pp. 350–53).

[26] Andrew Wachtel, *Making a Nation, Breaking a Nation: Literature and Cultural Politics in Yugoslavia*, Stanford, CA, 1998, pp. 53–63.

[27] 'Pravilnik o praznovanju praznika', p. 796.

in Serbia. Sava was born as Rastko, the third son of Stefan Nemanja, the twelfth century ruler of Raška — the forerunner of the medieval Serbian Kingdom — and founding father of the dynasty of Nemanjić. At a young age Rastko became monk under the name Sava on Mount Athos, where he established the first Serbian monastery. In 1219 Sava succeeded in securing autocephaly for the Orthodox Church in Serbia and became its first archbishop. After his death Sava was canonized. In the course of the nineteenth century political-national, folk-popular and religious elements were interwoven in the increasingly prominent national-religious cult of St Sava. As part of this cult St Sava had been celebrated as patron saint of schools in autonomous Serbia and the Serbian Orthodox schools in the Hungarian Vojvodina since the mid nineteenth century.[28]

The inclusion of a number of religious holidays in national education provoked bitter controversies between representatives of the most important religious institutions in the country and the state authorities, especially in the case of St Sava's Day. These controversies should be situated within a broader struggle between Yugoslav state authorities and religious institutions over the education and upbringing of 'their' children, which reflects the different ontologies of the nationalizing state and religious institutions. As I will show in the remainder of this article, these controversies also reveal the fundamental impact the state's policy on religion and nationhood and the controversies surrounding it had on the intertwining between various religious and national categories of identification. I shall first outline the strategies used by the state to establish St Sava's Day as a national holiday, before discussing the opposition to this policy from religious institutions and thinkers.

* * *

Soon after installing St Sava's Day as a school celebration the Ministry of Education issued regulations to guarantee 'that the celebration of St Sava would fully preserve its character of a general state-educational holiday'.[29] In schools with a homogeneously Orthodox pupil community, the festivities on St Sava's Day were co-organized by the school and the local church. In schools where Orthodox pupils were in the majority, the religious service should be separated from the school festivities, so

[28] Bojan Aleksov, 'Nationalism in Construction: The Memorial Church of St Sava on Vračar Hill in Belgrade', *Balkanalogie*, 7, 2003, 2, pp. 47–72 (pp. 49–51); Buchenau, 'Svetosavlje und Pravoslavlje', pp. 206–09; Rohdewald, 'Sava', p. 186.

[29] 'Proslava Sv. Save, način izvođenja', *Prosvetni glasnik*, 45, 1929, pp. 11–12 (p. 11).

that non-Orthodox pupils would not have to attend the religious part of the holiday. Where Orthodox pupils were in the minority, the religious celebration could not take place in school.

> In any case it should be made sure that the celebration of St Sava as national enlightener is understood and experienced by pupils and parents as a common national holiday. In that sense, especially in mixed schools attention has to be paid to the programme of the festivities (speeches, declamations, songs, et cetera) so that everything takes place in the wide spirit of religious tolerance and national unity.[30]

Educational authorities thus attempted to establish a strict distinction between the Orthodox religious celebration of St Sava, and the national commemoration of St Sava at school. However, the fact that this distinction was not made for schools with an Orthodox majority already hints at the fuzzy and problematic nature of this division.

In examples of typical Yugoslav national historiography, such as *Istorija Jugoslavije* (*History of Yugoslavia*) by Vladimir Ćorović, the leading historian at the University of Belgrade, or a model for popular lectures produced by the literary historian and publicist Pero Slijepčević, St Sava was celebrated as the personification of the national Serbian Church and a central figure in the consolidation of the independent Serbian state, and as the 'First Enlightener' of the Serbs. With regard to the former element, Sava was praised as the founder of the Serbian autonomous church, which had its own 'national' priests, used the national language and had very strong bonds with the Serbian state. In that way, it was argued, St Sava lay the foundation for the Serbian Church's national mission as the sole Serbian national institution after the fall of the medieval Serbian state.[31] Secondly, St Sava was praised as national enlightener: it was St Sava who had brought primitive Serbia to the circle of cultural Christian nations, who had first educated his people, and who had pointed to the importance of cultural progress for the fate of the nation.[32]

St Sava's direct relevance for the Yugoslav nation was essentially based on his credentials for the Serbian part of the nation. A typical article in the newspaper *Jugoslovenski dnevnik* explained:

[30] Ibid., p. 12.

[31] Vladimir Ćorović, *Istorija Jugoslavije*, Belgrade, 1933, p. 108; Pero Slijepčević, *O Svetoj Savi. Popularna predavanja sa 12 slikama*, Sarajevo, 1924, pp. 13–16.

[32] Ibid., pp. 19–22.

> If the history of the Serbian part of our nation had developed in a different direction, who knows how the history of our entire Yugoslav people would have developed. In that way the first Serbian Enlightener is also the leader of our national unification and as such of primary importance for all South Slavs.[33]

In an article in *Nova Evropa*, Aleksandar Donković complained about the neglect of St Sava and stressed that 'Sava's work has a popular-national character, and his Serbian ideology of that time played the same role of spiritually unifying regional and tribal mentalities as do Yugoslav ideals in our own society, so there is no reason not to establish Sava's work and cult on the present Yugoslav basis'.[34]

Another strategy to Yugoslavize St Sava was to link him to parallel figures in the history of the Catholic Church in the region. Two figures stand out in this respect: Gregory of Nin (Grgur Ninski) and Josip Juraj Strossmayer. Gregory of Nin was Bishop of Nin in the tenth century, who was mostly remembered as a propagator of the use of Glagolitic and Slavonic in liturgy and religious writings. He occupied a prominent place in curricula and textbooks of the period as the personification of the authentic national character of Yugoslav Catholicism. In 1929 the millennial anniversary of the death of Gregory of Nin was commemorated with the unveiling of a statue by Ivan Meštrović in the centre of Split. In a speech delivered on the occasion Ivo Tartaglia, head of the provincial authorities of the so-called Littoral *banovina*, comprising the largest part of Dalmatia and western Herzegovina, compared Gregory of Nin with St Sava. Just like St Sava, Tartaglia argued,

> Gregory of Nin introduced the educational idea of Cyril and Methodius along with their religious ideas, and brought about the final victory not only of the Slavonic language in our churches, but also of the mother tongue in our books, our huts and our palaces, thus saving our people and these shores from alienation and ruin, and protecting it through past centuries for our present great homeland.[35]

Josip Juraj Strossmayer was the Catholic Bishop of Bosnia and Srem with his seat in Đakovo. He was remembered as a supporter of South Slav

[33] 'Jugoslovenski značaj Sv. Save', *Jugoslovenski dnevnik* (Subotica), 29 January 1930, p. 1.

[34] Aleksandar Donković, 'Sava Nemanjić', *Nova Evropa*, 28, 1935, 3, pp. 67–77 (p. 77).

[35] 'Pred Meštrovićevim Grgurom Ninskim. Reč dra Tartalje pred kraljevim izaslanikom Nj. V. Knezom Pavlom pre otkrića spomenika', *Jadranska straža*, 7, 1929, 11, pp. 296–97.

unity in politics, in his capacity of leader of the People's Party in the 1860s and 1870s, and in culture, especially as the benefactor behind the Yugoslav Academy of Sciences and Arts in Zagreb. As a Catholic bishop who had explicitly supported the idea of the national unity of Serbs and Croats, as well as the necessity of religious tolerance between them, Strossmayer anitcipated the Yugoslav ideology of the interwar state and occupied a prominent place in the Yugoslav national discourse of the period.[36] As with Gregory of Nin, Yugoslav ideologues stressed the parallels between Strossmayer and St Sava. Frano Ivanišević for instance argued that both had had the goal of 'awakening the people's consciousness, which had almost disappeared under foreign yoke, to fight for its faith, its language, its physical and spiritual freedom'.[37] According to the initial regulations on school holidays the birthday of Josip Juraj Strossmayer (4 February) was to be annually commemorated with a special lecture in schools.[38] The clarifications on St Sava's Day of December 1928 installed the birthday of Josip Juraj Strossmayer as an additional day for cultural-educational festivities at school, clearly envisaged as a Catholic compensation to St Sava's Day.[39]

* * *

Regardless of these measures to embed the commemoration of St Sava within a broader Yugoslav framework and to detach the school holiday of St Sava from the Serbian Orthodox commemoration, at least for non-Orthodox children, the school celebration of St Sava's Day remained controversial throughout the interwar period and led to frequent disputes between the Yugoslav state authorities and representatives of religious institutions. Essentially, these controversies did not so much revolve around the Yugoslav national idea behind the state's educational policy, as around the appropriation of religious symbolic resources in definitions of Yugoslav national identity. The failure of the state authorities to take these criticisms and suggestions seriously and to align the use of Yugoslav

[36] Viktor Novak, *Antologija Jugoslovenske Misli i narodnog jedinstva*, Belgrade, 1930, pp. 215–29, 235–37; Ferdo Šišić, *Jugoslovenska misao: Istorija ideje jugoslovenskog narodnog ujedinjenja i oslobođenja od 1790–1918*, Belgrade, 1937, pp. 117–30.

[37] Frano Ivanišević, 'Dva velika narodna svetionika', *Narodna odbrana*, 10, 1935, 8, pp. 113–14 (p. 114).

[38] 'Pravilnik o praznovanju praznika', p. 797.

[39] 'Izmena pomenutih odredaba u pravilniku o praznovanju praznika P.br. 15.791 od 22. septembra 1928. god.', *Prosvetni glasnik*, 44, 1928, pp. 1076–77.

national language by religious thinkers and representatives with their own nationalizing policy explains the increasing prominence of alternative nationalizations of religion toward the end of the interwar period.

The Islamic Religious Community and St Sava's Day

In early 1930 the leader of the Islamic Religious Community of Bosnia-Herzegovina, Reis-ul-ulema Mehmed Džemaludin Čaušević, organized a boycott of the school celebration of St Sava's Day, urging Muslim parents not to send their children to school on that day. He explained to the state authorities that Islam forbids the celebration of mortal saints from any church and added that St Sava remained a saint of the Orthodox people instead of a Yugoslav national hero. He warned that in times of crisis and instability the state should avoid provoking religious turbulence among Muslims.[40] Čaušević also gave concrete examples of teachers who had forced Muslim students to attend the Orthodox celebration of St Sava's Day and of local authorities who had forced Muslim teachers to celebrate St Sava.[41]

Local authorities promptly intervened against Muslim teachers or parents who complied with Čaušević's call. On 11 March 1931, for example, two religious teachers in Srebrenica were fined with 150 dinars or three days in prison because they had led a local boycott.[42] Also in Srebrenica eight Muslim parents were sentenced to fines of 200–300 dinars, or three days in prison, for not sending their children to school on 27 January.[43] One of those sentenced took his case to the provincial authorities and explained that he had refused to send his children to school after inspecting the schools as head of the local school committee. According to him the local teacher had decorated the school and prepared the celebration in a strictly Serbian Orthodox religious way, as he had been used to doing in Užice, where he had worked before. Also, he claimed that Orthodox pupils were

[40] Belgrade, *Arhiv Jugoslavije*, Fond 66 (pov) of the Ministry of Education, fascicle 15, archival unit 39 (hereafter, AJ fond-fascicle-archival unit), Circular from Reis-ul-ulema Čaušević of 11 January 1930, quoted in a letter from the Ulema Medžlis in Sarajevo to the provincial authorities of Drina *banovina*, 29 July 1931 (the Ulema Medžlis was the highest religious council, responsible for the interpretation of Koran teaching in Bosnia-Herzegovina); AJ 66-258-500, letter from Reis-ul-ulema Čaušević to the authorities of Drina *banovina*, 20 January 1930.

[41] AJ 66-258-500, letter from Reis-ul-ulema Čaušević to Minister of Education Božidar Maksimović, 23 January 1930.

[42] AJ 66-15-39, report from the educational department of Drina *banovina* to the Ministry of Education, 14 September 1931.

[43] AJ 66-15-39, report from the Ulema medžlis to the authorities of Drina *banovina*, 29 July 1931.

not in the majority in the school, and that the religious celebration could thus not take place at the school.[44] In the meantime, Islamic religious authorities intervened in vain against the sentences on the basis of articles in the recently legalized Law on the Islamic Religious Community which stated that Muslim pupils could not be forced to attend 'exclusive celebration[s] of another faith'.[45]

In the reasoning of the state authorities these complaints were continuously discarded with the argument that the school celebrations of St Sava were not religious, but national:

> The commemoration of St Sava is not an act or a manifestation of one religion, it is a celebration of the school, which is a temple devoted to science, education and culture, and belongs to all faiths and classes. The celebration of 27 January is not a religious ritual, but the recognition by the school of a great historical figure, who has done the most for our national education and culture, and that celebration belongs to all faiths, not only the faith of our first national enlightener. Since the celebration takes place in school and not in the religious building of one specific faith, I will strictly punish every pupil who will not attend this commemoration, regardless of his faith.[46]

Continuing guidelines and reminders by the state authorities that Muslim pupils could not be forced to attend the religious part of the celebration of St Sava or to sing religious songs during the school commemoration indicate the ambivalence of the execution of this decree in practice.[47] Even higher state authorities were not always consistent. In January 1931 Velimir Popović, head of the provincial authorities of Drina *banovina* in eastern Bosnia, decreed that the school celebration of St Sava should be strictly separated from the religious celebrations and that all schools should send a detailed report about the programme to the provincial authorities. He

[44] AJ 66-15-39, complaint from Alija Selmanagić to the authorities of Drina *banovina*, 27 June 1931.

[45] AJ 66-15-39, complaint from the Ulema medžlis to the authorities of Drina *banovina*, 29 July 1931; report from the educational department of Drina *banovina* to the Ministry of Education, 14 September 1931; decision from the Ministry of Education, 21 September 1931.

[46] AJ 66-260-500, decree by the Ministry of Education of 12 January 1930, quoted in an internal report of 29 March 1934.

[47] Christian Axboe Nielsen, 'One State, One Nation, One King: The Dictatorship of King Aleksandar and his Yugoslav Project, 1929–1935', unpublished PhD dissertation, Columbia University, 2002, p. 226; 'Učenici islamske veroispovesti pri održavanju đačkih akademija, zabava i slično ne mogu učestvovati u horovima koji pevaju crkvene i pobožne pesme', *Prosvetni glasnik*, 47, 1931, p. 127.

added that the celebration should be ended with the national hymn and St Sava's Hymn.[48] The latter, however, strongly intertwined religious and national elements, with its glorification of St Sava as the head of the Serbian church, schools and people. As such, it perfectly illustrates the ambivalence of the state's division between the national and religious commemoration of St Sava.[49]

By the end of 1932 the Ministry had apparently realized that its policy was untenable. Muslim students were no longer expected to attend the 'state-school' part of the commemoration.[50] In 1935, however, this amendment was withdrawn, and Muslim pupils were again obliged to attend the school commemoration of St Sava.[51] The Ilmija, the hierarchy of Muslim law experts, rejected this decision, repeating that 'the commemoration of St Sava as a religious saint of the Orthodox church cannot be divided into a religious and a secular part'.[52] Finally, the amendments to the law on the Islamic Religious Community of February 1936, which had come about with the participation of the Yugoslav Muslim Organization, the main political representative of Bosnian Muslims, in the new governmental coalition of Milan Stojadinović, determined that Muslim citizens, including schoolchildren, could not be forced to participate in religious festivities or ceremonies of other religions. Crucially, it was added that the Islamic Religious Community had the right to determine to which ceremonies this ruling applied.[53]

The opposition of the Islamic Religious Community to the celebration of St Sava in school did not revolve around the Yugoslav national programme in the state's educational policy but rather around the intertwining of religion and Yugoslav nationhood. Indeed, Mehmed Džemaludin Čaušević himself consistently deployed the Yugoslav national idea in the framework of his reformist religious activism.[54] Although the inclusion only of

[48] AJ 66-15-39, letter from Velimir Popović to the district authorities in Drina *banovina*, 15 January 1931.

[49] Nielsen, 'One State', pp. 219–21.

[50] 'Proslava Sv. Save – način izvođenja', *Prosvetni glasnik*, 49, 1933, pp. 16–17.

[51] 'Pravila o vršenju verskih dužnosti učenika narodnih škola', *Prosvetni glasnik*, 51, 1935, p. 729.

[52] AJ 66-49-85, resolution of the Ilmija, 10 October 1935.

[53] Denis Bećirović, 'O položaju Islamske verske zajednice u Kraljevini Jugoslaviji (1929–1941)', *Historijska traganja*, 2, 2008, pp. 191–208; Adnan Jahić, 'Obnova autonomije Islamske zajednice u Bosni i Hercegovini 1936. godine', *Prilozi*, 37, 2008, pp. 95–111 (esp. p. 101, footnote 18); Dragan Novaković, 'Organizacija i položaj Islamske verske zajednice u Kraljevini Jugoslaviji', *Teme*, 27, 2003, 3, pp. 451–71 (pp. 469–71).

[54] Bougarel, 'Farewell to Ottoman Legacy'; Sabina Ferhadbegović, 'Fes oder Hut? Der Islam in Bosnien zwischen den Weltkriegen', *Wiener Zeitschrift zur Geschichte der Neuzeit*, 5, 2005, 2, pp. 69–85.

Christian symbolic resources in the calendar of school holidays indicates the peripheral position of Islam in definitions of Yugoslav national identity in education, the reformist voices that dominated Islamic religious institutions did not demand the addition of Muslim religious holidays as state-wide school holidays, but rather suggested a strict division between religion and national-building. At a congress of Muslim intellectuals in 1928 Mehmed Džemaludin Čaušević reported that Muslim pupils were alienated from elementary schools because they were forced to participate in Orthodox celebrations on holidays of St Sava, SS Cyril and Methodius or *Vidovdan*. He demanded that Muslims would no longer be forced to participate in religious holidays, because 'in the twentieth century it is no longer necessary to spread nationalism in a religious spirit'.[55] A resolution which was adopted at the end of the congress required:

> All religious ceremonies which have nothing to do with education and which can give our schools an undesired and incorrect characteristic should be removed [...]. As for any other faith, for Muslims the school has to be a temple for education, and not for religious ceremonies [...]. National holidays cannot be alienated from Muslims through such acts, in the interests of the idea of national unity and harmony.[56]

In a letter to the authorities of 15 January 1930 Čaušević again explained that it was not in the interest of the state 'to fuse church saints with the nation'.[57] In other words, reformist Muslim religious thinkers complained that the celebration of Orthodox holidays in schools denied South Slav Muslims their right of Yugoslav national education. Instead of the appropriation of religious symbolic resources, they demanded the removal of all religious elements from the state's nation-building programme, which would allow Muslims to participate fully in national education. The failure of the state authorities to take these remarkably secular suggestions — in the sense that they differentiate between the national and religious realms of human activity[58] — into consideration and to bring the appeal of Yugoslavism among Muslim intellectuals in agreement with their own Yugoslav nationalism helps to explain the growing nationalization of religion among Bosnian Muslims in the form of a one church-one nation oppositional model.

[55] 'Kongres muslimana intelektualaca', *Gajret*, 9, 1928, 19–20, p. 292.
[56] 'Završetak kongresa muslimana intelektualaca', *Gajret*, 9, 1928, 21, p. 349.
[57] Quoted and translated in Nielsen, 'One State', p. 222.
[58] Brubaker, 'Religion and Nationalism' (see note 2 above), p. 16.

The Catholic Church and St Sava's Day

In Catholic schools the celebration of St Sava also proved controversial. On 10 February 1930 the provincial authorities in Banja Luka reported that St Sava's Day had not been celebrated in Catholic schools in Jajce, Aleksandrovac, Delibašno Selo, Nazaret and Banja Luka.[59] In Šibenik, on the central Dalmatian coast, the district head started an investigation against the local Catholic religious teacher and priest because he had forbidden his pupils to buy stamps with the picture of St Sava, and had threatened to give them low grades if they did so. Several pupils confirmed the accusations and the school principal added that the stamp with the picture of St Sava had been much less popular than those with pictures of Karađorđe, the leader of the first Serbian uprising and founder of the Karađorđević dynasty, or Crown Prince Peter. To his own defence, the priest argued that he had mistakenly thought that the pupils were talking about an icon and not about stamps. He had only advised the pupils not to buy religious objects devoted to St Sava, and had not had the intention to make any claims about St Sava as the patron saint of education. On the contrary:

> I greatly value St Sava for his cultural meaning. [...] Each year I give a special lecture in which I stress that a scholar considers him a Catholic because he died in a monastery which recognized the unity of the church.[60]

Although formulated rather clumsily, this interpretation — which strictly separated St Sava as an Orthodox saint and St Sava as the patron of education — corresponded to the reasoning of the educational authorities. In his report the district head concluded that, taking into consideration the fact that the priest was known as a good citizen, 'this should not be considered as an anti-tribal or anti-state act, but as an ill-considered act inspired by his religious fanaticism'.[61]

On 11 May 1932 a teacher in the elementary school in Koprivnica, in northern Croatia, informed the school principal that his pupils had reacted very hostilely to a voluntary collection he had held for the church of St Sava in Belgrade, as had been decreed by the Ministry (see further). With great

[59] AJ 66-15-40, report from the educational department for Vrbas *banovina* to district authorities, 10 February 1930.

[60] AJ 66-15-39, quoted from the interrogation of Krste Stošić by the district authorities, 16 April 1931.

[61] AJ 66-15-39, report from the district chief of Šibenik to the educational department of Littoral *banovina*, 17 April 1931.

difficulties, he had collected only six dinars.[62] Interrogations of the pupils in question by the school principal confirmed that the scant success of the collection was caused by 'religious-tribal' intolerance. One of the pupils had even mumbled that he would give money for the Catholic Church, but 'not for the Vlachs'. Some pupils claimed that the teacher had threatened to beat everyone who would not pay for the church, but investigations revealed that the pupils had been instigated to tell such lies by students of the local gymnasium. The school principal concluded that harsh punishments for these pupils would have the opposite effect to that intended, given the tensions in Koprivnica. According to him, the pupils had been moved by the wider spirit of 'tribal separatism' among the population of Koprivnica, so the authorities should first act against those who were responsible for this atmosphere.[63]

St Sava celebrations also led to frequent discussions between the leadership of the Catholic Church and the state authorities. The Catholic Archbishop of Zagreb Antun Bauer first intervened against a decree of the Ministry of Education that special lectures had to be given about the building of the Church of St Sava in Belgrade and that pupils could make voluntary donations.[64] This decree was formulated on the suggestion of the Serbian Patriarch Varnava, who had stressed the importance of a large 'national' monument for St Sava and suggested that students could make a donation of one dinar to 'repay their first enlightener and teacher'.[65] Bauer objected that it was unacceptable for Catholic pupils to contribute to the building of an Orthodox Church. Such objections were legitimate within the reasoning of the educational authorities, as the decree did not make a clear distinction between the commemoration of St Sava as a religious and as a national figure. In response to this complaint Minister Kojić sent out an additional circular which explicated that the donations for the church of St Sava were voluntary, especially for non-Orthodox pupils.[66] On 10 December 1933 Antun Bauer presented the Ministry with

[62] AJ 66-12-32, letter from Dušan Dadasović to Gustav Ričl, 11 May 1932.

[63] AJ 66-12-32, report from Gustav Ričl to the district authorities, 20 May 1932.

[64] 'Podizanje hrama sv. Save u Beogradu – predavanja i skupljanje priloga na dan 10 maja ove godine', *Prosvetni glasnik*, 48, 1932, p. 33. This was the decree mentioned in the above given case of the Koprivnica elementary school. The church in question is the Church of St Sava on Vračar Hill in Belgrade, for which the first plans were made at the end of the nineteenth century but which is presently still unfinished. Aleksov, 'Nationalism in Construction'.

[65] AJ 66-59-500, letter from Patriarch Varnava to the Minister of Education, 2 January 1932.

[66] AJ 66-59-500, quoted in a telegram to Archbishop Bauer, undated.

a number of complaints about Catholic pupils who had been forced to attend commemorations of St Sava with a predominantly or exclusively Serbian Orthodox character. In most cases the complaint revolved around the fact that Catholic pupils had been obliged to sing the hymn to St Sava. Bauer concluded that these practices only led to bitterness among Catholic teachers and pupils and claimed that they violated the Ministry's decree that Catholic pupils should not participate in religious celebrations of St Sava.[67]

Bauer went a step further than these complaints against concrete violations and questioned the very possibility of distinguishing between the religious and national St Sava:

> I remark that St Sava is not a common Yugoslav saint, but just a tribal Serbian saint, and thus such an action leads to the destruction of religious peace and tolerance and provokes religious and tribal passions in the context of the present critical and tense relations among the school population, which is not in the least in the interest of the peaceful upbringing of youth. I add that, in these times of crisis, the collection of donations among schoolchildren, especially those that also insult religious sentiments, is very inconvenient. I don't know how the Orthodox school population would react to a decree to make donations, for instance, for the building of a Catholic cathedral in Belgrade.[68]

Similarly, the Catholic Archbishop of Bosnia-Herzegovina, with his seat in Sarajevo, Ivan Šarić, called it a serious anomaly to bring a religious celebration to school: 'If you want to give that celebration an all-national and educational meaning, it should be free of all religious elements, if not, it should be restricted to children of the Serbian Orthodox faith.'[69]

These comments clearly reveal accommodation to the Yugoslav national language of the period and indicate that, like the Islamic Religious Community, the Catholic Church did not oppose Yugoslav national education *an sich*, but rather its intertwining with symbolic resources related to Serbian Orthodoxy. This is not surprising for Antun Bauer, who had been a proponent of South Slav national unity and who had

[67] AJ 66-59-500, letter from Antun Bauer to the Ministry of Education, 10 December 1933.
[68] AJ 66-59-500, letter from Archbishop Antun Bauer to the Minister of Education, 30 April 1932.
[69] AJ 66-59-500, letter from the Archbishopric of Bosnia to the authorities of Drina *banovina*, 13 January 1934.

been connected to the Yugoslav-oriented wing in the Croatian Catholic Movement.[70] Ivan Šarić on the other hand represented the more exclusively Croatian branch of the Catholic religious thinkers in the region. His relations with the Yugoslav state authorities were extremely tense and he would become a firm supporter of the Independent State of Croatia during the Second World War.[71] Still, even Šarić accommodated himself to Yugoslav national discourse, opposing the usage of Serbian Orthodox symbolic resources in nation-building, and not Yugoslav nation-building as such.

The Ministry of Education time and again refuted these complaints by arguing that a strict division could and should be made between St Sava as an Orthodox saint, and St Sava as a national hero.[72] After Bauer's complaint of December 1933, for example, the Ministry acquitted the teachers involved because they had rightfully decided that all pupils could sing the hymn to St Sava, as this was not a religious but a national song.[73] As with the Islamic Religious Community, such a policy failed to align the accommodation to Yugoslav national discourse by Catholic religious thinkers with the Yugoslav nationalist agenda of the state and again explains the growing nationalization of religion in the form of a one church-one nation model for Croatia.

The Serbian Orthodox Church and St Sava

As if to make the circle complete, on 16 March 1934 Patriarch Varnava, the head of the Serbian Orthodox Church, warned that if Catholic pupils would no longer be obliged to participate in the commemoration of St Sava, the Orthodox pupils for their part should not have to take part in the celebration of Strossmayer's Day.[74] In 1935 Nikolaj Velimirović, one of the most important Serbian Orthodox theologians and activists of the period, who was at that time Bishop of Žiča, polemically rejected Archbishop Bauer's demand that non-Orthodox pupils should not participate in the celebration of St Sava. According to Velimirović St Sava lay the foundation for the Serbian medieval and modern state, and thus also for Yugoslavia.

[70] Krišto, 'Katoličko priklanjanje'; Jure Krišto, *Hrvatski katolički pokret 1903–1945*, Zagreb, 2004, pp. 103–20.

[71] Ibid., pp. 153–82, 233–42.

[72] AJ 66-59-500, letter from the Ministry of Education to Antun Bauer, 22 January 1934; letter from Minister of Education Kojić to Archbishop Bauer, 4 May 1932.

[73] AJ 66-59-500, internal report by the Ministry of Education on the commemoration of St Sava, 29 March 1934.

[74] AJ 66-59-500, internal report by the Ministry of Education on the commemoration of St Sava, 29 March 1934.

Therefore, St Sava was important for the entire Yugoslav population.[75] In a review of Vladimir Dvorniković's *Karakterologija* in the journal of Nikolaj Velimirović's bishopric of Žiča Ljubomir Ivančević contrasted the national Serbian Orthodox Church with the 'international' Catholic Church. From this point of view he criticized Dvorniković for not recognizing the national credentials of the Orthodox Church and for glorifying the Yugoslavism of Josip Juraj Strossmayer. Whereas the Orthodox Church had safeguarded Serbian and Yugoslav national interests throughout its history, the Yugoslavism of Strossmayer was a manoeuvre of the Roman Catholic Church to enslave the South Slavs in the Catholic 'cage' of the Austro-Hungarian Dual Monarchy:

> The figure of Bishop Strossmayer illustrates the failed attempt to merge nationalism with international Catholicism. He is the perfect proof in our Yugoslav history that it is impossible to be a good nationalist and a good Catholic at the same time.[76]

From the Serbian Orthodox point of view the installation of St Sava as a Yugoslav patron saint confirmed the close link between the Serbian Orthodox Church and the Yugoslav state, which continued the privileged position of the church in pre-First World War Serbia. The school celebration of St Sava's Day also reflected the unproblematic coexistence of the Yugoslav and Serbian categories of national identity in Serbian Orthodox thinking. Leading figures in the Serbian Orthodox Church enthusiastically greeted the establishment of the Yugoslav state and took over the Yugoslav national discourse of the period, but at the same time interpreted the unification of the Serbian Orthodox Church and the suffering of the Serbian nation and church during the Balkan Wars and the First World War within a strictly Serbian national framework.[77] The religious thinking of Nikolaj Velimirović, for example, was infused with Serbian and Yugoslav national discourse during the First World War and the immediate post-war period.[78] The enthronement of Patriarch Dimitrije in the Patriarchate of Peć on 28 August 1924 nicely illustrates this coexistence. In the royal charter, which

75 Buchenau, *Auf russischen Spuren*, p. 395.

76 Drago Roksandić, 'Karakterologija Jugoslovena Vladimira Dvornikovića i njezina recepcija u srpskoj i hrvatskoj kulturi (1939–1941)', in idem, *Srpska i hrvatska povijest i nova kultura*, Zagreb, 1991, pp. 257–81 (pp. 275–77, quotation on p. 277).

77 Falina, 'Pyrrhic Victory', pp. 89–95.

78 Jovan Byford, *Denial and Repression of Antisemitism: Post-Communist Remembrance of the Serbian Bishop Nikolaj Velimirović*, Budapest and New York, 2008, pp. 29–30.

was read out by Prime Minister Ljubomir Davidović, the state authorities acknowledged the national credentials of the Serbian Orthodox Church from the Middle Ages until the First World War. After leading Dimitrije to the patriarchal throne, King Alexander handed him an icon of St Sava and kissed the cross of Emperor Dušan, under whose rule the medieval Serbian Kingdom reached its territorial peak and the Serbian Archbishopric was promoted to a Patriarchate. Patriarch Dimtrije compared the ceremony to the enthronement of Patriarch Janićije by Emperor Dušan, and referred to the national tradition of St Sava, Karađorđe and Prince Miloš, leader of the Serbian uprising and first ruler of the autonomous Serbian Principality. However, the one thing missing in this typical Serbian national enactment was a direct reference to the Serbian nation. Instead, Dimitrije claimed that 'the long desired brotherly embrace of all tribes of our nation has shone today from this sanctuary'.[79]

Although the Orthodox Church leadership did not oppose the state-wide celebration of St Sava, it did object to the strict division between religious and national celebrations of St Sava, arguing that St Sava celebrations had always consisted of a combination of school festivities and a church service, because St Sava personified the strong bonds between church, nation, state and school.[80] Serbian Orthodox thinkers rejected any interpretation of St Sava in which his religious role did not occupy a central place or was subordinated to his national importance. In the course of 1935, for example, the theologians Đoko Slijepčević and Milutin Devrnja strongly opposed a number of publications about St Sava by prominent intellectuals like Stanoje Stanojević, Miloš Crnjanski or Savić Marković Štedimlija, because they downplayed Sava's religious role and instead focused on his political-national role.[81]

In 1935 the Serbian Orthodox Church commemorated the 700th anniversary of the death of St Sava with St Sava's Year. The Patriarchate stressed that the commemorations should have an 'all-national' character, and that the church would make great efforts to impress the figure of St Sava 'in the heart and mind of our nation', again indicating the vague concurrence of Serbian and Yugoslav national categories in the religious agenda of the Orthodox Church. For the complete success of St Sava's Year the Patriarchate demanded the cooperation of the Ministry of Education.

[79] 'Dimitriju Patriarhu svih srpskih i pomorskih zemalja mnogaja ljeta', *Politika* (Belgrade), 29 August 1924, pp. 1–3 (quotation on p. 1).

[80] AJ 66-260-500, letter from Patriarch Varnava to the Ministry of Education, 23 January 1933.

[81] Buchenau, *Auf russischen Spuren*, pp. 394–95; Falina, 'Pyrrhic Victory', pp. 198–99.

St Sava's Day had to be celebrated more festively than ever before. During the school year students should make excursions to places which were connected to the figure of St Sava, and travelling teachers of the Orthodox Church should be allowed to hold lectures in schools. Finally, Orthodox pupils and parents should make donations for the Church of St Sava.[82]

The assassination of King Alexander in October 1934 seriously complicated the celebration of St Sava's Year. The Ministry of Education informed the Patriarchate that it had commissioned all schools to celebrate St Sava's Day humbly in the light of the general mourning over Alexander's death and suggested to postpone the special celebrations of St Sava's Day to the next year.[83] More fundamentally, the Ministry rejected the merging of religious and national elements in the proposal of the Orthodox Church. It stressed that special lectures by representatives of the Patriarchate, collections, excursions and the distribution of books could only apply to Orthodox pupils.[84] As the lectures on 27 January were intended for all pupils they could only 'speak about the life, work, meaning and personality of St Sava as a national enlightener and as one of the most important figures in the history of our people'.[85] In other words, whereas the Serbian Orthodox Church envisaged the nationalization of the essentially religious commemoration of St Sava, the state authorities held on to a clear division between the religious and national celebration of St Sava.

The rhetoric of the Serbian Orthodox Church leadership with regard to St Sava's Day presented above reveals the appropriation of Serbian and Yugoslav national categories in the framework of the church's religious ontology. Analogically, as Klaus Buchenau has shown, in its earliest phase during the first half of the 1930s the ideas of *Svetosavlje* were not exclusively linked to the Serbian nation, but reached out to the Yugoslav, Slav and even all-human level. In that regard, it can be seen as the religious counterpart to the secular Yugoslav interpretation of St Sava of the state authorities.[86] In the second half of the 1930s Serbian Orthodox thinkers, of whom Nikolaj Velimirović was the most important, appropriated St Sava as the basis of a fundamentally Orthodox and anti-Western definition of Serbian national culture and increasingly refuted any openness to the Yugoslav

82 AJ 66-260-500, letter from the Serbian Orthodox Patriarchate to the Ministry of Education, 26 November 1934.

83 AJ 66-260-500, letter from the Minister of Education to Patriarch Varnava, 26 December 1934.

84 'Uputstva u vezi sa svetosavskom godinom', *Prosvetni glasnik*, 51, 1935, pp. 8–9.

85 'Proslava Sv. Save', *Prosvetni glasnik*, 51, 1935, p. 8.

86 Buchenau, 'Svetosavlje und Pravoslavlje', pp. 209–14.

category of collective identification.[87] The rejection of the Yugoslav element in these alternative interpretations of St Sava has to be understood as a reaction against the secular nationalist policy of the Yugoslav state, which discredited the coexistence of Yugoslav and Serbian categories in the national discourse which had been deployed by the Serbian Orthodox Church in the context of the euphoria and hopes associated with the establishment of the Yugoslav state.

* * *

The nation-building policy of the interwar Yugoslav state gave a place to religious diversity within Yugoslav nationhood by pointing to the common national character of different religious traditions, and made a distinction between the more superficial, religious character and the fundamental, national character of symbolic resources like St Sava. Religious authorities objected to the secularization of what they conceived as fundamentally religious resources, repeatedly arguing that it was impossible to make a distinction between the religious and the national St Sava. The leaders of the Catholic Church and the Islamic Religious Community continuously warned that the merging of religious symbols like St Sava with the Yugoslav nation only discredited the Yugoslav national idea among Catholics and Muslims, precisely because St Sava remained a Serbian Orthodox saint. These warnings were in fact confirmed by the Serbian Orthodox Church's rejection of any national interpretation of St Sava in which his Orthodox religious meaning was downplayed or put aside, and also by the fact that for Orthodox pupils the educational authorities did not consider it necessary to make a distinction between church and school celebrations of St Sava's Day. Thus, in essence, these disputes reveal the fundamentally different ontologies of religion and nationhood: the essential point of reference for interpreting St Sava in nationalist thinking is the nation, in religious thinking religion.

The Yugoslav state authorities failed to take into consideration suggestions made by leaders of the Islamic Religious Community and the Catholic Church to delineate and separate the domains of religion and the Yugoslav nation, which clearly indicate a considerable concession to national modernity on their part, as they acknowledged the restriction of religion's domain of influence. The consequent nationalization of religion, which was a prominent feature of Catholic and Muslim religious thinking

[87] See note 17 above. For Velimirović see, specifically, Byford, *Denial*, pp. 40–42.

in Yugoslavia by the end of the interwar period, should be seen as a more confident appropriation of the nation within the all-encompassing domain of religion. Additionally, it was an accommodation to the close intertwining between nationhood and religion in the nationalities policy of the Yugoslav state. However, in opposition against what they conceived as the intertwining of Orthodox symbolic resources and Yugoslav nationhood in the state's educational policy, Catholic and Muslim religious thinkers and authorities appropriated alternative Croatian and Bosnian Muslim categories of national identification and turned away from Yugoslavism. The Orthodox leadership rejected the differentiation of the religious and the national in the state policy on St Sava's Day from a similar ontological point of departure but with a different, more confident agenda, and demanded the merging of the religious and the national. Their oppositional strategy, however, was analogical to that of Muslim and Catholic religious thinkers: the Serbian nationalization of Orthodoxy and the rejection of secular Yugoslavism.

I have argued that these shifting alliances have to be related to the failure of the nationalizing state to bring together various ontologies and interests under a shared model for the intertwining of religion and nationhood. In the pre-war Serbian Kingdom and Serbian community in South Hungary the intertwining of religion and nationhood, of which the celebration of St Sava's Day in school was the ultimate expression, had accommodated the ontologies of the nationalizing state, secular nationalists and the church. In the context of the dynamic relation between various categories of national and religious identification available in interwar Yugoslavia, however, such a policy alienated the agendas of the religious institutions in the country from that of the nationalizing state. In response to the state authorities' institutionalization of religion and nationhood, religious thinkers deployed alternative nationalist languages in pursuit of their essentially religious claims. Orthodox, Catholic and Muslim religious thinkers increasingly rejected Yugoslavism and turned towards delineated, one-to-one religious-national narratives. By doing so, they formed a heterogeneous alliance with the nationalist opposition against the nationalizing state.

The Peculiar Prosperity of Psychoanalysis in Socialist Yugoslavia

MAT SAVELLI

GENERALLY speaking, the psychoanalytic movement did not fare well in most of the Marxist-Leninist world. Historians and observers of psychoanalysis have identified a confluence of events — Freud's own criticisms of Communism, Trotskii's erstwhile public support, and the decision to throw official favour upon the more materialist ideas of scientists such as Ivan Pavlov and Vladimir Bekhterev — which all condemned the movement in the Soviet Union and elsewhere in Communist Europe.[1] Aside from these particular episodes (which, as consequences of individual decisions, could perhaps have been avoided), strong ideological reasons worked against a wide-scale adoption of psychoanalysis.

Such a development is perhaps not surprising when considering the basic tenets of the theories constructed by Freud and his associates. The 'unmeasurables' of psychoanalysis could hardly blend well with the fierce materialism that reigned in most of the Communist world. To accept the unseen (and scientifically undetectable) elements of id, ego and superego as the core components of personality structure could be tantamount to conceding the existence of the soul; unobservable forces of mystery

Mat Savelli is a postdoctoral fellow at the Chemical Heritage Foundation in Philadelphia. This research was primarily conducted as a doctoral student at the University of Oxford (St Antony's College) and the article was written while at McMaster University and the Chemical Heritage Foundation.

[1] Mark G. Field, 'Psychiatry and Ideology: The Official Soviet View of Western Theories and Practices', *American Journal of Psychotherapy*, 22, 1968, 4, pp. 602–15; Martin A. Miller, 'Freudian Theory under Bolshevik Rule: The Theoretical Controversy during the 1920s', *Slavic Review*, 44, 1985, 4, pp. 625–46; Martin A. Miller, *Freud and the Bolsheviks: Psychoanalysis in Imperial Russia and the Soviet Union*, New Haven, CT, 1998; Alexander Etkind, *Eros of the Impossible: The History of Psychoanalysis in Russia*, Boulder, CO, 1997.

could hold no place in the atheistic-materialist world that these societies were (theoretically) striving to create. Specifically, the violent and selfish desires of the id were totally at odds with the Marxist-Leninist perception of man as fundamentally collective and good-willed. These characteristics were usually explained by ideologues as the leftover by-products of capitalist greed, but Freud insisted they derived from innate instinctual drives.[2] Freudian stress upon unconscious processes as the guiding force behind behaviour also clashed violently with the exalted place of (class) consciousness in the Marxist-Leninist narrative.[3] Beyond these factors, that psychoanalysis extended far beyond a mere treatment modality into a full-blown world-view dealt a crushing blow to psychoanalytic movements in these countries. Such a quality put it squarely at odds with the monopoly enjoyed by Marxist-Leninism when it came to explaining the world.

As a consequence of these and other barriers, psychoanalysis — as a treatment modality and broader psychological theory — was severely repressed across Communist Europe. Soviet officials tarnished Freudianism as a 'weapon of bourgeois reaction', with one official citing the movement's popularity in the United States as proof of its imperialist nature.[4] Despite a period of lively debate on the subject in the 1920s, the controversial nature of psychoanalysis meant that Russian translations of Freud's works were halted by 1930, effectively spelling the end of psychoanalysis in the USSR.[5] Although greater consideration was given to psychotherapeutic approaches in the thaw after Stalin's death, theorists frequently justified their conclusions in Pavlovian terms and knowledge of psychoanalysis remained threadbare.[6] This lack of psychoanalytic familiarity had diagnostic implications as certain disorders (particularly those related to the neuroses) were consequently less likely to be acknowledged by psychiatrists.[7] Although repression was harshest in

[2] Arthur Kleinman and David Mechanic, 'Some Observations of Mental Illness and Its Treatment in the People's Republic of China', *Journal of Nervous and Mental Disease*, 167, 1979, 5, pp. 267–74; Mark G. Field, 'Soviet Psychiatry and Social Structure, Culture, and Ideology: A Preliminary Assessment', *American Journal of Psychotherapy*, 21, 1967, 2, pp. 230–43.

[3] Of course, many theorists did attempt to blend the ideas of Marx and Freud, notably Wilhelm Reich, Otto Fenichel, Herbert Marcuse and Erich Fromm. In the same way that Marxist-Leninists took to attacking Freudianism, many psychoanalysts were also critical of those who attempted to fuse Freud's ideas with those of Marx.

[4] Field, 'Psychiatry and Ideology', p. 604.

[5] Miller, *Freud and the Bolsheviks*.

[6] Boris M. Segal, 'The Theoretical Basis of Soviet Psychotherapy', *American Journal of Psychotherapy*, 29, 1975, 4, pp. 503–23.

[7] Agita Luse, 'From Social Pathologies to Individual Psyches: Psychiatry Navigating

the USSR, it extended to the satellite states as well. Writing in Ari Kiev's edited volume on psychiatry within the Communist world, a group of prominent Czechoslovak psychiatrists expressed pride in the fact that 'no extravagant doctrines were accepted, as was the case [...] in foreign psychiatry', which ensured that Czechoslovak psychiatry would 'retain its scientific foundations and [...] not slip into doubtful theories and practices that only formally resemble the scientific approach'.[8] In the GDR, the former psychoanalyst Alexander Mette (who took up the mantle of Pavlov after the Second World War) argued that 'Freud's rejection of the scientific and clinical scope of experience [...] has resulted in an overgrowth of the weeds of speculation'.[9] In short, psychoanalysis was under attack on both ideological and scientific grounds.

Recently, however, historians and medical practitioners have begun to qualify the depiction of psychoanalysis under Communism. In Czechoslovakia, for example, some therapists were able to incorporate psychoanalytic theories into their practice by coding the language they used to talk about their work. Underground communities of Freudian devotees persisted to such an extent that psychoanalysis was a prominent force in shaping psychotherapy after the Velvet Revolution.[10] It seems that repression, in the Czechoslovak case, was not a constant force, but came in waves depending on the ideological climate of the time.[11] In the case of the GDR, former psychotherapeutic practitioners attested to a 'gap between "official" theory and "unofficial" practice' that began to emerge in the 1970s as psychoanalytic concepts entered the therapeutic discourse with greater frequency.[12] Although group therapy continued to dominate, individualistic approaches started to become more common in this era. After an initial period of violent repression in Hungary, the movement's supporters found respite by the mid 1970s. Members of the psychoanalytic community were thus able to use state funds to travel to the Sigmund

Socio-Political Currents in 20th-Century Latvia', *History of Psychiatry*, 22, 2012, 1, pp. 20–39.

[8] Josef Prokupek, Jaroslav Stuchlik and Stanislav Grof, 'Czechoslovak Psychiatry', in Ari Kiev, *Psychiatry in the Communist World*, New York, 1968, pp. 125, 128.

[9] Alexander Mette in Dietfried Muller-Hegemann, 'Psychotherapy in the German Democratic Republic', in Kiev, *Psychiatry in the Communist World*, p. 58.

[10] R. J. Decarvalho and Ivo Cermak 'History of Humanistic Psychology in Czechoslovakia', *Journal of Humanistic Psychology*, 37, 1997, 1, pp. 110–30.

[11] S. Hoskovcová, J. Hoskovec, A. Plháková, M. Sebek, J. Svancara and D. Voboril, 'Historiography of Czech Psychology', *History of Psychology*, 13, 2010, 3, pp. 309–34.

[12] Christine Leuenberger 'The End of Socialism and the Reinvention of the Self: A Study of the East German Psychotherapeutic Community in Transition', *Theory and Society*, 31, 2002, 2, p. 258.

Freud Institute in Frankfurt and present their work in 1974.[13] In the case of the Soviet Union, the Georgian Dimitri Uznadze respected the ban on psychoanalysis but continued to rely on the unconscious in his research, later inspiring a 1979 conference in Tbilisi (to which many Western psychoanalysts were invited) which helped generate domestic knowledge and interest in Freud's theories.[14] It should be stressed that these studies do not suggest that psychoanalysis blossomed under Marxist-Leninism but rather reveal instances in which its methods and presumptions filtered through the cracks of what was ideologically acceptable. In the face of this new research, historians must revaluate the fate of psychoanalysis in Eastern Europe.

So how did psychoanalysis fare in the particular conditions of Socialist Yugoslavia which was scientifically and culturally more liberal than the rest of the Eastern Bloc but remained an ideologically-driven authoritarian state? While it would be an exaggeration to state that the movement truly thrived during the Titoist era, it would have been equally incorrect to label it dead or dormant. The basic tenets of psychoanalysis informed major debates in Yugoslav psychiatry and prompted the expansion of psychotherapy as an important method of treatment. The progression of psychodynamic thought and practice in the post-war period could roughly be summarized as the evolution from a fringe movement of dubious ideological standing to a commonly understood and applied theory of conceiving mental disease.[15] Although 'true' analysts were few and far between, a system of 'semi-psychoanalysis' emerged which relied heavily on practical alterations to fit the Yugoslav landscape — namely shorter-term psychotherapy and widespread use of group analysis.[16] The underlying

[13] B. Buda, T. Tomcsanyi, J. Harmatta, R. Csaky-Pallavicini and G. Paneth, 'Psychotherapy in Hungary During the Socialist Era and the Socialist Dictatorship', *European Journal of Mental Health*, 4, 2009, 1, pp. 67–99.

[14] Alberto Angelini, 'History of the Unconscious in Soviet Russia: From Its Origins to the Fall of the Soviet Union', *International Journal of Psychoanalysis*, 89, 2008, 2, pp. 369–88.

[15] The major landmarks in the evolution of Yugoslav psychoanalysis will be explored in another article.

[16] For more on the gulf between 'legitimate' or 'proper' psychoanalysis and the variants practised under socialist conditions, see Leuenberger, 'The End of Socialism and the Reinvention of the Self'. While in the East German example, the shift toward group therapy was an attempt to conform to prevailing ideological conditions, the Yugoslav case was based primarily on pragmatism. A number of psychoanalytically-oriented practitioners trained under West European pioneers of group analysis such as Siegfried Heinrich Foulkes and Henry Ezriel. Moreover, treating patients in a group setting was also economically more viable than individual treatment. Yugoslav practitioners (across the psychiatric spectrum) almost never made reference to ideological dogma in their

ethos of the movement was the pursuit of a more human(e) psychiatry against the backdrop of the growing strength of the biomedical model of mental illness; to this end, they experienced some success. Alongside the social psychiatry movement, psychoanalytically-oriented psychiatrists carved out a substantial portion of the Yugoslav psychiatric world in which human experience, rather than biochemistry, guided patient care and psychiatric research.[17] In Belgrade, Dragiša Mišović Hospital and the Institute for Mental Health would employ scores of practitioners who relied heavily on psychoanalytic research to guide their practice. In Zagreb, first at the Psychotherapeutic Department of Rebro Hospital and later at the Centre for Mental Health, psychoanalytic techniques heavily informed patient care. Adherents of the movement organized and published one of the country's leading medical journals (*Psihoterapija*). Biannual training seminars in Mokrice, Plitvice and elsewhere attracted some of the brightest psychiatric minds in Yugoslavia and helped educate hundreds of practitioners in psychoanalytically-inspired psychiatric practice. In short, the theoretical principles of Freud and his associates became well known across the country's psychiatric spectrum. This development, it must be stressed, was by no means a foregone conclusion. This article outlines the substantial barriers against the survival and expansion of psychoanalysis in Yugoslavia and attempts to explain the reasons for its persistence.

Methodology and Scope

Although this article examines the fate of psychoanalysis in Yugoslavia from the end of World War Two through to the country's collapse in 1991, the primary focus is on its evolution from a threatened and marginal subdiscipline in the immediate post-war period through the mid 1970s, by which time its conceptual impact on Yugoslav psychiatry was apparent. Although some of the barriers identified in the first part of this article began to recede by the early 1950s, others persisted until the country's dissolution. The nuances of psychoanalytic evolvement in Yugoslavia are not the concern of this article (these will instead be explored in a subsequent article). Here the focus is primarily on highlighting the threats posed to psychoanalysis and explaining how the adherents of Freud's ideas were able to persist in making a remarkable contribution to Yugoslav psychiatry.

published works.

[17] On the social psychiatry movement in Yugoslavia, see Mat Savelli, 'Diseased, Depraved or Just Drunk? The Psychiatric Panic over Alcoholism in Communist Yugoslavia', *Social History of Medicine*, 25, 2012, 2, pp. 462–80.

Regarding terminology, I use 'psychoanalytic', 'psychodynamic' and 'Freudian' interchangeably and the writings of many Yugoslav practitioners reveal a tendency to use these terms in a similar fashion. I retain use of the word 'psychoanalysts' to describe a core group of roughly fifteen to twenty individuals centred around the figures of Vojin Matić, Vladislav Klajn and Stjepan Betlheim. These women and men self-identified as 'psychoanalytically-oriented psychotherapists' (rather than psychoanalysts) since the International Psychoanalytic Association did not recognize Yugoslavia as a member group. In addition to these figures, by the mid 1970s there were a few hundred mental health practitioners who used psychodynamics in their research and therapeutic work without necessarily seeing themselves as members of the more intimate 'psychoanalytic family'.

Oral interviews and personal correspondence form an important part of the source base for this research. They date primarily from between 2008 and 2010 and were conducted in English, French and Serbo-Croatian. Figures interviewed and consulted included psychoanalytically-oriented therapists (Alek Vuco, Tamara Štajner-Popović, Vesna Brzev-Curcić, Svetomir Bojanin, Nevenka Tadić, Ljubomir Erić, Eugenija Cividini-Stranić, Vesna Vidović) and psychiatrists without psychoanalytic leanings (Vukosav Žvan, Vlado Jukić). Other mental health workers, medical historians and sociologists were interviewed for a larger project, and although their comments proved useful in gaining a greater understanding of psychiatry in Yugoslavia they were not relevant to this particular paper. Oral history is the subject of much discussion and an interviewee's reconstruction of the past is affected by a diversity of factors including the natural deficiencies of memory, the desire to recast the past through the prism of the present, and the tendency to personalize wider events. The author has been mindful of the dilemmas facing the historian when conducting and analysing the research.[18] Those interviewed were asked

[18] On the use of oral interviews in the history of medicine, see Nancy Tomes, 'Oral History in the History of Medicine', *Journal of American History*, 78, 1991, 2, pp. 607–17, and Paul Thompson, 'Oral History and the History of Medicine: A Review', *Social History of Medicine*, 4, 1991, 2, pp. 371–83. The issues of memory, nostalgia and the challenges of oral interviews in the former Yugoslavia are addressed in Zala Volčić, 'Yugo-nostalgia: Cultural Memory and Media in the Former Yugoslavia', *Critical Studies in Media Communication*, 24, 2007, 1, pp. 21–38; Tanja Petrović, 'Nostalgia for the JNA? Remembering the Army in the Former Yugoslavia', in M. Todorova and Z. Gille (eds), *Post-Communist Nostalgia*, New York, 2010, pp. 61–81; Nicole Lindstrom, 'Yugonostalgia: Restorative and Reflective Nostalgia in Former Yugoslavia', *East Central Europe*, 32, 2005, 1–2, pp. 231–42.

primarily about their own experiences but also volunteered information about psychoanalysis and psychiatry in Yugoslavia more generally. One gets the sense that the tightness of the community during the Socialist period engendered a sense of shared history. I often heard the same stories and anecdotes from different interviewees and most were very eager to share their experiences.

Papers in medical journals, psychiatric textbooks and conference proceedings form the other major sources for this article. Between 2007 and 2009, I digitized more than 30,000 pages of material relating to psychiatry in Yugoslavia, mainly collected at Vrapče Psychiatric Hospital (Zagreb), Koševo Hospital (Sarajevo) and the Institute for Mental Health (Belgrade). It is not difficult to see the tremendous influence that psychoanalytic assumptions had on Yugoslav psychiatry as hundreds of articles, book chapters and conference presentations were littered with bibliographies recalling the names and ideas of key psychoanalytic figures both domestic and international. A simple chronological reading of this material reveals a snowballing proliferation of psychoanalytic knowledge, but first it is necessary to understand why such a development was remarkable.

Barriers to the Vitality of Psychoanalysis

In the immediate years of post-war Yugoslavia, a number of institutional, ideological and economic factors stood as obstacles to the survival of psychoanalysis. These impediments would not prove insurmountable but unquestionably they served to impede psychoanalytical evolution in Yugoslavia. To begin, it is remarkable to note how few individuals possessed any sort of psychoanalytic knowledge in the aftermath of the war. Prior to the Second World War, fewer than a dozen medical professionals had anything to do with psychoanalysis, let alone used it as a primary treatment modality. Small psychoanalytic groups met in Belgrade and Zagreb and attempted to popularize the works of Freud, Jung and others. Primary figures in this endeavour included Nikola Sugar, Stjepan Betlheim, Hugo Klajn, Vojin Matić and several others. By the conclusion of the war, the number of practising psychoanalysts who had actually completed their training was reduced to two individuals — Stjepan Betlheim in Croatia and Vojin Matić in Serbia.[19] Nikola Sugar,

[19] The only other figure with any kind of pre-war training in psychoanalysis that would come to play a decisive role in the post-war preservation of the movement was Sugar's student Vladislav Klajn. Prior to the war, however, Klajn was only a student and had neither qualified as a psychiatrist nor completed his psychoanalytic training.

a Jew like most other practitioners at this time, had been killed in the concentration camp at Theresienstadt. Hugo Klajn, on the other hand, had committed the crime of falling in love with a patient and was forced to give up medical practice for the world of the theatre. The further development of psychoanalysis in Yugoslavia would depend on the work of these few remaining individuals. Perhaps more than any other single factor, the sheer dearth of analysts would make the movement's eventual survival all the more astonishing.

Like elsewhere in the Communist world, ideological and political opposition effectively constrained psychoanalysis in Yugoslavia, at least in the early years. In some cases, political opposition was outspoken in attacking the theory. Belgrade-based Tamara Štajner-Popović recounted that Vojin Matić was at one point thrown out of the University of Belgrade's medical faculty and branded a 'psychoanalytic danger to society' because of his psychoanalytic leanings.[20] In Croatia, Jakov Blažević, a high-ranking party and government official, insisted that proper socialist consciousness was completely incompatible with the basic tenets of Freudianism.[21] One practitioner described the decision to pursue psychoanalysis during this early era as resulting in a 'social kiss of death', whereby one might subsequently encounter problems in certain work and social environments.[22] In these sorts of instances, one cannot speak of outright repression or forbiddance of psychoanalysis, but a gentler and more subtle indication that not all figures in authority had tolerant attitudes towards Freud's theories. As one analyst related, 'there existed a verbal message that psychoanalysis was not to be a treatment option among psychiatric patients'.[23] For another, 'psychoanalysis was not always smiled upon'.[24] Nevenka Tadić, meanwhile, recounted an episode from her time studying medicine to illustrate that 'of course many people thought that psychoanalysis was a capitalistic, bourgeois science'. Once, while reading

[20] Interview with Tamara Štajner-Popović, Belgrade, 28 February 2008. While finding written evidence confirming this claim has proven impossible, a number of other interviewees indicated that Matić had experienced problems with certain authority figures. In contrast, Nevenka Tadić believed that the main reason the authorities had such an issue with Matić was his refusal (or inability) to 'play the bureaucrat'. In her view, Matić was an incredibly disorganized man who simply would not bother with the paperwork and 'proper' terminology required of a 'correct boss' under the Communist system. Interview with Nevenka Tadić, Belgrade, 24 August 2010.

[21] Interview with Vlado Jukić, Zagreb, 28 Feburary 2008.

[22] Interview with Alek Vuco, Belgrade, 28 February 2008.

[23] Private email from Eugenija Cividini-Stranić, 21 January 2010.

[24] Interview with Svetomir Bojanin, Belgrade, 26 February 2008.

some of Freud's work, she was accosted by a young party member who told her that Freud's theories were 'useless' and 'not suitable' for reading.[25]

The denouement to Tadić's story, however, involved neither punishment nor any other further action. In her mind, psychoanalysis was 'discouraged, but not forbidden'. Political opposition, it seems, was neither monolithic nor permanent. As her career progressed and she became the director of various psychiatric units and departments, not once did any figure from either the Party or the government attempt to interfere in her work. Given that her husband (Ljubomir Tadić) was a well-known dissident, this is all the more remarkable.[26] This notion of non-interference was echoed by Vesna Brzev-Ćurčić, a trainee of Vojin Matić and a staff member under Vladislav Klajn at Mišović Hospital. In her experience, psychoanalysis was neither supported nor forbidden by the authorities. Instead, practitioners were left to develop treatments on their own.[27] In the words of Vesna Vidović, a child psychotherapist at the Centre for Mental Health at Zagreb's Rebro Hospital: 'we were not so important; nobody cared what we were doing!'[28] Such freedom was perhaps typical for psychiatrists where, according to one practitioner, 'Thank god, in this profession, they [the authorities] didn't really interfere like they did elsewhere'.[29] This is not to suggest that psychoanalysis was entirely free from the political and ideological critiques that occurred elsewhere in Eastern Europe (and indeed in other authoritarian regimes) — anti-Freudian sentiment continued to exist — but rather that political issues were not necessarily the only (or most significant) obstacles to the treatment's success.[30]

Although party and government officials represented one source of potential opposition to psychoanalysis, fellow medical professionals were another, perhaps more vociferous, force of anti-Freudian sentiment. The first years of Yugoslav Socialism witnessed attempts to 'Stalinize' medicine

[25] Interview with Tadić.

[26] Ibid.

[27] Private correspondence with Vesna Brzev-Ćurčić, 8 January 2010.

[28] Interview with Vesna Vidović, Zagreb, 28 November 2012.

[29] Interview with Vukosav Žvan, Ljubljana, 1 March 2008.

[30] For more on the efforts to establish psychoanalysis in authoritarian and totalitarian conditions, see Joy Damousi and Mariano Ben Plotkin (eds), *Psychoanalysis and Politics: Histories of Psychoanalysis under Conditions of Restricted Political Freedom*, Oxford, 2012; Mitchell G. Ash (ed.), *Psychoanalyse in totalitären und autoritären Regimen*, Frankfurt am Main, 2010; Heike Bernhardt and Regine Lockot (eds), *Mit ohne Freud. Zur Geschichte der Psychoanalyse in Ostdeutschland*, Giessen, 2000; Christine Leuenberger, 'Socialist Psychotherapy and Its Dissidents', *Journal of the History of the Behavioral Sciences*, 37, 2001, 3, pp. 261–73.

and replicate the Soviet approach to health care.[31] In psychiatric terms, this meant a rejection of psychoanalysis and a focus instead on materialistic approaches to mental illness — in practice, a concentration on organic psychiatry. During this period, the neurologically-focused research of men such as Vladimir Vujić (the undeclared leader of Yugoslav psychiatry in the immediate post-war period) was paramount. This focus on organic psychiatry contributed to a dearth of psychoanalytical research in medical literature from the mid 1940s to the mid 1950s.[32] Stjepan Betlheim, while not shying away from biological neuropsychiatric research, sought to keep the psychoanalytic flame burning by reminding his colleagues that 'psychological factors play an important part even in cases of organic lesions'.[33] Nonetheless, psychological approaches and their chief concern, the neuroses, were essentially ignored during the early years of the Socialist period.[34] Eventually social-psychological approaches to understanding mental illness would take root but in these early years one can easily see the precarious position of non-biological interpretations of aetiology.

While these social-psychological theories would eventually become central to mainstream Yugoslav psychiatry, psychoanalytic approaches were themselves less protected from criticism. For example, Viktor Komarecki attacked the 'dogmatic tendencies' of psychoanalytic supporters by noting that Freud's theories came to light in a time and place very different from contemporaneous Yugoslavia. Thus, it was time to stop treating Freudianism as 'true faith' and end strict adherence to these theories.[35]

[31] The virtues of Soviet medicine were extolled in a series of anonymous editorials in the first issues of *Medicinski Glasnik* in 1946. See also, Nikola Nikolić, 'Vladimir Iljić Lenjin i Zaštita Narodnog Zdravlja', *Medicinski Glasnik*, 1, 1947, 5; G. Nikolic, 'Oktobarska Revolucija i Razvoj Sovjetske Medicine', *Vojno-Sanitetski Pregled*, 4, 1947, 11–12; V. Stojanović, 'Velika Oktobarska Revolucija i Zaštita Narodnog Zdravlja u SSSR', *Medicinski Glasnik*, 2, 1947, 2, and the series of four articles by Nikola Nikolić on the virtues of Soviet medicine, beginning at Nikola Nikolić, 'Razvice Sovjetske Medicine', *Medicinski Glasnik*, 1, 1947, 9.

[32] For example, see the special issue on psychiatry in *Medicinski Glasnik*, 8, 1954, 11–12. The opening editorial wasted little time in trying to make the case that psychiatry was, in fact, 'real' (meaning organic) medicine. Although the anonymous editorialist granted that psychological factors were a significant element of mental health, these factors were, he explained, merely by-products of a material process in the brain. Thus, 'understanding neurology is a sine qua non for practising psychiatry' (p. 401).

[33] Stjepan Betlheim, 'O Radnoj Sposobnosti Neurotika', *Druga Naucna Sastanka Neuro-Psihijatrija FNRJ*, Opatija, 1949.

[34] Stjepan Betlheim, 'Mogucnosti Preventivnog Rada Liječnika na Području Neuroze', *Medicinski Glasnik*, 18, 1964, 12, pp. 401–04. The one exception to the rule was 'war neurosis' — probably because of the large number of Partisans who suffered from the condition.

[35] Viktor Komarecki, 'O Neki Dogmatskim Tendencijama u Psihoterapeutskoj

Josip Berger echoed these thoughts, stating that 'macrotheoretic systems' like psychoanalysis belonged to a historical era of 'heroic psychiatry' — such approaches were surely no longer relevant in the Yugoslavia of the 1970s.[36] Slavka Morić-Petrović, chief of the powerful Institute for Mental Health, once indicated to a young doctor at the Institute that she did not want her 'spending time on Matić's couch' — a reference to Vojin Matić's clandestine teaching of psychoanalytic methods.[37]

Some psychiatrists hypothesized that a certain amount of professional jealousy may have been behind some of the attacks on psychoanalysts. Petar Klajn, for example, described how Vojin Matić was attacked for his 'decadent, capitalist techniques' and his 'bourgeois' approach to treating patients. These criticisms, coming from Matić's rivals, came at a time when he was breaking new ground with his psychoanalytically-oriented Medical-Pedagogical Counselling Centre (Medicinsko-Pedagoško Savetovalište).[38] Eventually, the authorities decided to close his institution and the staff was dispersed to other centres in the city, notably the Institute for Mental Health.[39] Vesna Brzev-Ćurčić concurred that a degree of professional envy existed towards psychoanalysts. In her view, there existed a current of thinking which maintained that psychoanalysts were 'chosen' and thus granted special treatment.[40] In any case, the attitude of some physicians stood as a bulwark against the widespread acceptance of the theory in its totality — a situation whose ramifications will be further examined later in the paper.

Training and education formed another considerable obstacle to the growth and prosperity of the psychoanalytic movement. As noted earlier, one could count on precisely two fingers the number of post-war practitioners who had completed their psychoanalytic training in the classical fashion.

Metodologiji', *Prvi Naučni Sastanak Psihijatrijara Srbije*, Vrnjacka Banja, 1970.

[36] Josip Berger, 'Savremena Kretanja Kliničke Psihologije Uopšte i Posebno u SR Srbiji', in ibid.

[37] Interview with Tadić. Apparently, however, Morić-Petrović's attitude towards Matić's psychoanalytic tutoring changed once she hired him at the Institute for Mental Health. She would go on to employ several of his psychoanalytically-oriented students as well, including Nevenka Tadić and Svetomir Bojanin.

[38] Petar Klajn, *Razvoj Psihoanalize u Srbiji*, Subotica, 1989, p. 82.

[39] Alek Vuco presumed that the decision to close the institute may have come at the behest of Slavka Morić-Petrović who was then able to poach Matić's best personnel. Interview with Alek Vuco.

[40] Private correspondence with Brzev-Ćurčić. This belief is particularly interesting given that many psychoanalysts testified that they felt somehow alienated from mainstream psychiatry. The primary point here is that, for better or worse, psychoanalysts believed that other psychiatrists viewed them as a somewhat distinct and separate group.

If one includes Vladislav Klajn (who was active in psychoanalytic circles without ever being fully trained), only three individuals were able to provide psychoanalytic education for the entire country. Added to this problem was a negative attitude towards psychoanalysis (being considered both theoretically and practically dubious) which meant that those wishing to pursue psychoanalysis did not receive financial assistance for classical individually-oriented training.[41]

These circumstances combined to create a situation in which substantial training in psychoanalytic methods had to occur in 'unofficial' or 'atypical' settings. In Belgrade, for example, Vojin Matić taught a small group of students in meetings at his flat. The group was never more than three or four students, and Matić conducted their psychoanalytic education in a rather indirect and unusual fashion. Nevenka Tadić recalled the 'magical' atmosphere that permeated these regular meetings: 'we could discuss anything — god, sex, religion, politics, culture, literature... *this* is how we learned psychoanalysis!'[42] Matić might orient the meeting around a story, book or myth and then relate the tale in psychoanalytic terms to teach fundamental principles. He set up a special room and mirror to allow his students to watch themselves as they conducted therapeutic sessions.[43] In contrast to classical psychoanalytic training (where each person must undergo individual analysis with a trainer), students learned via group psychoanalysis — each person presenting cases and having their own case discussed.[44] This deviation would have crucial repercussions for the evolution of Yugoslav psychoanalysis as group-centred analysis became the dominant treatment modality within the psychoanalytic realm. Students received no official credit for these weekly sessions, and Matić did not receive an official salary. Instead, Tadić, Bojanin and other students would leave token amounts of money on Matić's table from time to time — both to supplement his living conditions (since his pedagogical clinic had been closed) and as a sign of respect for their cherished teacher.[45] Many of his students revered him as a father figure and he was known colloquially as 'Father Mata'.[46] In Zagreb, on the other hand, Vesna Vidović fondly

41 Private correspondence with Cividini-Stranić.
42 Interview with Tadić.
43 Interview with Bojanin.
44 Interviews with Bojanin, Tadić and Vidović.
45 Interviews with Bojanin, Tadić.
46 The Serbian phrase is the more endearing 'Tata Mata'. See Tamara Štajner-Popović and Alek Vuco, 'Vojin Matić, 1911–2000: Čovek Kome Se Ispunio San', *Vreme*, 18 March 2000.

recalled a daily ritual at the Centre for Mental Health where staff would break from their work to discuss culture, philosophy and literature, often through the lens of psychoanalysis. She remembered 'incredibly well read and brilliant people' such as Duška Blažević, Eduard Klain or Eugenija Cividini-Stranić, leading 'very sophisticated conversations — not small talk' where 'people possessed so much knowledge it could make you feel small'.[47] The pursuit of psychoanalysis in these conditions was truly a labour of love, both for students and instructors.

Such training, although undoubtedly meaningful to those pursuing it, was of course problematic as it was limited to those within the 'inner circle'.[48] Vladislav Klajn and Djordje Bogičević underscored the pedagogical problems of training new therapists in a 1970 presentation about psychodynamic psychiatry where they bemoaned the lack of solid training structures. Even if those outside the small groups orbiting Matić and Betlheim could grasp key theoretical precepts, the overall quality of therapy was liable to be very low because of the absence of formalized and practical apprenticeship. Consequently, the only people privy to instruction in good psychotherapeutic and psychoanalytic technique were those working at institutions where psychotherapy was held in high esteem — namely places where Betheim, Matić and (Vladislav) Klajn himself worked.[49] Additionally, since Yugoslav psychoanalysis did not have any formal ties to the major international or European psychoanalytic associations, students could not easily appeal to a higher body and thus had to learn in a climate of 'semi-isolation'.[50] An attempt was made to rectify this problem in Croatia during the 1970s when four practitioners from the Centre for Mental Health were sent abroad to undergo psychoanalytic training in 'official settings' with the understanding that they would then return to impart their knowledge of 'proper' psychoanalysis to other therapists. Ultimately, this scheme failed when only Staniša Nikolić

[47] Interview with Vidović.

[48] Apparently the Croatian group originally 'tried to follow the strict psychoanalytic rules' by neither analysing each other nor their students, but practicality eventually forced them to reconsider this policy. Interview with Vidović.

[49] Vladislav Klajn and Djordje Bogičević, 'Tokovi Dinamičke Psihijatrije Uopšte i Posebno u Sr Srbiji', *Prvi Naučni Sastanak Psihijatrijara Srbije*, Vrnjačka Banja, 1970.

[50] Interview with Štajner-Popović. Vidović believes that the focus on group analysis in Yugoslavia stemmed largely from the failure of the IPA to recognize individual analysts in Yugoslavia. When it became apparent that the IPA was not going to grant Yugoslavia member status, leading figures such as Blažević, Klain and Cividini-Stranić turned instead to (largely British) practitioners of group analysis who eagerly recognized their Yugoslav colleagues and provided assistance with organizing training. Interview with Vidović.

returned to Yugoslavia, the others choosing to remain abroad.[51] It is not difficult to perceive how substantial a barrier the teaching climate (or lack thereof) must have been for the healthy advancement of Yugoslav psychoanalysis, but as later sections of this article will demonstrate, a dedicated corps of practitioners was able to navigate around the problem.

One critical challenge facing Yugoslav psychoanalysis differed greatly from the institutional and ideological hindrances that have thus far been elucidated — a shortage of 'appropriate' patients. To begin, those eager for 'proper' psychoanalysis would have to pay out of pocket since state medical insurance did not cover treatment in private settings.[52] It is unlikely that substantial numbers of citizens would have been prepared to make such a financial sacrifice. Additionally, there existed something of a 'cultural challenge' to psychoanalysis. It is worth keeping in mind that Yugoslavia was in a phase of transition from a rural and uneducated society to one far more urbanized and educated. This transition, however, remained very much a work in progress. One practitioner claimed that 'psychoanalysis was accepted the way a savage accepts a sorcerer', alluding to a combination of fear and scepticism on the part of the population.[53] When members of the general population did embrace psychoanalytic principles, the results could end disastrously.[54] Svetomir Bojanin likened the early efforts to popularize psychoanalysis as a sort of 'civil conflict' between highly-educated and cosmopolitan practitioners and the patriarchal and uneducated masses.[55]

[51] While in Paris, Nikolić studied with Diatkine and Lebovici and was responsible for introducing psychoanalytic psychodrama to Yugoslavia. Interview with Vidović.

[52] Private correspondence with Cividini-Stranić. Private practice, in most forms, was essentially illegal. Of course, some people did choose to pay out of pocket by visiting practitioners outside of regular working hours (paying under the table) while others were able to obtain a form of state-financed psychodynamic treatment if they visited an institution (such as Mišović Hospital in Belgrade) where the staff took an enthusiastic attitude to psychoanalysis.

[53] Interview with Vuco.

[54] For example, people often misunderstood key concepts and took a literal interpretation of psychodynamic explanations. Vojin Matić once delivered a public lecture on psychoanalysis (during the 1950s or 1960s) and, having concluded his talk, asked the audience if there were any questions or points needing clarifying. One man (a teacher), stood up and wondered: 'I've been listening to you and I've done everything just like you said. When I had sexual intercourse with my wife, I held my five-year-old son on my shoulders so that he could see what we were doing. Was that a good thing to do?' Interview with Bojanin.

[55] Practitioners tended to be trained in Western Europe and came from upper middle-class families in the pre-war period while the urban population of post-war Yugoslavia was growing largely on the basis of immigration from rural areas. The 'cultural conflict' between patients and practitioners found earlier expression in the Yugoslav debates over war neurosis. See Ana Antić, 'Psychiatry at War: Psychiatric Culture and Political Ideology

The sort of patients these early practitioners would have encountered would likely have differed greatly from Freud and Jung's famous case studies they had read about during their training. Betlheim warned that it was fundamental that a potential patient be of sufficient intelligence. One simply could not treat a patient of 'embarrassing primitiveness' or even one who had done a bit of schooling but failed to augment their education in any way. Because Yugoslavia possessed so few analytically-oriented psychotherapists, they did not have the luxury of choosing inappropriate or overwhelmingly difficult patients for fear of wasting psychotherapeutic resources.[56]

A final barrier worth considering was also the simplest — the problem of time. Classical psychoanalysis demands that clients and therapists work together for a period of at least four to five hours per week. Ideally this would occur one hour per day over a number of years. Vojin Matić's preference was to work with two or three patients per day but the reality of the situation in post-war Yugoslavia was that levels of mental illness were far too great to permit such intensive work with individual patients.[57] Psychiatry, rather than employing long-term psychoanalytic approaches, could instead only respond to 'psychiatric emergencies' as practitioners were few and far between.[58] Josip Dojč, a psychiatrist holding the rank of major in the Yugoslav People's Army (JNA), used a 1952 article to warn of the extremely high levels of mental illness that were threatening Yugoslavia.[59] In the country's flagship medical journal, Dojč took a psychoanalytic approach to explaining illness and urged GPs to gain a basic familiarity of Freudian ideas and treatments so that they stopped directing every case of nervousness to psychiatrists who were vastly overburdened with patients. Feeling this time pressure, Stjepan Betlheim concluded that practitioners still wishing to employ psychoanalytic methods (as opposed to simple somatic treatments and restraint) needed to consider less-intensive forms of psychodynamic treatment which might require only a few hours per week for a couple of months.[60] This suggestion, coming from a senior

in Yugoslavia under the Nazi Occupation', unpublished PhD thesis, Columbia University, 2012.

[56] Stjepan Betlheim, 'O Indikacijama Za Psihoterapiju', *Medicinski Glasnik*, 8, 1956, 11–12, pp. 411–15.

[57] Interview with Bojanin. He claims that practitioners had to see between ten to fifteen patients per day if they were to come close to meeting the demand.

[58] Klajn and Bogičević, 'Tokovi Dinamičke Psihijatrije'.

[59] Josip Dojč, 'Savremeno Gledanje na Problem Psihonervnih Smetnji', *Medicinski Glasnik*, 6, 1952, 10, pp. 289–97.

[60] Betlheim, 'O Indikicijama Za Psihoterapiju', p. 411.

member of the small psychoanalytic community, would prove prophetic as Yugoslav therapists started adopting and adapting approaches to therapy that were far less time-consuming.

Thus, the barriers to psychoanalytic development in Yugoslavia were considerable and diverse. The negative attitudes of fellow professionals and the strength of somatic traditions, combined with the challenges of navigating the ideological minefield laid out by some authorities, ensured a struggle to demonstrate the legitimacy and value of the psychoanalytic approach. Poor training structures and a lack of qualified instructors threatened the possibility of future generations of analysts, while a sceptical and ill-suited public reduced the potential patient base substantially. Finally, the economic realities of post-war Yugoslavia with its high levels of mental illness (on account of large-scale migration, the devastation of the war and widespread poverty) guaranteed a ratio of patients to physicians that made long-term and intensive psychoanalysis a practical impossibility. Although the political and ideological impediments receded with time, discoveries in somatic psychiatry (such as new psychiatric medications) and an explosion in the patient population posed further challenges to the movement's health throughout the duration of the Socialist period. Yet despite these formidable obstacles, psychoanalysis persevered and in some ways even thrived. The next section will detail how exactly psychoanalysis was able to prosper during the Socialist era.

Reasons for Survival and Prosperity

The survival of the psychoanalytic movement was never a certainty and, at one point, looked highly unlikely. In the immediate days after the Second World War, the psychoanalytic community consisted of three or four individuals in a climate somewhat hostile to the 'bourgeois' and 'medically vacuous' ideas of Freud. In contrast, by the 1970s psychoanalytic ideas were being vibrantly discussed in medical journals and hundreds of practitioners were borrowing from the theory in their therapeutic work with patients. Practically speaking, perhaps the paramount factor explaining its survival during this period can best be summarized by the adage, 'it pays to have friends in high places'. It is entirely plausible to suggest that psychoanalysis would not have survived as a treatment modality had it not been for the efforts and interventions of a few powerful supporters. Chief among these 'protectors' of psychoanalysis was Vladislav Klajn, himself a psychiatrist. Klajn had been a Communist agitator in POW camps in Albania and Italy during the Second World War and actively joined the Partisans in 1943. One year later, he returned to Belgrade and began working with the security services UDBA and OZNA.[61] He then headed up the psychiatric section of Dragiša Mišović Hospital (which became a bastion of psychoanalytic thought) while retaining a position within the Ministry of the Interior. Mišović Hospital was, according to one long-term staff member, 'an UDBA hospital', meaning that high-ranking members of the Party and security services received treatment there.[62] With such a lofty profile, Klajn's influence helped protect psychoanalysis from its ideological critics. He described the uncertain situation surrounding the founding of the psychotherapeutic ward at Mišović in a 1979 presentation, noting that 'dogmatic vulgar materialistic attitudes' lay behind a series of ideological attacks on the institution. Klajn turned the tables on his critics, citing their 'poor knowledge of dialectical materialism' in refutation. Psychoanalysis, he insisted, did in fact possess a scientific basis.[63] Besides, any methodological approach that improved the mental health of the population was worthy of consideration.[64] Having been a member of the small pre-war psychoanalytic circle, Klajn was a rare point of continuity between the pre-war and post-war eras and helped to ensure that the legacy of those early psychoanalysts survived in the 'new' Yugoslavia.

If Klajn helped safeguard psychoanalysis in Serbia, Stjepan Betlheim and Duška Blažević were its guarantors in Croatia. Betlheim joined the Partisans in 1943 as a medical officer, eventually moving to Kovin Hospital to become one of the main contributors to the study of war neurosis — the primary psychiatric concern of the authorities in the late-war and early post-war years.[65] The success of psychoanalytic psychotherapy in treating

[61] Klajn, *Razvoj Psihoanalize u Srbiji*.

[62] Private correspondence with Brzev-Ćurčić. She worked at the hospital from 1974 until 2005. Vladeta Jerotić, a Jungian psychiatrist at Mišović from 1961 until the mid 1980s, also stated that it was 'well known' that the hospital 'belonged' to UDBA. Despite this high-profile nature, the overwhelming majority of the psychiatric department (handpicked by Vladislav Klajn) were not even party members. According to Jerotić, himself an influential contributor to psychodynamics in Yugoslavia, staff at Mišović were free to conduct psychodynamic research and treatment without fear of interference under the auspices of Klajn. See his autobiography at <http://www.rastko.rs/filosofija/jerotic/vjerotic-autobiografija_c.html>.

[63] Vladislav Klajn, 'Prilog Izučavanju Razvoja Psihoterapije u Jugoslavije', *III Kongres Psihoterapeuta Jugoslavije*, Belgrade, 1979. Klajn's conference presentation was an incredibly rare example of a psychiatrist actually bringing Marxist-Leninist discourse into the discussion. In his eyes, the attacks were not so much ideologically-motivated but stemmed from personal and professional vendettas.

[64] This was the message that Vladislav Klajn delivered to Ljubomir Erić as a young psychiatrist. Interview with Ljubomir Erić, Belgrade, 10 September 2007.

[65] The other chief psychiatrist entrusted by the authorities to deal with the problem of

many of those suffering from the condition doubtlessly enhanced the reputation of psychoanalysis. Betlheim's student Duška Blažević, like her mentor, had joined the partisan effort during the war. Blažević earned a medal of courage for her medical deeds during wartime and was also renowned for her political work, serving on a number of government health committees. Like Vladislav Klajn, she participated in psychiatric seminars organized by the JNA (Yugoslav People's Army).[66] Blažević brought these credentials to the table when she helped co-found the Psychotherapeutic Department at Zagreb's Rebro Hospital, an institution priding itself on its use of psychoanalysis.[67] Only 'connected people' such as Blažević and Betlheim 'could make new buildings appear like that'.[68] In effect, the partisan and political credibility of these pioneers made attacks on the ideological foundation of psychoanalysis much more difficult.

A substantially higher profile guardian existed in the form of Konstantin 'Koča' Popović. Born to a wealthy family, Popović spent his childhood split between Belgrade and Switzerland, later studying philosophy in Paris where he aligned himself with the Left Bank intellectual circle. Returning to the Kingdom of Yugoslavia, he began a career as a 'progressive journalist' and surrealist poet. He joined the Communist Party in 1933 and fought in the Spanish Civil War. Despite his bourgeois background, Popović became one of the most trusted figures within Tito's inner circle and commanded the First Proletarian Brigade during the Second World War.[69] Popović began post-war life as the Chief of the General Staff and later took up the position of Foreign Minister and eventually Vice-President of Yugoslavia. Given his liberal leanings and status as one of the most respected figures in Yugoslavia (and a close personal friend of Tito), Popović was virtually beyond reproach. According to one psychoanalyst, he was instrumental in protecting the status of psychoanalysis, a subject he wrote about as a prominent member of the Serbian surrealist movement.[70]

Finally, one can perhaps speculate that a sort of collective credibility existed in the psychoanalytic community given the fact that the majority of

war neurosis at Kovin was Hugo Klajn — himself a psychoanalyst and psychiatrist before his move into the theatre world.

[66] See for example their presentations at the *Prvi Jugoslovenski Simpozijum o Psihotrauma u Vanrednim Situacijama*, Belgrade, 1970.

[67] Suradnici, 'In Memoriam Prof Dr. Duška Blažević', *Psihoterapija*, 11, 1981, 2, pp. 113–14.

[68] Interview with Vidović.

[69] Slobodan Stanković, 'Koca Popović: A Tough Eastern Proletariat Raised by Western Governesses', Radio Free Europe Research, 1966.

[70] Interview with Alek Vuco.

psychoanalysts were Jews. For obvious reasons, Jews were probably the only ethnic group that did not collaborate on some level with the fascist puppet regimes set up on Yugoslav territory during the Second World War. Some psychoanalysts (i.e. Nikola Sugar) perished while most of the others either lost family in concentration camps (i.e. Jasenovac) or narrowly avoided doing so by joining the Partisans. As Jews had been targeted to varying degrees by the three Partisan bogeymen (Germans, Ustaše and Četniks), antisemitism did not enjoy much currency in officially multiethnic Yugoslavia.[71] Betlheim tried to tap into this current in a 1956 article entitled 'What is the Stance of Doctors towards Psychoanalysis?'. Using language familiarly associated with the Partisans, he depicted Freud as a 'warrior' who struggled for his ideals. The rejection of psychoanalysis, Betlheim insisted, owed itself more to antisemitism than any rational explanation.[72] By associating Freud with Partisans and the critics of psychoanalysis with antisemitism, Betlheim was helping to forestall attacks on the movement.

In addition to having well-situated defenders and protectors, psychoanalysis in Yugoslavia owed much of its survival to the general wave of liberalism that swept the country, first after the country's expulsion from the Cominform in 1948, and later after hardliner Aleksandar Ranković's fall from grace in 1966. Even though Yugoslavia never came close during the 'Stalinist years' to approaching the sort of intellectual single-mindedness that characterized the excesses of Stalin's USSR, the fate of psychoanalysis was still up in the air in the mid-late 1940s. As Yugoslavia made friends with the West and set out on the path of non-alignment, a plurality in thought otherwise unthinkable in most Marxist-Leninist regimes came to light. Psychoanalysis benefited from this climate, as did many other aspects of cultural and intellectual life.[73] While it is

[71] The extent of Četnik antisemitism is debated. In this instance, it matters less whether Četniks actively pursued an antisemitic agenda so long as they were perceived to have been antisemitic by the Communists. For one account of Četnik antisemitism, see Marko Attila Hoare, *Genocide and Resistance in Hitler's Bosnia: The Partisans and the Chetniks, 1941–1943*, Oxford, 2006.

[72] Stjepan Betlheim, 'Kakav Je Stav Lekara Prema Psihoanalizi', *Novi Vesnik, List Omladine Srbije*, March 30 1956. Muradif Kulenović also published an article in celebration of Freud's 120th birthday in which he drew a favourable comparison between Marx and Freud. He claimed that Freud revealed the struggle between conscious and unconscious in *The Interpretation of Dreams* with the same persuasiveness that Marx had exhibited in detailing the struggle between social structures in the historical process in *The Communist Manifesto*. See M. Kulenović, 'Izgnanstvo i Smrt – u Tudjem Gradu', *Psihoterapija*, 6, 1976, 2, pp. 192–97.

[73] For manifestations of Yugoslavia's liberal cultural and intellectual climate, see the essays in Breda Luthar and Marusa Pusnik, *Remembering Utopia: The Culture of Everyday*

undoubtedly true that, as Kristie Makrakis has argued, '[a]lthough politics influences science in every modern industrialized country, the interaction is particularly magnified in countries in which the state dominates society', political authorities in Yugoslavia paid far less attention to mental health care than their equivalents elsewhere in Communist Europe.[74] As such, no official line or decree on psychoanalysis ever came to light, leaving any battles over psychoanalysis to take place mainly within the medical community.

Amidst the climate of paranoia and uncertainty that gripped Yugoslavia during the break from the Cominform in the late 1940s, Yugoslav propagandists frequently invoked the dangers of 'dogmatism'. In paving the country's own path to Communism, Tito asserted that Yugoslavia would not get bogged down by a slavish devotion to any philosophical or ideological stance. Against this backdrop, defenders of psychoanalysis skillfully fired back against their critics by levying charges of dogmatism.[75] In a book on neuroses published in 1962, Vladislav Klajn was responding to unnamed critics within the medical community when he argued that psychoanalysis was not in conflict with the principles of dialectical materialism. He savaged the 'mechanistic tendencies' of 'reflexologists' who depended too much on Pavlov (the Soviet favourite) for their conceptualization of mental processes. Although psychoanalysis had an 'inconsistent' ideological basis, it was important not to reject it holistically but instead criticize individual components and improve upon them.[76] The forensic expert Dušan Jevtić, meanwhile, acknowledged the great advances brought about by 'materialistic sciences' but wanted to avoid any sense of dogmatism in his textbook on psychopathology. He introduced psychoanalysis as one of the 'natural sciences' and discussed Freudian beliefs at length, despite clearly not being associated with the movement himself.[77] Nikola Peršić, a famous Zagreb-based physician, used his introductory remarks at the

Life in Socialist Yugoslavia, Washington, D.C., 2010.

[74] Kristie Macrakis, 'Interpreting East German Science', in K. Macrakis and D. Hoffmann, *Science Under Socialism: East Germany in Comparative Perspective*, Cambridge, MA, 1999, p. 1.

[75] In his work on Soviet cybernetics and computers, Slava Gerovitch demonstrates how ideological precepts could be used to tarnish rival scientific claims. See Slava Gerovitch, '"Mathematical Machines" of the Cold War: Soviet Computing, American Cybernetics, and Ideological Disputes in the Early 1950s', *Social Studies of Science*, 31, 2001, 2, pp. 253–87.

[76] Vladislav Klajn, *Neuroze Teorija i Klinička Praksa*, Belgrade, 1962. Klajn also attacked Western researchers for discarding Communism as a system that destroys the spiritual life of man. See Klajn and Bogičević, 'Tokovi Dinamičke Psihijatrije'.

[77] Dušan Jevtić, *Sudska Psihopatologija*, Belgrade, 1960.

Symposium on Psychiatry and Neurology in 1969 to warn that dogmatic approaches to the concept of mental disease and illness were bound to fail — only 'interdisciplinary' approaches (meaning approaches that combined biochemical, psychological and sociological theories) could truly solve the greatest problems of psychiatry.[78]

Of course, avoiding dogmatic interpretations themselves proved vital for the movement's survival. In addition to allowing them to adapt their methods to the circumstances dictated by the reality of life in Yugoslavia, many analysts made substantial contributions to other fields as well. Looking at the research careers of the principal psychoanalytic figures, biology and neurology featured prominently in much of their work.[79] The biological underpinnings of Freudian theory and the instinctual drive process were frequently invoked as evidence of the scientific pedigree of psychoanalysis.[80] As Klajn and Bogičević suggested, biological and genetic interpretations were not underestimated by psychoanalysts, but simply not dominant.[81] Since man's physical, psychological and social life were inherently connected, the only real answers could be achieved by taking into consideration all three aspects. Although they themselves were sometimes painted as inflexible, most psychiatrists with psychoanalytic leanings involved themselves in research of a biological or, more often, social nature.[82] In the early period, when conducting psychoanalytic research was far more suspect, their openness to other methods probably maintained their careers. Once psychoanalytic concepts became commonplace, their willingness to work with other interpretations earned valuable allies, respect and research capacity.[83] In his case study

[78] Nikola Persić, 'Uvodne Rijeci', *Simpozij o Neurologiji i Psihijatriji*, Ljubljana, 1969.

[79] As examples, see Stjepan Betlheim and Duška Blažević, 'Neka Zapazanja Pri Terapij Elektrošokom', *Druga Naucna Sastanka Neuro-Psihijatrija FNRJ*, Opatija, 1949; S Betlheim, A. Matić, and V. Kovacević, 'Nasa Iskustva Kod Liječenja s Glutaminskom Kiselinom', *Neuropsihijatrija*, 1, 1953, 1–4, pp. 32–38; Sergije Dogan and Duška Blažević, 'Funkciolna Organizacija Kore Velikog Mozga', *Neuropsihijatrija*, 1, 1953, 1–4, pp. 192–204.

[80] See, for example, Klajn, *Neuroze Teorija i Klinička Praksa*, pp. 126–27; Slobodan Stojilković, *Psihijatrija sa Medicinskom Psihilogijom*, Belgrade, 1962, p. 129; Jevtić, *Sudska Psihopatologija*, pp. 150–60.

[81] Klajn and Bogičević, 'Tokovi Dinamičke Psihijatrije'.

[82] Viktor Komarecki, especially, attacked the cult of personality surrounding Freud, despite being very open to psychoanalysis himself. He acknowledged the contribution of psychodynamic thought to modern psychiatry but considered it high time that psychiatrists moved on and stopped reading Freud as if it were 'true faith'. See Komarecki, 'O Neki Dogmatskim Tendencijama u Psihoterapeutskoj Metodologiji'.

[83] Probably the best example in this regard was the Institute for Mental Health in Belgrade. Headed by a geneticist (Slavka Morić-Petrović) and full of social psychiatric advocates, the Institute served as the home for a number of psychoanalytically-oriented

of the German psychologist Kurt Gottschaldt, Mitchell G. Ash has aptly demonstrated how practitioners were able to navigate the ideological and institutional changes that occurred in Germany from the Weimar period through to the GDR by proving highly adaptable and flexible.[84] Psychoanalytically-minded psychotherapists in Yugoslavia, although not facing the same kind of ideological dictums, pursued similarly adaptive strategies which might go some way in explaining their longevity and influence within Yugoslav psychiatry.

Naturally, Yugoslavia's comparative openness towards the world beyond its borders (both culturally and in the sense that citizens could more easily obtain passports to travel, work and train abroad) served as a substantial boost for the advancement of psychoanalysis. The regular exchange of knowledge between Yugoslav analysts and foreign practitioners throughout the Socialist era was a pivotal factor in the flourishing of psychoanalysis and Stjepan Betlheim was crucial in promoting these ties. The only Socialist-era analyst with formal membership in the International Psychoanalytic Association (IPA), Betlheim, who trained under Paul Schilder and Sandor Rado, maintained personal and working relationships with some of the most renowned figures in the psychoanalytic world. A selection of his correspondence revealed ties with Schilder, Rado, Karl Abraham, Helen Deutsch, Heinz Hartmann and others. In particular, he had a very close friendship with Edith Jacobson; in their letters the two of them frequently addressed each other with nicknames and playful banter.[85] Essentially, Betlheim remained connected to the psychoanalytic circle he had joined while training in Vienna during the pre-war era. The tone of a report he filed from London on the centenary celebration of Freud's birth made clear that he was very much part of the 'inner family' of European psychoanalysis, and he spent much of the weekend renewing these old friendships.[86] Notably, he informed readers about his thirty-year working relationship with Hartmann, at that time President of the IPA. In addition to the celebrations, Betlheim attended seminars and clinics led by prominent analysts such as Anna Freud. On later trips abroad, Betlheim would bring his students along and introduce them into the international

researchers including Vojin Matić and Nevenka Tadić.

[84] Mitchell G. Ash, 'Kurt Gottschaldt and Psychological Research in Nazi and Socialist Germany', in Macrakis and Hoffman, *Science Under Socialism*.

[85] For the correspondence, see Ruth Betlheim and Gordana Lerotić, *Stjepan Betlheim: Radovi, Pisma, Dokumenti 1898–1970*, Zagreb, 2006.

[86] Stjepan Betlheim, 'Sigmund Freud: Impresije Povodom Proslove Stogodisnjice Freudova Rodjenja u Londonu', *Neuropsihijatrija*, 4, 1956, 1, pp. 130–34.

psychoanalytic fold.[87] Betlheim's expertise was also clearly respected internationally and he served on the WHO Expert Committee on Mental Health in the 1950s.[88] These activities kept him (and consequently his students) in constant contact with psychoanalytic developments outside Yugoslavia's borders.

Yugoslav integration and involvement with the wider psychoanalytic community extended far deeper than the occasional seminar. Many therapists had opportunities to undergo extensive training abroad during the Socialist years. Paris and London were the most common ports of call for psychiatrists learning their craft outside of Yugoslavia. Usually receiving a state stipend, these young professionals were expected to go abroad for a period of several months to a year and frequently sent back reports to their colleagues. In some instances, these reports were descriptive, perhaps aiming to show the way in which the writer was enveloped within the world of 'famous psychiatry'. The journal, *Neuropsihijatrija*, for instance, published Maja Beck-Dvoržak's 'Letter from Paris', in which she discussed her daily walk to La Salpetrière, remarking on the statue of the humanitarian Philippe Pinel and the 'old feel' of the place. She took care also to mention that the hospital was the site of Freud's tutelage under Charcot.[89] In her second letter, she continued her physical depictions of Paris but concentrated on the progress being made in terms of patient rights, noting that those forcibly confined could petition the prefecture of Paris if they wanted to leave and that the patients of some psychiatric hospitals had even begun forming unions and publishing newsletters.[90] In other cases, reports were more technical in nature, advising colleagues back home of the latest discoveries in psychoanalytic and psychiatric care. Eugenija Cividini-Stranić, for example, made repeated trips to London over a two year period to study at the Institute for Group Analysis (under Siegfried Foulkes) and the Tavistock Clinic in London. She described in detail the methods employed by her trainers which, in this case, were of particular interest to Yugoslav analysts on account of their affinity for

[87] Eduard Klain, 'Uvod', in Betlheim and Lerotić, *Stjepan Betlheim*.

[88] Betlheim was not alone in terms of Yugoslav psychoanalysts in this regard. Vojin Matić also did extensive work abroad, serving the WHO at one point and even being invited by Diatkine to spend a year in Paris so that he could gain full IPA membership — an offer Matić declined. Interview with Alek Vuco.

[89] Maja Beck-Dvoržak, 'La Salpetriere: Pismo iz Pariza', *Neuropsihijatrija*, 3, 1955, 3–4, pp. 261–63.

[90] Maja Beck-Dvoržak, 'Centar za Liječenje i Socijalni Readaptaciju u Duševnoj Bolnici Ville-Edward: Pismo iz Pariza', *Neuropsihijatrija*, 4, 1956, 2, pp. 135–37.

group treatment.[91] Muradif Kulenović, one of Zagreb's psychoanalytically-oriented therapists, also reported back from the Tavistock, detailing his impressions of Henry Ezriel's group psychotherapy.[92] Even in instances where the methods were not entirely novel from the Yugoslav perspective, evoking these famous names in psychoanalysis leant legitimacy to their practices and provoked new insights and interpretations into the world of the subconscious.

Psychoanalytic traffic, it must be said, did not merely travel in one direction — whether because of personal friendships, established training exchanges or just curiosity about psychoanalysis under Communism — foreign professionals regularly travelled to the country for professional purposes, helping to enrich domestic psychoanalysis. Numerous international conferences hosted in Yugoslavia brought in psychotherapists from various corners of the world.[93] At the famous Praxis Summer School on the island of Korčula, Herbert Marcuse spoke on his psychoanalytically-oriented re-imagination of Marxism. The Austrian Cultural Centre in Zagreb, meanwhile, hosted a combined seminar of Austrian and Yugoslav psychoanalysts to commemorate the 120th anniversary of Freud's birth.[94] The editorial board of *Psihoterapija*, the primary journal for psychoanalysts, included Serge Lebovici (who trained a number of Yugoslav analysts in Paris), Edith Jacobson (the close friend of Stjepan Betlheim) and Raymond Battegay. Although the IPA did not recognize the Yugoslav psychoanalysts during the Socialist era, the ties between international and domestic practitioners during these years resulted in recognition of the Belgrade Study Group in 1996. Of course, the level of international contact during the Socialist period was not nearly what most psychoanalysts would have hoped for, but one can easily see the benefits that their semi-integration in the wider psychoanalytic world provided.[95]

[91] Eugenija Cividini-Stranić, 'Gdje Je Danas Grupna Analiza?', *Psihoterapija*, 6, 1976, 2, pp. 217–55.

[92] Muradif Kulenović, 'Metoda Grupne Psihoterapije u Tavistock Klinići', *Psihoterapija*, 15, 1985, 1, pp. 89–97.

[93] For example, the 1972 International Symposium on Psychiatry in Belgrade brought in physicians from dozens of countries (both East and West) as did the Thirteenth International Congress of Psychotherapy in Opatija in 1985. These are merely representative examples as foreign practitioners regularly attended Yugoslav meetings.

[94] See the seminar's programme found in *Psihoterapija*, 7, 1977, 1.

[95] In the words of Štajner-Popović, 'we weren't Russia, but we weren't Hungary either'. Hungarian analysts received recognition from the IPA in 1983. Interview with Štajner-Popović. For more on psychoanalysis in Hungary during the Socialist period, see Bela Buda, Teodora Tomcsanyi, Janos Harmatta, Roger Csaky-Pallavini and Gabor Paneth, 'Psychotherapy in Hungary During the Socialist Era and the Socialist Dictatorship',

One final reason that likely contributed to the prosperity of the psychoanalytic movement was the sense of community that pervaded those keen in psychodynamics. Although few in number, psychoanalysts (more so than other groups of psychiatrists) cultivated strong support networks. This fact quite likely owed itself to their status as 'outsiders' involved with a theory that, although not forbidden, was definitely not encouraged or understood by authorities or other medical practitioners. In addition to meeting regularly (at the so-called Mokrice seminars) and publishing in their journal *Psihoterapija*, psychotherapists were the only subsection of Yugoslav psychiatry to establish their own specialist organization, the Association of Yugoslav Psychotherapists. The language these analysts used to describe each other reflected a strong sense of emotional connection. On Betlheim's death, his colleagues wrote about how

> they didn't want to believe that one day, he would no longer exist! That one day he wouldn't be sitting in his room, as always ready to teach us, to instruct us on the importance and beauty of psychotherapy. It's difficult for us to write about him in the past tense... 'he was', 'he lived', 'he said', 'he taught',...[96]

With the passing of Duška Blažević, her students and fellow analysts mourned 'our dear Duška, our longtime leader, our teacher, our colleague, and our friend... Psychotherapy for her was not merely a professional activity but the consequence of her entire person'.[97] Vesna-Brzev Ćurčić, in her eyes, was merely 'carrying on the family tradition' when she took up psychoanalysis with Vojin Matić and Vladislav Klajn: 'I think I told you everything. But, it is obvious that I loved both of my teachers, Matić and Klajn. They were always very warm and kind.'[98] These personal connections strengthened the sense of family that pervaded the inner circle of psychoanalysis, contributing to its endurance through less than ideal conditions.

European Journal of Mental Health, 4, 2009, 1, pp. 67–99.

[96] Suradnici, 'Prof Dr. Stjepan Betlheim 1898–1970', *Neuropsihijatrija*, 18, 1970, 2–3, pp. 119–20.

[97] Suradnici, 'In Memoriam Prof Dr. Duška Blažević', p. 114.

[98] Private correspondence with Vesna Brzev-Ćurčić. Her mother had also studied with Matić and focused on paediatric psychiatry. In fact, many of the most dedicated psychoanalysts were related in some way. Alek Vuco and Tamara Štajner-Popović were spouses, Milan Popović was Vuco's uncle, Vlasta Rudan is Blažević's daughter, Petar Klajn was a relative of Melanie Klein, etc. In the words of Alek Vuco, 'all of us people are connected' (interview).

Conclusion

Psychoanalysis represented a potent force in the evolution of Yugoslav psychiatry. Despite the ideological and practical barriers to its survival, the theories of Freud and his followers ensured that psychotherapy remained one of the most vibrantly researched treatment options for the country's mental health workers. It formed the theoretical basis for a major journal, dominated treatment in specialist psychotherapeutic wards and departments, and informed the very manner in which hundreds of mental health workers understood the nature of psychiatric disease. Yet this was not psychoanalysis in the classical sense; 'proper' analysts were few and far between. Instead, psychoanalytic tenets penetrated mainstream understandings of symptomology and aetiology and a select group of physicians began to view themselves as 'psychoanalitically-oriented psychotherapists'. To counter the imbalance between patient and practitioner, they employed shorter-term therapy and conducted group-oriented sessions. The consequences of this approach shaped the direction of psychoanalytic research and the dynamics of group treatment came to represent a cardinal concern. This flexibility of interpretation was a pivotal reason for the movement's survival, but highly-regarded 'defenders' of psychoanalysis also contributed vitally. Through strong connections to the international psychoanalytic world and a sense of communal purpose, psychoanalysis, in a way, flourished under Yugoslav conditions. Consequently, the theories frequently believed to be inherently in conflict with Marxism came to represent one of the most significant undercurrents of psychiatric thought in Socialist Yugoslavia.

Practically speaking, the proliferation of psychoanalytic thinking had important ramifications for the psychiatric profession's overall orientation. By demanding that practitioners conduct regular psychotherapy with patients, it encouraged a more humanistic (as opposed to mechanistic) conception of mental illness. Rather than concentrating on cortical structures or alterations in neurochemistry, Yugoslav psychoanalysis promoted an approach to treatment that focused on problems specific to individuals' psychological and emotional experience. In this way, it served as a useful adjunct to the country's prodigious social psychiatry movement. These twin movements (social psychiatry and psychoanalysis) combined to create an environment that situated the origins of mental illness in the problems of the individual and how one interacted with the wider social milieu. Given the vast social changes transforming Titoist Yugoslavia, this focus on the individual's place in the social environment was significant. Many practitioners concentrated on mental health problems that seemed to present the greatest threat to social well-being; Yugoslavia's psychiatrists placed particular emphasis on social issues such as alcoholism and suicide. The relative strength of psychoanalysis was vital in illuminating the individual at the heart of these overarching psycho-sociological investigations.

The example of Yugoslavia adds to the complex story of psychoanalysis within the Communist world. Previous case studies have concentrated on the ways in which the psychoanalytic movement was stunted or silenced by authorities on the basis of ideological inappropriateness. This article has highlighted additional types of hindrances faced by psychoanalysts and has demonstrated how Freud's ideas could survive and proliferate in a climate that was politically, socially and economically harsh. Doubtlessly, the intellectual freedom enjoyed by Yugoslavs was greater than elsewhere in Eastern Europe but, as this article has argued, the threats to psychoanalysis were more numerous and diverse than mere political opposition, and the extent to which psychoanalytic concepts informed psychiatric practice remains remarkable. Thus, the prosperity of Yugoslav psychoanalysis is peculiar not so much because of its ability to survive ideological attacks (although these did occur as well), but rather because of the size, strength and variance of obstacles blocking its path.

Caught between Germany and Russia: Memory and National Identity in Poland's Right-Wing Media Post-2004

EWA STAŃCZYK

Recently, there has been a growing interest in issues of memory and practices of remembrance, along with their impact on the redefinition of national identity in contemporary Poland. Many have observed that the process of transforming collective memory has been thwarted by historical controversies surrounding both World War Two and the Communist era, preventing old wounds from healing and delaying closure.[1] In addition to the challenge of reworking its communal traumas, Poland has had to deal simultaneously with competing narratives of its national past as articulated by the political elites.[2] Following the electoral success of the conservative Law and Justice Party (Prawo i Sprawiedliwość, PiS) in 2005, the country witnessed a rapid revival of officially sanctioned debate about the importance of preserving national identity. This was to be achieved through the commemoration of historical traumas, in particular Poland's subjugation by 'Others' and the suffering this inflicted on the Polish nation. Simultaneously, Law and Justice forged the notion of the 'Fourth

Ewa Stańczyk is Thomas Brown Assistant Professor in Polish Studies in the Department of Russian and Slavonic Studies at Trinity College Dublin.

The author would like to express her deep gratitude to Andy Arnold, Balázs Apor and *SEER*'s anonymous reviewers for their helpful comments and suggestions on early drafts of this article.

[1] See, for example, Gregory Slysz, 'Poland: History as Crucible', *Transitions Online*, 22 September 2009 <http://www.tol.org/client/article/20858-history-as-crucible.html> [accessed 16 April 2012]; Ewa M. Thompson, 'Ways of Remembering: The Case of Poland', *Toronto Slavic Quarterly*, 12, 2005 <http://www.utoronto.ca/tsq/12/thompson12.shtml> [accessed 11 January 2012].

[2] See Paweł Machcewicz, 'Polityka historyczna to nic nowego', *Gazeta Wyborcza*, 20 April 2006.

Republic' which was to complete the 'unfinished revolution' of 1989 by undertaking an organized de-Communization of the country, tackling corruption and instigating extensive purges of former Communists.[3] As a way of countering and lessening the impact of imposed silencing of memory in Communist Poland, it established a culture of 'historical reinvention', emphasizing both Nazi and Communist crimes as well as the resilience of the nation in light of oppression.[4] This was accompanied by a reluctance to look to the future, particularly where relations with Russia and Germany were concerned. As a result, a governing narrative of the past, produced from above, took centre stage in this politics of memory. While stressing Polish martyrdom, it aimed at steering clear of alternative interpretations of history and pluralization of memory.[5]

In stark contrast, the conservative-liberal Civic Platform Party (Platforma Obywatelska, PO), which came to power in 2007, prompted a discussion on the importance of multivocal and multivalent articulations of memory, respectful of Poland's past and based on democratic principles.[6] Also the role of intercultural dialogue in transforming Polish culture from 'the culture of traumas to the culture of acknowledged memories',[7] to borrow Ewa Thompson's phrase, was highlighted. Polish-Russian reconciliation proved to be an important point on its agenda, and so did the development and strengthening of economic and political ties with Germany.[8] Upon taking office in 2007, Donald Tusk gave an indication of these efforts, proposing the creation of a museum of war in Gdańsk, formerly Danzig, which would leave aside the notion of Polish victimhood and present a view of the past that captured the universal experience of war, being equally acceptable to Poles, Germans and Russians.[9] As James Mark rightly points out, those debates over identity and ways of remembering the past were to 'play important roles in defining both domestic political cleavages and new geopolitical orientations'.[10] The media, in particular, have become instrumental in this process of enforcing new visions of Polishness by

3 James Mark, *The Unfinished Revolution: Making Sense of the Communist Past in Central-Eastern Europe*, New Haven, CT and London, 2010, p. 15.

4 Ibid., p. 215.

5 Ibid., pp. 56–59.

6 Tomasz Nałęcz, 'Polską rządzą historycy', *Polityka*, 27 August 2010.

7 Thompson, 'Ways of Remembering'.

8 See the election programme of the Civic Platform Party from 2007: *Polska Obywatelska*, 25 <http://www.po.org.pl/program/> [accessed 2 April 2012].

9 Jo Harper, 'Negating Negation: Civic Platform, Law and Justice, and the Struggle over "Polishness"', *Problems of Post-Communism*, 57, 2010, 4, pp. 16–36 (p. 28).

10 Mark, *The Unfinished Revolution*, p. xii.

moulding, re-forging and transmitting often disparate images of the past and pointing to the differing ways in which Germany and Russia feature in it.

In Poland, the cultural tradition of othering Germany and Russia is rich in evocative images of the two countries. The representations of Germans, for example, date as far back as the beginnings of Polish nationhood, when *Niemiec* typified any foreigner who was difficult, or impossible, to understand and communicate with, becoming, in turn, a universal figure for the 'Other'.[11] During the sixteenth and seventeenth centuries, cultural and religious differences were often highlighted, as exemplified by the dislike of the traditional German attire and the usage of the surname 'Luther' as a derogative term denoting nationality.[12] With time, and especially in the nineteenth century, the perception of Poland's Western neighbour grew to be more ambiguous. Wojciech Wrzesiński argues that, regardless of political circumstances and mutual conflicts, Germans tended to be viewed as representatives of a higher civilization which was also culturally more sophisticated. On the one hand, they were pictured as brutal, ruthless, pugnacious, predatory, contemptuous and arrogant, which reflected Polish attitudes after the Partitions of 1772–95, in which Prussia was involved. On the other hand, however, they were presented as dynamic, self-disciplined, hard-working, rational and pragmatic.[13] Not surprisingly, World War Two strengthened the former notion which was revised only in the 1990s when the idea of an affluent, industrious and cultured German came to dominate the opinion polls.[14]

Representations of Russia have an equally long history, although they became more widespread only in the eighteenth century, following the Partitions, when Russia was viewed chiefly as an aggressor and annihilator of Poland's independence. This portrayal subsequently merged with and was eventually dominated by images of a barbaric and despotic nation, contrasted with the messianic mission of Poland and its highly important role as the most western outpost of civilized Europe.[15] Being popular in the Romantic period, the identification of Russia with the wild Asian hordes returned with redoubled force after the 1917 Revolution.[16] Later on, the

[11] Jerzy Bartmiński, 'Jak zmienia się stereotyp Niemca w Polsce?', *Przegląd Humanistyczny*, 5, 1994, pp. 81–104 (p. 82).

[12] Ibid., p. 83.

[13] Wojciech Wrzesiński, *Sąsiad czy wróg? Ze studiów nad kształtowaniem obrazu Niemca w Polsce w latach 1795–1939*, Wrocław, 1992, p. 713.

[14] Bartmiński, 'Jak zmienia się stereotyp Niemca w Polsce?', p. 98.

[15] Maria Janion, *Niesamowita Słowiańszczyzna*, Kraków, 2006, pp. 191–93.

[16] Marek Kornat, 'Między wyobraźnią i wiedzą. Rosja w polskiej myśli historycznej',

infamous Molotov-Ribbentrop Pact of 1939 which was followed by World War Two, was presented as 'a knife in Poland's back', while the decades of political subjugation to Moscow after 1945 restored the dichotomy of Russia as the aggressor and Poland as the victim. These concerns, however, did not publicly resurface until after the fall of Communism, when derogatory images and suppressed memories re-emerged.[17]

Although considerable research has been devoted to the practices of remembrance in Poland, most notably in the last ten years, rather less attention has been paid to the ways in which memory transpires in print media from 2005 onwards. One prominent line of research into the relationship between memory and identity in Poland focuses on the role of the post-Communist transition in regaining 'the freedom to remember'. Several studies have analysed the eruption and commodification of memory in the post-1989 period and the ways in which specific historical events, for example, the Warsaw Uprising, the emergence of Solidarity and Martial Law, function within collective remembering.[18] Others have attempted to draw a landscape of contemporary memory culture in Poland, stressing on the one hand the country's fixation with the past and its inability to work through historical traumas[19] and, on the other, the lack of propitious circumstances to achieve closure.[20] A number of studies have also looked at the institutionalization of collective remembering[21] and Poland's sites of memory, including the contentious ones, such as the Red Army memorials.[22] Conspicuously absent in most of this research is an assessment of how representations of Poland's two external 'Others', Germany and Russia, are employed in the process of redefining national identity in media discourse. Even though several studies have explored the framing of Russia in Polish public discourse, including articles by Tomasz Zarycki and Ekaterina Levintova, they have not explored the interplay

in Magdziak-Miszewska et al., *Polacy i Rosjanie: 100 kluczowych pojęć*, Warsaw, 2002, pp. 34–50 (pp. 49–50).

[17] Ekaterina Levintova, 'Good Neighbours? Dominant Narratives about the "Other" in Contemporary Polish and Russian Newspapers', *Europe-Asia Studies*, 62, 2010, 8, pp. 1339–61 (p. 1343).

[18] See, for example, Barbara Szacka, *Czas przeszły – pamięć – mit*, Warsaw, 2006–07; Piotr T. Kwiatkowski, *Pamięć zbiorowa społeczeństwa polskiego w okresie transformacji*, Warsaw, 2008.

[19] Slysz, 'Poland: History as Crucible'.

[20] Thompson, 'Ways of Remembering'.

[21] Mark, *The Unfinished Revolution*.

[22] See, for example, Ewa Ochman, 'Soviet War Memorials and the Re-Construction of National and Local Identities in Post-Communist Poland', *Nationalities Papers*, 38, 2010, 4, pp. 509–30.

between those images and the editorial policy of the specific media. Neither have they attempted to examine those representations in light of the broader politics of memory in Poland.[23]

This article will, therefore, explore the interaction between media representations of Germany and Russia and the process of delineating national identity in relation to them. In particular, it will investigate how the memory of both World War Two and the years of Communism, among other historical events, fuels right-wing media discourse in the period after Poland's accession to the European Union in 2004 and, as a result, reinforces specific interpretations of the past. By concentrating on cover stories published between 2005 and 2009 by the then right-wing opinion weekly news magazine, *Wprost* (*Straight Talk*), this article will seek to answer two key questions: first, how did the right-wing print media view Poland's two powerful neighbours in the period between important historical anniversaries and second, what image of collective memory and national identity did these representations project in the period between the country's momentous accession to the EU in 2004 and the tragic crash of the presidential plane near Smolensk on 10 April 2010?

Why 'Wprost'?

For many years *Wprost* has been an important feature in the landscape of the Polish media. After being founded in 1982 as a regional magazine in Greater Poland it gained nationwide prominence in 1989, becoming the flagship right-wing weekly news magazine in the country.[24] Throughout the 2000s, together with the centre-left *Polityka* and the centrist *Newsweek Polska*, it was part of the 'Holy Trinity' of the weekly press, which had circulation figures amounting to 176,400 (*Polityka*), 147,500 (*Wprost*) and

[23] See Levintova, 'Good Neighbours?', and Tomasz Zarycki, 'Uses of Russia: The Role of Russia in the Modern Polish National Identity', *East European Politics & Societies*, 18, 2004, pp. 595–627.

[24] In the Polish context the distinction between right- and left-wing politics is not always clear-cut. For example, from its inception, Solidarity has promoted left-liberal political ideals along with traditional, Christian values. In addition, part of the opposition intelligentsia aligned with Solidarity created a conservative right-wing current within the movement, which included the Kaczyński brothers, Jan Olszewski and Marek Jurek among others, forming one group, and Donald Tusk, Jan Bielecki and Janusz Lewandowski, who promoted a liberal stance on the economy while fostering Christian democratic values, comprising another group. Equally, nowadays, while the Law and Justice Party supports nationalist-Catholic tradition, normally associated with right-wing ideology, its social policies are more left-wing than those of the Civic Platform Party. See, for example, Stanislav Holubec and Gavin Rae, 'A Conservative Convergence? The Differences and Similarities of the Conservative Right in the Czech Republic and Poland', *Contemporary Politics*, 16, 2010, 2, pp. 189–207 (pp. 196 and 199).

146,000 (*Newsweek Polska*) in 2005, leaving other popular weeklies such as the Catholic *Gość Niedzielny* (*Sunday's Guest*) and the liberal Catholic *Tygodnik Powszechny* (*The General Weekly*) far behind.[25] In terms of readership, the three major news magazines have been surpassed only by influential daily newspapers, such as the centre-left *Gazeta Wyborcza*, the most popular daily in Poland with an average issue readership of just over 300,000 and the centre-right *Rzeczpospolita*, selling approximately 150,000 copies.

Wprost had been owned by the Warsaw-based Publishing and Advertising Agency *Straight Talk* (Agencja Wydawniczo-Reklamowa *Wprost*, AWRW) until the end of December 2009, when 80 per cent of its shares were bought by another Polish enterprise — Media Platform Point Group (Platforma Mediowa Point Group, PMPG). Following the takeover and subsequent changes in editorial staff and policy, *Wprost* has been rebranded into a centrist weekly and, since May 2010, when the highly accomplished journalist Tomasz Lis was appointed editor-in-chief, the magazine has been veering between its newly prescribed centrist identity and a more liberal stance. Devoid of the conservative voice of the pre-2010 *Wprost*, the weekly press in Poland had become more homogeneous and unequivocal until the immediate aftermath of the Smolensk plane crash, when the readership of the far-right *Gazeta Polska* rocketed to 63,579, increasing by 160 per cent in just a few months.[26] However, as Wojciech Kosc has observed, the magazine seems unlikely to attract mainstream readership due to its fixation on the accident and its links with circles promoting conspiratorial interpretations of the crash.[27] In stark contrast, the emergence of a new weekly, *Uważam Rze*, in February 2011, established by journalists attached to the daily, *Rzeczpospolita*, and described by them as 'the only conservative-liberal voice in the public debate about important contemporary events', marked another change in Poland's weekly press market, with the magazine rapidly becoming the best-selling weekly and its readership soaring to nearly 137,000 in 2011.[28]

[25] See, for example, 'Tygodniki opinii: *Polityka* liderem sprzedaży', *Gazeta.pl* <http://wiadomosci.gazeta.pl/wiadomosci/1,114873,2903367.html> [accessed 15 November 2012].

[26] These figures come from July 2010. See '"Gazeta Polska" zwiększyła sprzedaż o 160 proc.', *Gazeta.pl* <http://wiadomosci.gazeta.pl/wiadomosci/1,114873,8409975,_Gazeta_Polska__zwiekszyla_sprzedaz_o_160_proc_.html.html> [accessed 15 November 2012].

[27] Wojciech Kosc, 'Publishing Takeover Rattles the Polish Right', *Transitions Online*, 22 August 2011.

[28] The magazine's readership figures fell by 6.25 per cent in 2012, making *Uważam Rze* the fourth popular weekly. See '"Uważam Rze" rok temu był najpopularniejszym tygodnikiem. W lipcu spadł z podium', *TokFm.pl* <http://wiadomosci.gazeta.pl/

As of February 2012, when Tomasz Lis was replaced by Michał Kobosko, the future of *Wprost* remains unclear. However, with experience in *Newsweek Polska*, among other news magazines, the new editor is very likely to continue the agenda of his predecessor, which was intended to please the Civic Platform Party voters, as opposed to aligning itself with supporters of the Law and Justice Party, which was a distinct feature of the pre-2010 *Wprost*, particularly at the height of PiS's popularity between 2005 and 2007.[29] After all, it was in 2005 that Jarosław Kaczyński was awarded the Person of the Year Prize by the news magazine, while his then fellow party affiliate and Minister of Justice, Zbigniew Ziobro, was given the title in 2006. The gradual waning of the party's popularity from 2008 onwards was marked by the weekly's takeover in 2009 and an increasingly PO-sympathizing agenda.[30] This was consistently continued by Lis who gave the Person of the Year 2011 title to Tusk, making this his final undertaking as editor-in-chief, before leaving to develop his own project — the Polish counterpart of the American news website *Huffington Post* and taking over, shortly after, the editorship of *Newsweek Polska*.

Although *Wprost*'s contentious political agenda has become a thing of the past, it is still urgent to analyse, question and explore it given how representative it is of the wider conservative discourse in contemporary Poland. This is especially important considering the political and cultural changes that took place after 2005, including the eruption of the PiS-controlled *polityka historyczna*, or 'historical politics', along with the ideological battles between Poland's two main parties. More importantly, both 2005 and 2009 marked several anniversaries, including the sixtieth anniversary of the end of World War Two, the seventieth anniversary of the outbreak of the war and the twentieth anniversary of the end of Communism. The remembrance of those events, which had a particularly strong impact on Polish-German and Polish-Russian relations, resulted in a proliferation of cover stories concerning both neighbours. Having

wiadomosci/1,114873,12526603,_Uwazam_Rze__rok_temu_byl_najpopularniejszym_tygodnikiem_.html> [accessed 15 November 2012].

[29] *Wprost* between 2005 and 2009 as well today can be viewed as a classic example of a news magazine which has been affected by shifting patterns of ownership. This, in turn, has made the weekly largely subservient to issues of profitability and forced its owners to present the perspective of the dominant political establishment.

[30] For example, in 2008 and 2009 the Person of the Year titles were given to two Civic Platform members Donald Tusk and Jerzy Buzek, respectively. In comparison, the highly acclaimed TV prizes 'Wiktory' awarded in several categories, one being the most popular politician of the year, went to PiS's Kazimierz Marcinkiewicz in 2005, and two PO members Radosław Sikorski in 2006 and Donald Tusk in 2007.

considered the total of 255 cover stories published in *Wprost* during this five-year period, ten out of twenty-one stories that made explicit reference to both countries were selected and analysed, based on how representative they were of Poland's public discourse at the time and whether or not they alluded to historical events. For example, in 2005 there were three covers out of a total of fifty-two that referred to each of the countries, all of which contained a discussion of the past. Both 2007 and 2008 saw an explosion of interest in Germany (four and three covers respectively) and a continued preoccupation with Russia (one and two covers respectively). In total, during this five-year period, Germany featured on *Wprost*'s covers thirteen and Russia eight times.[31]

The use of cover stories as case studies has been primarily motivated by their importance in the editorial policy of the weekly opinion press in that they tend to be representative of its wider political agenda. *Wprost*'s lead stories in particular were indicative of the weekly's grappling with Poland's past and present, in addition to projecting its visions of future Polish national identity. They were often accompanied by highly controversial, graphically manipulated covers. These notorious representations were aimed at grabbing and captivating the imagination of the public, while boosting readership figures. Its daring covers made *Wprost* distinct from other weeklies, perpetuating, to some extent, national stereotypes and reflecting shared fears in regard to Poland's external 'Others'. Not only did this shed new light on collective traumas, as viewed by the news magazine, but it also indicated important differences in the mechanisms involved in representing the two countries.

Media, Politics and National Identity

Although the extent to which the media affects the construction of national identities has been subject to numerous debates, it is almost universally acknowledged that there is a strong relationship between the two. Benedict Anderson argues that the daily 'mass ceremony' of newspaper reading constituted a driving force in the mental construction of nations as imagined communities.[32] In particular, he points to the emergence of industrial-scale printing in the nineteenth century, which initiated the spread of vernacular languages and unified previously disparate

[31] This comprises covers with overt references to both countries. See issues 5/2005, 17/2005, 27/2005, 35/2006, 45/2006, 24/2007, 26/2007, 35/2007, 38/2007, 5/2008, 10/2008, 42/2008 and 36/2009 for representations of Germany, and 16/2005, 27/2005, 36/2005, 2/2006, 3/2007, 34/2008, 37/2008, 36/2009 for representations of Russia.

[32] Benedict Anderson, *Imagined Communities*, London, 2006, p. 36.

communities.[33] Similarly, Anthony Smith asserts that it is the mass media that ensures the existence of common values, traditions, ideas and aspirations by producing a shared culture and, consequently contributes to the creation of nations.[34] By comparison, Ernest Gellner argues that it is not the specific message conveyed by the media that matters but the

> pervasiveness and importance of abstract, centralized, standardized, one to many communication, which itself automatically engenders the core idea of nationalism, quite irrespective of what in particular is being put into the specific messages transmitted.[35]

The media therefore constitutes a 'powerful ideological apparatus' which has the potential to influence large audiences by deploying a politicized agenda as a lens through which to report and comment on contemporary events.[36] As shown previously, the political spectrum of the most influential print media in Poland ranges from right to centre-left, with far right media outlets such as *Gazeta Polska* and *Nasz Dziennik* being equally vocal, but located on the margins where readership figures are concerned. In the Polish context, defining the political alignment of a media outlet proves to be increasingly problematic due to certain ideological convergences, such as the attachment to the Polish-Catholic model of national identity, especially within centrist and right-wing discourses. Analysing the language of constitutional debates of 1996 and 1997, and in particular the articulations of national identity by various political camps, Geneviève Zubrzycki pinpoints the disparities between those different discourses:

> The Center-Left speaks of 'citizens,' 'civil society,' and the 'civic nation,' and aims at creating a modern Poland open to Europe, oriented toward the future, and based on universal human values. In contrast, the conservative Center and the Right speak of 'Poles' and their 'ancestors' and reach to the past, to Poland's thousand years of history. It aims at preserving a national tradition, emphasizing the national-Christian heritage and values. The first is legitimized according to rational-legal principles, the other by the weight of tradition.[37]

[33] Ibid., p. 44.
[34] Anthony D. Smith, *National Identity*, Reno, NV, 1991, p. 11.
[35] Ernest Gellner, *Nations and Nationalism*, Oxford, 2006, p. 122.
[36] Norman Fairclough, *Media Discourse*, London, 1995, pp. 46–47.
[37] Geneviève Zubrzycki, *The Crosses of Auschwitz: Nationalism and Religion in Post-Communist Poland*, Chicago, IL and London, 2006, p. 94.

Zubrzycki's distinctions are also true of the Polish print media. For example, she points out elsewhere that over the years intellectuals associated with *Gazeta Wyborcza*, most notably its long-term editor-in-chief Adam Michnik, have been fostering the idea of Polish national identity founded on 'social justice' and 'civic rights and duties'.[38] This is perhaps one of the reasons why the newspaper has often been seen as an arch-enemy of the PiS project and an example of liberal discourse in need of re-polonization.[39] Using similar distinctions, this article posits that the pre-2010 *Wprost* was a medium through which conservative values and opinions concerning national history were promoted and transmitted, concurrently unifying and dividing communities. It suggests that by creating and replicating particular images of its external 'Others' the news magazine enforced both a centralized politics of memory and a compelling vision of Polish national identity. By looking into the mechanisms of producing and disseminating those views, the article shows how concerted efforts to pervade public discourse with seemingly collective notions of the past served the weekly in the process of endorsing specific political viewpoints.

First explored will be the representations of Germany between 2005 and 2009, followed by an examination of images of Russia during the same period. The article will then provide a brief overview of the portrayal of each country in the days leading up to important historical anniversaries, to then conclude by comparing *Wprost*'s visions of both countries and assessing the magazine's new political agenda post-2010.

From Unrequited Love to Severe Tuskophobia: Representations of Germany

Following the collapse of Communism in 1989 and Poland's accession to the EU in 2004, Polish-German relations at least appeared to have begun to improve. Beginning with Bonn's, and then Berlin's, backing of Poland's 'return to Europe', through the increased cooperation of the two countries on both the international and regional scales, to the attempts of successive governments to work through historical grievances, reconciliation seemed to be in sight. However, mutual relations deteriorated rapidly under the Kaczyński twins, who made anti-German/Russian policy their calling card. At the height of their popularity from 2005 to 2007, when Jarosław Kaczyński was Prime Minister and Lech President, their rhetoric of the 'enemies at the gates' seeped into the right-wing press and elevated prejudice to an officially sanctioned form of discourse. With extensive

[38] Ibid., pp. 81–82.
[39] See, for example, Harper, 'Negating Negation', p. 30.

experience in hand, *Wprost* readily followed this trend, providing a wide array of cover stories concerning the complex issues of Polish-German history. Woven into those discussions was Poland's position in the EU and the effect the past has had on the two states' partnership, as well as power dynamics within the wider European community.

One of the most notorious cover stories, exploring the Polish-German collaboration within the EU, appeared in the summer of 2007. Issue 26/2007 followed the European Council's negotiations on the Treaty of Lisbon that took place in Brussels on 21 and 22 June 2007. The most controversial part of the negotiations was Poland's rejection of the proposal on voting weights, which met with strong opposition from Germany, then presiding over the EU. Although the Lisbon Treaty eventually changed voting in the Council of Ministers so that more decisions are now made by Qualified Majority Voting (QMV), rather than unanimous voting, the negotiations had demonstrated, according to *Wprost*, that Germany was incapable of treating Poland as an equal political partner. The authors of the article claimed that it was not Warsaw's refusal to accept the proposed voting weights that led to the conflict but the 'German mentality and its intrinsic *postcolonial* attitude towards Poland'.[40] It seems that the authors meant a '*colonial* attitude' here, which, as they implied, was a remnant of the Second World War that underpinned German decisions on European policy and shaped contemporary relations between the two nations. Despite applying postcolonial terminology in a casual manner, the article demonstrates how the reductive dichotomy of colonizers and colonized can become a powerful weapon in the right-wing media. It revitalizes the idea of repetitive patterns of history with both the perpetrator and the victim seemingly re-enacting their assigned roles. Simultaneously, the narrative of German guilt and Polish oppression, which has been one of the cornerstones of memory discourses in post-war Poland, came to life once more.[41]

The image that appeared alongside this story presents Angela Merkel, the German Chancellor, and between January-June 2007 also President of the EU Council, breastfeeding the Kaczyński twins. Perhaps one of *Wprost*'s most controversial covers to date, this graphically manipulated photograph employed a salient symbol in Polish national mythology — that of the nourishing mother. This mode of representation, originating from the cult

[40] All translations are mine. Krzysztof Rak and Mariusz Muszyński, 'Macocha Europy', *Wprost*, 1 July 2007, p. 20. Emphasis added.

[41] Eric Langenbacher, 'Twenty-First Century Memory Regimes in Germany and Poland', *German Politics and Society*, 89, 2008, 26, pp. 50–81 (p. 63).

of the Virgin Mary, has dominated Polish national discourse throughout the centuries and idealized the role of the mother in society.[42] However, the caption, 'Macocha Europy' (The Stepmother of Europe), subverts this archetypal representation, denying religious connotations and stripping Merkel of any positive characteristics that the act of breastfeeding may have invoked. By introducing the word 'stepmother', *Wprost* presents the Kaczyński brothers, and by association perhaps even the Polish nation as a whole, as the neglected and unwanted children of Europe who are rejected by the one who should be their closest ally. The twins' supposed striving for Polish-German partnership and cooperation within wider European structures is emphasized here by the ambiguous 'V' sign, gestured towards the German leader by one of the brothers. On the one hand this might be interpreted as begging for peace and on the other as a sign of victory, a reference to the outcome of the European Council negotiations mentioned above.

The symbolically charged act of breastfeeding, which brings associations with Polish conceptions of perfect femininity, is subverted here and used in order to provide a highly ambiguous portrayal of Germany. As Norman Fairclough asserts, in the media 'the images have primacy over the words in the sense that the events related happen first visually'.[43] Here the seemingly positive cover image comes first and it is only the story, clearly critical of Germany, which brings out the inconsistencies and tensions in the overall message that is projected. As such, the news magazine replicates here some of the enduring representations of Germany found in Polish culture and historiography, which often combined a mixture of respect and contempt. At the same time *Wprost* presents the Polish nation as one that attempts to establish a peaceful dialogue with Germany but is constantly rejected and disregarded by the latter. This apparent re-enacting and re-telling of historical enmities within a new European setting may be read as a way of alleviating shared traumas and crystallizing collective memory, each being an inseparable part of the healing process.[44]

However, the wider political context of this story suggests deeper-rooted phobias on the part of the Polish right. As a document bringing the Charter of Fundamental Rights of the European Union into full legal

[42] For a longer discussion of the trajectory of this archetype see, for example, Elżbieta Ostrowska, 'Matki Polki i ich synowie. Kilka uwag o genezie obrazów kobiecości i męskości w kulturze polskiej', in Małgorzata Radkiewicz (ed.), *Gender. Konteksty*, Kraków, 2004, pp. 215–27 (pp. 217–18).

[43] Fairclough, *Media Discourse*, p. 7.

[44] See, for example, Jennifer Cole, 'Painful Memories: Ritual and the Transformation of Community Traumas', *Culture, Medicine and Psychiatry*, 28, 2004, pp. 87–105 (p. 88).

effect, not only was the Lisbon Treaty to result in a professed 'moral decline' by legalizing civil partnerships but it was to lead to the increase of compensation claims from German expellees who were forced to leave the so-called 'Recovered Territories' following World War Two. According to the Law and Justice Party, the Treaty was to undermine both Poland's interests and its traditional ethical values. These debates led, in turn, to ironic reactions from the liberal media, such as *Gazeta Wyborcza*, who later described the apprehension of the Kaczyński brothers as *strachy na Lachy*, a phrase used for unjustified fears.[45]

Similar representations of Polish-German relations appear in other cover stories from that period. Issue 10/2008, for instance, asks a rhetorical question: 'Jak pokochać Niemcy' ('How to Love Germany'). The absence of a question mark in the title of this issue brings to mind how-to or self-help books which guide their readers through perplexities of modern life; in this case the matters of intercultural tolerance being the key predicament. The image on the cover presents a Polish woman kissing the Mercedes-Benz logo. Nationality is indicated here by the Polish flag, a bicolour of white and red, painted on her cheek. While the company emblem would normally be viewed as a figure for German prosperity, here it symbolizes innate Germanness. The intimate relationship the woman has with a product of German manufacturing industry illustrates the central theme of the cover story: Polish anti-Germanness is a myth. According to research conducted for the magazine in Poland, 'Poles love the Germans; the latter however do not reciprocate those feelings'.[46] *Wprost* further claimed that it was in fact anti-Polish sentiment spreading through its neighbouring country that was to blame for the estrangement of the two nations.

The narrative that emerges from the two stories discussed above is, ostensibly, one of attempted reconciliation, a process which nonetheless is impeded by a difficult and uncooperative partner. On the surface, *Wprost* seeks to embrace the mainstream debates of the Warsaw-Berlin rapprochement, which have dominated public discourse post-2004. This is illustrated by numerous examples of Poland's willingness to restore cordial relations between the two countries, including the survey conducted for the magazine, which confirms Poles' affinity with their Western neighbour. In truth, some of the methods used to achieve this had the exact opposite effect. Ambiguous covers, in particular, including the one presenting bare-chested Merkel breast-feeding the Kaczyński brothers, which proved

[45] Dominik Uhlig, 'Strachy na Lachy', *Gazeta Wyborcza*, 25 March 2008.
[46] Grzegorz Sadowski and Karolina Woźniak, 'Jak pokochać Niemcy', *Wprost*, 9 March 2008, p. 22.

to carry negative undertones when juxtaposed with the accompanying articles, suggest deeply suppressed resentment and a latent inferiority complex. These stories seem, in effect, to run counter to the opinions of scholars who claim that traumas stemming from a painful Polish-German history have, unlike those concerning Russo-Polish relations, reached their closure.[47] As a result, *Wprost* projects a highly fragmented image of the Polish nation which on the one hand has already begun to heal, but on the other is reopening old wounds.

A different strategy used by the news magazine for expressing a highly ambiguous view of Germany in the period under discussion is closely tied to representations of Donald Tusk, the leader of the Civic Platform Party and Poland's Prime Minister since 2007. 2007–08 in particular was characterized by an increased media visibility on the part of the Prime Minister who is also a staunch supporter of the creation of a lasting peace as well as the strengthening of political and economic relations between the two nations.[48] The strongly pro-German orientation of his government had often been exploited by the magazine in their constructions of the 'Other', as in issue 9/2007. The cover presents Tusk, a few months before he was elected Prime Minister, and one of the Civic Platform Party members, Jan Rokita. They stand side by side, holding hands, smiling and wearing matching blue shirts. In other words, they are portrayed as a model gay couple. This graphically manipulated image invokes pictures used in the 'Niech nas zobaczą' ('Let Them See Us') photographic campaign which took place in Poland in 2003.[49] The project featured posters and billboards presenting fifteen gay and fifteen lesbian couples displayed in major cities in Poland, which aimed at making homosexuality more visible in the public space. The cover story discusses the recent reconciliation of the two politicians whose past misunderstandings, described in the article as the 'clash of characters', had often led to problems within the party. Their reunion is depicted as a 'love parade' or 'equality parade', in order to demonstrate that the party has now several equal leaders.[50] By using this particular phrase, the article explicitly refers to the *Loveparade* that originated in Berlin. The combination of an image epitomizing an equality campaign with phrases such as 'love parade' reveals the belief widespread

[47] See, for example, Thompson, 'Ways of Remembering'.

[48] In this respect, worthy of special mention is the key role of Poland's Foreign Minister, Radosław Sikorski, in implementing these policies of reconciliation.

[49] This is reiterated by the title on the cover of that issue.

[50] Marcin Dzierżanowski and Katarzyna Nowicka, 'Niech nas zobaczą!', *Wprost*, 4 March 2007, p. 20.

in right-wing discourse that moral destruction, represented here by homosexuality, came with gay pride parades from Germany. *Wprost*'s supposed inability to distinguish the German *Loveparade*, which from its inception has not been associated with any specific sexual orientation, from equality parades is symptomatic of the way in which Western, and German in particular, cultural influences are viewed by the Polish right. Often intentionally distorted, they are aimed at fuelling nationalistic feelings and polarizing society along political lines. Hence, if we take into account Tusk's strong pro-German orientation, this representation of the two politicians as a gay couple is not only homophobic but also xenophobic. Analysing gender issues in the Polish press, Agnieszka Graff claims that Polish homophobia has a strong anti-German element to it and argues that 'it is in fact a neurotic nationalism'.[51] This echoes the controversies surrounding the prohibition of the Equality March in 2005 by the then mayor of Warsaw, Lech Kaczyński, who claimed to have been protecting the religious feelings of the inhabitants of the city, while implying the anti-Catholic and anti-Polish nature of the march.[52] What *Wprost* alludes to here is the more recent history of sexual emancipation post-1989, when German culture became an attractive alternative to the culture of sexual repression, characteristic of Communist and, to some extent, also post-Communist Poland. The story also seeks to deride Tusk as a leader of the Civic Platform Party in anticipation of the general election.

Anti-German sentiment is often linked by *Wprost* with representations of Donald Tusk; his image, however, appears in a variety of contexts and serves a range of purposes. For example, the cover story in issue 5/2008 focuses on the forced population transfers at the end of World War Two, during which time German inhabitants of regions such as Silesia and Pomerania, including Tusk's home town of Gdańsk/Danzig, were forcibly resettled in present-day Germany. The article argues that those Germans have no right to demand compensations and their expulsions should be treated as a natural aftermath of World War Two. In order to further undermine those claims, the authors recall the population transfers that took place between 1939 and 1945 which displaced an estimated 1.7 million Poles from Nazi occupied territories as a means of accommodating the arriving SS forces.[53]

[51] Agnieszka Graff, *Rykoszetem. Rzecz o płci, seksualności i narodzie*, Warsaw, 2008, pp. 101 and 141.

[52] See Anika Keinz, 'European Desires and National Bedrooms? Negotiating "Normalcy" in Postsocialist Poland', *Central European History*, 44, 2011, pp. 92–117 (p. 114).

[53] Mariusz Muszyński and Krzysztof Rak, 'Kogo wypędzić', *Wprost*, 3 February 2008,

The cover story is supplemented with an evocative image of Tusk as a deportee being expelled from his native country. Showing him out is the president of Germany's Federation of Expellees (Bund der Vertriebenen, BdV), Erika Steinbach, dressed in an SS uniform. Born in the Pomeranian town of Rumia/Rahmel, where her father was stationed as a Luftwaffe officer, Steinbach is here the metaphor for all Germans who were expelled from those territories from the mid 1940s onwards. The imagery and rhetoric used present the expellees as a powerful group that could reappropriate the land and lead to mass deportations of Poles.[54] Employing here once more the idea of history's cyclical nature, the magazine's portrayal of Steinbach brings to mind Hitler's concept of *Lebensraum*, or 'living space', which was the foundation of the expansionist policy of Nazi Germany. In view of that, not only can this particular cover story be seen as an expression of *Wprost*'s opposition to German compensation claims but also as a way of deepening societal prejudice against the Federation of Expellees and presenting them as a threat to Polish sovereignty. In addition, the title of the article, 'Kogo wypędzić' ('Who Should be Expelled'), and the placement of Donald Tusk in this photograph are indicative of the magazine's 'Tuskophobia', and concurrently, are clear markers of *Wprost*'s political sympathies. In this respect, the story replicates some of the views of the leader of PiS, Jarosław Kaczyński, who has often described PO's pro-German stance as servile and damaging to Polish interests. More recently, he proposed declaring Steinbach *persona non grata*, which would prevent her from entering Poland.[55]

On the level of memory and identity construction, the story shows the striving of the conservative elites aligned with PiS for a monopoly on suffering, where World War Two is concerned. These attempts seem to be underpinned by a fear of de-legitimization and a belittling of Polish traumas, and perhaps even their eventual obliteration. As controversies surrounding plans to build the Centre against Expulsions in Berlin which

p. 40.

[54] Worthy of special mention is another of *Wprost*'s cover stories featuring Erika Steinbach, published before 2005, in issue 38/2003. Similar to the article from 2008, the story refuses to accept German compensation claims and perpetuates the narrative of German guilt by presenting Steinbach dressed in an SS uniform, riding Chancellor Schröder. See Sławomir Sieradzki, 'Niemiecki koń trojański', *Wprost*, 28 September 2003, p. 16.

[55] PAP. 'Kaczyński dla PAP: jeśli zostanę premierem Steinbach będzie persona non grata', 4 October 2011 <http://wiadomosci.gazeta.pl/wiadomosci/1,114873,10409488,Kaczynski_dla_PAP__jesli_zostane_premierem__Steinbach.html> [accessed 9 December 2012].

resurfaced a few years earlier have shown, the issue of German wartime suffering is often viewed in Poland as an attack on Polish interpretations of history and a means of presenting Germans as the main victims of World War Two.[56] As such, actions of the League of Expellees are seen by the weekly as undermining the narrative of Polish victimization and German culpability which has been dominant in Poland since the end of the war.

The analyses above have indicated that *Wprost*'s representations of Germany constitute the locus where the issues of World War Two and European integration intertwine, clash and grapple. Interestingly, some of these representations keep up the appearance of embracing reconciliation between the two nations in the spirit of enlarged Europe, yet spectacularly fail to sustain such a narrative when examined in-depth. This is evident in the stories featuring both Angela Merkel and the Mercedes-Benz emblem. There are also covers which skilfully disguise anti-German sentiment, as exemplified by the story presenting Tusk and Rokita as a gay couple. This multitude of themes and approaches to Germany as well as the attempts to picture Poland's Western neighbour in a nuanced way suggest the complexity of *Wprost*'s perspective. This corresponds to a large extent with the tradition of othering Germany in Poland, which is characterized by the intertwining of contempt and deference. If viewed in a more positive light, however, these representations may also be interpreted as miniature steps towards genuine rapprochement. As the next section will demonstrate, right-wing discourse on Russia is nowhere near taking similar steps.

The Expansionist Neighbour: Representations of Russia

After the fall of Communism, Russia has been conventionally 'othered' in Poland, leading to negative societal reactions, in particular where foreign security issues are concerned. Since its inception in 2001, the Law and Justice Party has maintained a strong anti-Communist stance, while exploiting the Katyń discourse in an attempt to foster the victim-and-hero status of Poland.[57] This narrative intensified following the plane crash with the memory of those who were killed in the accident becoming an important point on PiS's anti-Russian agenda.[58] Having a more reconciliatory stance towards Russia, the Civic Platform Party, and especially Poland's Foreign

56 Pawel Lutomski, 'The Debate about a Center against Expulsions: An Unexpected Crisis in German-Polish Relations?', *German Studies Review*, 27, 2004, 3, pp. 449–68 (p. 452).

57 Harper, 'Negating Negation', p. 28.

58 See, for example, *Program PiS 2011*, p. 53 <http://www.pis.org.pl/dokumenty.php?s=partia&iddoc=157> [accessed 22 November 2012].

Minister Radosław Sikorski, have repeatedly stressed the need for a wider EU-Russia cooperation and the Polish government's readiness to enter into a dialogue with Russia.[59] Admittedly, PO's fierce criticism of the Russo-German gas pipeline under the Baltic Sea, chiefly in the early stages of the project, has been reminiscent of traditional 'othering' discourses, but the gradual warming of Polish-Russian relations after 10 April 2010 marked an important shift in perceptions of this particular country.

Although Russia features in *Wprost* less often than Germany, it is certainly more visible, with the majority of the eight covers published between 2005 and 2009 reiterating the notion of Russia as a threat. Such a perception of this 'Other' has been an important feature of conservative and nationalist discourses in post-Communist Poland, particularly within the last few years. Recent events such as the Russo-Georgian conflict in 2008 served *Wprost* as examples of Moscow's expansionist policy, further demonizing the country and feeding Polish anti-Russian sentiment.

Indeed, dominant representations of Russia convey an image of a country driven entirely by its imperial ambitions, which uses its gas resources as a political weapon. One example of this is a cover story on the North European Gas Pipeline in issue 27/2005.[60] Completed in 2012 and running from the Russian city of Vyborg to Greifswald in Germany, it is the longest submarine pipeline in the world. Since its inception in the late 1990s, the project has been fervently supported by Vladimir Putin and Gerhard Schröder, who is currently the chairman of the board of Nord Stream GA, the consortium responsible for implementing the project.[61] The undertaking has been controversial from the start, due to various environmental and political issues. It was noted, for example, that the pipeline construction and operation:

> may disturb fish breeding grounds and disrupt fisheries in construction areas. Traditional fishing areas may be permanently displaced if a no fishing zone is implemented in the pipeline area to prevent just such

[59] Radosław Sikorski, 'Informacja rządu na temat polskiej polityki zagranicznej w 2008 roku', *Rocznik Polskiej Polityki Zagranicznej*, 2009, pp. 9–26 (p. 15).

[60] Jerzy M. Nowakowski and Piotr Woźniak, 'Gazowe okrążenie Polski', *Wprost*, 17 July 2005, p. 84.

[61] The majority shareholder is the state-owned Russian Gazprom, which owns 51 per cent of the outstanding shares, while two German-based companies, Wintershall and E.ON Ruhrgas, control 20 per cent of the shares each. The remaining 9 per cent is owned by a Dutch company N.V. Nederlandse Gasunie. It has been announced recently that a French energy company GDF Suez has signed an initial agreement with Gazprom to acquire a 9 per cent stake of its shares.

damage. Gas leaks may harm or kill fish, their eggs, larvae and fry. Natural gas can also affect other marine organisms, such as zooplankton.[62]

In addition, concerns of a political nature have been expressed. Poland and the Baltic States in particular have viewed the pipeline, which bypasses their territories, as the Kremlin's attempt to restore its influence in the region. Depending heavily on Russian gas,[63] these countries feared that Moscow would pressurize them to adopt favourable stances towards it. This would manifest itself in state-controlled Gazprom breaking existing agreements, raising prices and threatening to cut gas supplies, without having to affect its Western European customers.[64]

Wprost voiced similar concerns shortly after the initial Russo-German agreement was signed. In 'Gazowe okrążenie Polski' ('The Gas Encirclement of Poland'), Jerzy Marek Nowakowski and Piotr Woźniak discussed the project in the context of Poland's history, emphasizing the impact the cooperation of both states had on its past. The authors claimed that Nord Stream would seriously threaten Poland's energy autonomy and lead to its political marginalization in the region. This Russo-German 'love affair', as they describe the undertaking, is compared here to important historical events that marred Poland's relations with its two neighbours over past centuries, including the Partitions of Poland in the eighteenth century and the Molotov-Ribbentrop Pact (1939). While it has been widely acknowledged that all these events affected significantly Poland's sovereignty in the past, the influence of the pipeline on the original transit countries remains yet to be determined. The article leaves no doubts, however, as to its assessment of the project, by suggesting its deeply political nature and describing the pipeline as 'political shackles'.[65] This message is reinforced by the compelling cover image which presents Vladimir Putin and Gerhard Schröder shaking hands, or rather shaking pipelines that spread across the map of the Baltic Sea. Accompanying the title of this issue is a meaningful caption, 'Pakt Putin-Schröder' ('The Putin-Schröder Pact'), which alludes to the 1939 Soviet-German non-aggression pact.

[62] Ellen Karm, 'Environment and Energy: The Baltic Sea Gas Pipeline', *Journal of Baltic Studies*, 39, 2008, 2, pp. 99–121 (p. 108).

[63] On average up to 72 per cent of Poland's gas is imported; in 2010 nearly 90 per cent of imported gas came from Russia, and approximately of 10 per cent from Germany. See *PGNiG Raport roczny 2010*, 31, 43 <http://www.pgnig.pl/reports/raportroczny2010/> [accessed 23 April 2012].

[64] See, for example, Maria Mälksoo, *The Politics of Becoming European: A Study of Polish and Baltic Post-Cold War Security Imaginaries*, London, 2010, p. 76.

[65] Nowakowski and Woźniak, 'Gazowe okrążenie Polski'.

Tomasz Zarycki claims that the view of Russia as a threat is entrenched in the dominant model of Polish historiography,[66] to the extent that negative representations have 'become institutionalized in the formal discourse of textbooks or media'.[67] This is largely derived from the anti-Communist paradigm of Polish national identity,[68] which has become one of the factors affecting official politics of memory following the electoral success of the Law and Justice Party in 2005. The idea of a Russo-German alliance adds another dimension to *Wprost*'s constructions of identity and memory, namely in its allusion to a Romantic vision of Polishness as marked by incessant suffering and victimization.[69] Comparing the gas pipeline to the Molotov-Ribbentrop Pact aims to revive historical traumas and, consequently, generate deep distrust and moral condemnation of both countries. This historical analogy also reveals what Qi Wang describes as the 'directive function' of collective memory, whereby past feuds and failures are used by the elites in the process of educating the community on the ways of avoiding risks and securing future safety.[70] However, the powerful nature of these analogies makes them often, as is visible in this case, susceptible to political manipulation.

The question of Moscow's energy policy appears again almost a year later in issue 2/2006.[71] This time, however, the weekly discusses the roots of Poland's dependence on Russian gas. Nowakowski, the author of the article, believes that for years Russia has been paying for lobbyists to infiltrate Polish politics and prevent decisions leading to diversification of gas suppliers being taken. The author maintains that this 'Soviet lobby', consisting of leading politicians of the Democratic Left Alliance (Sojusz Lewicy Demokratycznej, SLD), pressured the government of Jerzy Buzek to break initial agreements with Norway and stay with the Russian supplier. Here, once again, Nowakowski suggests that the Kremlin's 'energy terrorism' is symptomatic of its anachronistic foreign policy which is based on territorial expansion and spheres of political influence. Being heavily based on the political programme of the PiS Party from 2005, the article largely replicates its views on energy and economic security. For example, aside from criticizing Russia, it also denigrates left-wing

[66] Zarycki, 'Uses of Russia,' p. 608.

[67] Ibid., p. 598.

[68] Ibid.

[69] For a longer discussion of the Romantic paradigm of Polish national identity, see, for example, Janion, *Niesamowita Słowiańszczyzna*, pp. 192–94.

[70] Qi Wang, 'On the Cultural Constitution of Collective Memory', *Memory*, 16, 2008, 3, pp. 305–17 (p. 310).

[71] Jerzy M. Nowakowski, 'Miotacz gazu', *Wprost*, 22 January 2006, p. 22.

politicians originating from former Communist elites, accusing them of continued subjugation to Moscow and subsequently, attempting to deepen the political divide in society.[72] *Wprost* obliquely recalls here the notion of incomplete de-Communization post-1989, put forth by the Law and Justice Party, and stresses the need for removing ex-Communists from political life. The article fails to mention, however, that it was the social-democrat president, Aleksander Kwaśniewski, an ex-Communist himself, who challenged the environmental security of the North European Gas Pipeline and argued that it 'does not satisfy economic and political criteria, which should be taken into serious consideration before starting such projects'.[73]

The cover of this particular issue is equally controversial. It presents Vladimir Putin spewing gas from his mouth. The personification of Russia as Putin is a common strategy used by *Wprost*, even after 2008 when his second presidential term ended. Described here as 'the flamethrower', not only is he portrayed as a powerful figure that fully controls Russia's natural resources, but he is also compared to a dangerous weapon that has the ability to destroy anything in sight. This sends out a clear message: Moscow uses its gas resources as a political weapon. Similar concerns have been raised by Western media on several occasions, most notably during the Russian-Ukrainian gas rows in 2006 and 2009. However, it was also observed that Gazprom's supply to the West was stable even during the Cold War and it is still a more trustworthy source than the, potentially unreliable, alternative providers in Central Asia.[74] *Wprost*'s inward-looking rhetoric is nowhere near the carefully balanced tone of coverage offered by these media. In contrast, by alleging the Kremlin's ferocious imperial ambitions and hyperbolizing the level of threat posed to national security, it reveals a fully fledged Russophobia. Also conspicuous is the way in which the past is exploited in order to demonize Putin, which suggests that Polish-Russian relations, as perceived by *Wprost*, are constantly straddling the borders of history and geopolitics.

[72] See, for example, *Program PiS 2005*, pp. 48–49 <http://www.pis.org.pl/doc.php?d=unit&id=3> [accessed 9 December 2012].

[73] Fatih Ozbay and Bulent Aras, 'Polish-Russian Relations: History, Geography and Geopolitics', *East European Quarterly*, 1, 2008, pp. 27–42 (p. 37).

[74] See, for example, Ziba Norman, 'Russia's Gas Weapon', *New York Times*, 21 December 2005 <http://www.nytimes.com/2005/12/20/opinion/20iht-ednorman.html> [accessed 22 March 2012]; Adrian Blomfield, 'Russia's Powerful Weapon: Oil and Natural Gas', *The Daily Telegraph*, 29 August 2008 <http://www.telegraph.co.uk/news/worldnews/europe/russia/2645890/Russias-powerful-weapon-oil-and-natural-gas.html> [accessed 20 January 2012], and BBC News, 'Q&A: Russia-Ukraine Gas Row', 20 January 2009 <http://news.bbc.co.uk/2/hi/europe/7240462.stm> [accessed 27 March 2012].

This corresponds with Iurii Solozobov's observations on these contentious energy issues. He rightly points out that Poland is Gazprom's ninth largest trade partner, one that is, however, very reluctant to continue its dependence on Russian gas, viewing it as a 'voluntary submission to slavery'. He claims that these historically motivated tensions can only be defused by increased cooperation and participation in joint projects, such as the construction of the second leg of the Yamal-Europe gas pipeline. Solozobov also underlines the importance of a peaceful political dialogue between the two countries that would bring about reconciliation and end the wars of memory.[75]

Wprost's other articles relating to Russia focus almost exclusively on the Russo-Georgian conflict in South Ossetia in August 2008. The cover article in issue 34/2008 stresses the long-standing tradition of Russian imperialism, arguing that:

> Russia has always grown in strength by the means of conquest [...]. In fact, Russia does not produce anything but weapons and soldiers. Russian rulers have always used its massive army in order to conquer non-Russian territories and subsequently sell their natural resources. They do it up to this day.[76]

The article's telling title, 'Adolf Putin', also appears on the magazine cover which presents the former Russian president stylized as Hitler. Aside from alluding to the violent territorial expansion of Nazi Germany, which by now has become an almost universal symbol of oppression and devastation, the cover story suggests Putin's continuing influence on Russia's foreign policy. Paradoxically perhaps, it also stresses his importance as the representative figure in Russian politics, even though his presidential term ended a few months prior to the conflict. As indicated by the quotation above, the article uses economic figures, including the strategic importance of Russia's defence industry, to sustain the narrative of the evil empire. By recalling the size and military prowess of the Russian army, it revitalizes the stereotypical vision of this country as the ferocious Asian horde, well-established in Polish historiography and literature. Concurrently, it suggests that Moscow's expansionist policy poses a serious threat to Europe and its allies. Further, the author asserts that Putin is the first Russian politician since Peter the Great to display both high political intelligence and a

[75] Iurii Solozobov, 'An Answer to the "Polish Question"', *Russian Politics and Law*, 48, 2010, 6, pp. 51–63 (pp. 59–61).

[76] Ewa M. Thompson, 'Adolf Putin', *Wprost*, 24 August 2008, p. 18.

'*truly Russian* ruthlessness'.[77] By alluding to 'true' Russianness, the article seems to reveal a strong belief in the fixed and unchangeable nature of the Russian national character, reinforcing the notion of Russia as a merciless predator, who thrives on invading, exploiting and destroying others.

Another cover article from the period of the Russo-Georgian war criticizes Europe's soft approach to Russia and the futile nature of the EU's 'verbal' pressure for a ceasefire. According to the author, Andrzej Nowak, the reaction of Western politicians and media to the Russian encroachment on Georgia can be compared to a similar debate that took place in 1919 as the Polish-Soviet War began. Nowak maintains that at the time both the British Labour and Liberal Parties accused Poland of a violent invasion of Russia. Similarly, as stated by Nowak, the Russian offensive in Georgia has been described by some, including a member of the German Social Democratic Party (Sozialdemokratische Partei Deutschlands, SPD), Gernot Erler, as a defensive action against Georgia's attack on Ossetia. The author observes that Europe has become mentally subjugated by Russia and wonders whether it can be considered a Russian colony.[78] This story is supplemented by a graphically manipulated image on the cover presenting Putin putting Nicolas Sarkozy, then president of the European Union, over his knee and spanking his bottom. Once again the former Russian president personifies Moscow and this saturation of stories relating to Russia with images of Putin seems to be mocking the alleged fascination of the West with this political figure. The image also belittles Europe by implying its helplessness when confronted with the Russian 'aggressor', which concurrently discloses *Wprost*'s euroscepticism.

Interestingly enough, a year later a report commissioned by the Council of the European Union investigating the origins of this conflict was published. It concluded that it was Georgia which started the war; however the attack was preceded by months of provocation, and both sides breached international law.[79] When analysed in the light of the report, *Wprost*'s stories reveal a style of coverage that is deeply biased and often impetuous in its assessment of Kremlin foreign policy, while its view of Europe, especially where Russia is concerned, discloses insistence on the repetitive patterns of history, as illustrated by the alleged pro-Soviet/Russian response to both the Polish-Soviet War of 1919–21 and the Russo-Georgian conflict of 2008 respectively. In fact, the article refuses to acknowledge the

[77] Ibid., emphasis added.

[78] Andrzej Nowak, 'Partnerstwo dla pokoju', *Wprost*, 14 September 2008, p. 22.

[79] Independent International Fact-Finding Mission on the Conflict in Georgia, <http://www.ceiig.ch/Report.html> [accessed 4 April 2012].

EU's mediation in the latter case which resulted in a preliminary ceasefire agreement signed only several days after the start of the war. To a large extent, this mode of journalism comports with the political manner of the Law and Justice Party, including its views on Poland's foreign and intra-European policy that have often been guided by anti-Russian sentiment, even if the price to be paid was self-induced isolation in the EU.

In respect of *Wprost*'s politics of memory, the story demonstrates how the events of the national past, in this case the Polish-Soviet War, were renegotiated and restructured in light of modern-day conflicts featuring Russia. By stressing, on the one hand, the need for solidarity with Moscow's enemies, and on the other cautiousness towards its potential allies, *Wprost* added a new significance to its articulations and interpretations of Polish national history. As mentioned above, these powerful analogies between past and present reflect the instructive nature of collective memory that *Wprost* was striving to construct. In this case, its open manipulation of the past was an attempt to raise awareness about the Kremlin's purported imperialism and, by alluding to the shared experience of 'unprovoked violence', to create an imagined community capable of bonding emotionally with Russia's 'victims'.

As shown above, *Wprost*'s representations of Russia in the period under discussion focus predominantly on demonstrations of Moscow's imperial yearning, whether actual or imaginary, and its potential consequences for Poland and other European states. Central to those debates is Poland's ostensible 'expertise' in the Kremlin's foreign policy, derived from the long-standing interaction between the two countries, which is often contrasted with the West's superficial knowledge of Russia.[80] The magazine skilfully concealed anti-Russian sentiment in West European media, creating an image of a Europe infatuated with Russia and blind to the threat it poses. As a result, not only does it reveal its own anti-Russian sentiment but also a strong anti-European agenda, presenting Poland as the lonely preacher of the 'truth' and a potential victim of more powerful polities. Both its vulnerability and uniqueness perpetuate historical traumas and restore Romantic ideas about a national identity which thrives on pain and suffering, thus resurrecting the ghosts of the past and refusing to look to the future. As the next section will demonstrate, a similar rhetoric became profuse in the days leading up to important historical anniversaries.

[80] Tomasz Zarycki comes to a similar conclusion while analysing discourses on Russia in Poland. See Zarycki, 'Uses of Russia', p. 617.

'Apologize for World War II!': On the Eve of Important Anniversaries

The seventieth anniversary of the start of World War Two provoked some evocative stories about the period, suggesting ways in which *Wprost* wanted its readers to remember the past. Issue 36, published in August 2009 on the anniversary of the signing of the Molotov-Ribbentrop Pact has perhaps one of the most contentious covers to date, employing a graphically manipulated photograph of the event. In the original image, Molotov is sitting at a desk signing the document while closely behind him stand, among others, Ribbentrop and Stalin, who are posing for the photograph under an image of Lenin. In *Wprost*'s version of the photograph the Soviet Foreign Minister is replaced by Vladimir Putin, while Angela Merkel takes the place of the German Minister. The cover title demands: 'Przeproście za II wojnę!' ('Apologize for World War II!'), while the article lists the numerous achievements and failures in Poland's struggle against the Nazis:

> It was us, Poles, who were the first ones to say 'No!' to Hitler. It was us who fought on all the fronts of this war. It was us who inspired the whole world. [...] But everyone, including every single Pole, also knows that we lost that war. [...] We lost being ill commanded, ill equipped, without intelligence, and alone. More importantly, we lost deceived and betrayed by our allies.[81]

Here the narrative of suffering intertwines with that of heroism, one rarely employed by the weekly.[82] The Romantic rhetoric, identified in some of the cover stories discussed above, also appears in this article, transpiring most strongly in its recollection of the alleged deceit of and betrayal by the Western allies. The use of personal pronouns adds force to the message and suggests the author's deep connection to national history. This demonstrates the workings of memory at grass-roots level and as such, individualizes what is an elite-validated account of the past.

While the story commemorating the beginning of World War Two concerns both Germany and Russia, asking for apologies from the former, as indicated in the title, and thanks from the latter for delaying the Nazi invasion for two years, issue 16/2005, remembering the sixtieth anniversary of the end of the war, focuses exclusively on Polish-Russian relations. More precisely, it provides an overview of 'myths' relating to the two nations

[81] Dariusz Baliszewski, 'Przeproście za II wojnę!', *Wprost*, 6 September 2009, p. 70.

[82] Eric Langenbacher makes a similar observation in relation to collective memory discourses in contemporary Poland more generally, showing that Polish victimization during World War Two has been emphasized more often than heroism. See Langenbacher, 'Twenty-First Century Memory Regimes in Germany and Poland', p. 63.

that, according to the author, still function in Poland. These include their deep-rooted 'natural' alliance, civilizational proximity, strong economic ties and willingness to cooperate. One by one, the article examines each of these points, with the aim of proving them false. Further, the author asserts that cordial Warsaw-Moscow relations can only be established if Poland gives up its sovereignty to Russia. The image on the cover leaves no doubt as to *Wprost*'s assessment of the dealings between the two countries, presenting them as a boxing match. Interestingly enough, Poland is assigned a blue and Russia a red boxing glove, alluding to the most basic colour symbolism, where blue stands for calm and peace, and red for action and aggression.[83] If drawn even further however, red, the colour of Russia here, would evoke associations with Communism, the ultimate incarnation of evil.

If cultural memory has, as both Maurice Halbwachs and Jan Assmann argue, the capacity to reconstruct and retell the past in relation to the present, then the magazine's reconfigurations of Russo-Polish and German-Polish history project a gloomy picture of the Polish nation on the eve of important historical anniversaries.[84] *Wprost*'s rhetoric on the commemoration of World War Two, which rests on scrutinizing and reliving of a painful past, shows a nation that is unable and/or unwilling to move on. As such, the weekly makes apt use of theoretical discourses surrounding trauma. After all, 'to be traumatized is precisely to be possessed by an image or event', to experience it repeatedly, and more important, to become the medium through which history writes back.[85]

Conclusions

Examining *Wprost*'s references to Germany and Russia between 2005 and 2009, it can be concluded that its articulations of Polishness relied heavily on old notions of power, presenting Poland sandwiched between Germany and Russia. As such, those representations suggested that right-wing media discourse in Poland still suffers from a postcolonial inferiority complex. In some instances, this was translated into xenophobia, proving that the weekly's politics of memory were to a great extent anchored in past fears.

Wprost's depiction of both countries revealed that its Russophobia was often complemented by more restrained, and often ambiguous,

[83] Jerzy M. Nowakowski, 'Polska – Rosja', *Wprost*, 1 May 2005, p. 24.

[84] Jan Assmann and John Czaplicka, 'Collective Memory and Cultural Identity', *New German Critique*, 65, 1995, pp. 125–33 (p. 130).

[85] Cathy Caruth, 'Trauma and Experience: Introduction', in eadem (ed.), *Trauma: Explorations in Memory*, Baltimore, MD, 1995, pp. 3–12 (pp. 4–5).

representations of Germany. While its anti-Russian rhetoric was transparent and rested almost exclusively on superficial historical analogies, the magazine's portrayal of Germany painted a more complex image. On the one hand, it presented a traumatized, neurotic country gripped by an irrational fear of its stronger neighbour. On the other hand, however, it disclosed what could be described as a psychological projection, whereby negative feelings and thoughts are assigned elsewhere. Indeed, the recurring idea of being disregarded, unheard and unloved by Poland's Western neighbour indicated *Wprost*'s refusal to recognize and openly admit its anti-German sentiment. Hence, while Russophobia remains in the sphere of acknowledged emotions, the othering of Germany is, to a certain extent, a taboo subject in right-wing media discourse. This seems to be largely motivated by Poland's accession to the EU in 2004, when some of its long-standing antagonisms had to be revised in the spirit of a united Europe. *Wprost* thus pointed to different shades of conservative memory discourse, consisting of both the intentional/explicit and the repressed/hidden forms of othering. Both of them, however, were a manifestation of the same phenomenon — a reductive notion of patriotism based on a compulsive need to cling to a painful past.

As already mentioned, 2010 brought about important editorial changes in the news magazine, ending its long and close alignment with the right. While Romantic notions of identity were being put to rest in *Wprost*'s archives, Poland began to mourn the victims of the presidential plane crash of 10 April 2010. The rhetoric of suffering, sacrifice and victimhood erupted with redoubled force, revealing new layers of anti-Russian sentiment in the pro-Law and Justice media and generating antagonism towards Tusk's government.[86] Nonetheless, *Wprost*'s metamorphosis continued and still continues, with its editorial team seeking to dismantle ossified and reductive ideas of national identity and patriotism, and to bring forth a more balanced politics of memory. Issues published following the takeover in the late 2009, such as 50/2010 featuring an interview with the then Russian president Dmitry Medvedev and 4/2011 which refuted the

[86] An interesting discussion of the right-wing discourse of mourning following the crash can be found in an article by Joanna Niżyńska, 'The Politics of Mourning and the Crisis of Poland's Symbolic Language after April 10', *East European Politics & Societies*, 24, 2010, pp. 467–79. For an analysis of media discourse following the accident, see, for example, Jakub Zieliński, '"Nie jestem wrażliwa na wzniosłą symbolikę polskiego patriotyzmu". Dyskurs o patriotyzmie po katastrofie smoleńskiej na przykładzie publikacji "Gazety Wyborczej"', in Piotr Goliński and Jacek Wasilewski (eds), *Katastrofa smoleńska. Reakcje społeczne, polityczne i medialne*, Warsaw, 2011, pp. 264–87.

conspiracy theories surrounding the Smolensk plane crash, are indicative of an effort to free existing discourses of history from bias and animosity.[87] One would hope to view those changes as heralding a wider process of healing both media and political discourses in Poland that would consequently cure the Polish psyche and lead to the achievement of long-awaited closure.

[87] Tomasz Lis, 'Inna twarz Rosji', *Wprost*, 5–11 December 2010, p. 16; Rafał Kalukin, 'We władzy demonów', *Wprost*, 23–29 January 2011, p. 26.

Reviews

Del Gaudio, Salvatore. *On the Nature of Suržyk: A Double Perspective.* Wiener slavistischer Almanach, 75. Otto Sagner, Munich, Berlin and Vienna, 2010. 328 pp. Map. Tables. Figures. Notes. Bibliography. Appendix. CD-rom. €36.80 (paperback).

Salvatore del Gaudio's study, which aims to revise the contemporary theory of *suržyk*, the Ukrainian-Russian mixed language, is based on his German-language doctoral dissertation, submitted and approved by the University of Vienna in 2008. Despite its significant research scope, it nevertheless leaves much to be desired.

The volume includes a bibliography in which non-Cyrillic and Cyrillic publications are set apart, two resumés in German and Russian and a CD-rom containing samples of *suržyk* tape-recorded in Kyiv, Kharkiv and Chernihiv. The disorganized presentation of the book's materials, however, is immediately distracting, particularly the Romanization of all Cyrillic-based references cited in the text, as against their listing in the bibliography in their original script. The text contains a horde of 'ghost references' not found in the bibliography, for example, Taranenko 2004, Feller 1994, Lesjuk 1998, Masenko 2001 and many others. The use of linguistic transliteration is sloppy, for example, *Kyjiv* (p. 51), *Charkiv* (p. 54), *Peresopnyca* (p. 182) next to *Kiev* (p. 53), *Kharkiv* (p. 326), *Peresopnycja* (p. 186). Among other inconsistencies is the translation of all non-English citations, save for those in German and French.

Del Gaudio, however, should be given credit for attempting to break the spell of politically-biased interpretations of *suržyk* that prevail in Ukraine and beyond and for questioning the contemporary 'research tendency according to which *suržyk* is ultimately the result of Ukrainian-Russian language contact or the outcome of exclusively socio-linguistic and psycho-cultural factors' (p. 141). Del Gaudio rightly argues that the Ukrainian dialectal substratum, traceable back to early Middle Ukrainian, must have played a fundamental role in determining the basic structure of *suržyk* (pp. 40–41). The author fails, however, to demonstrate the real extent of the Ukrainian substratum not only in *suržyk* which, according to him, emerged in the second half of the nineteenth century (p. 224), but also in literary Russian. The latter 'continued to develop on the basis of [...] the *slov"janorus'ka mova*', in use until the appearance of Ivan Kotljarevs'kyj's *Enejida* (1798) (p. 223), a 'Latin-Ukrainian mixture' with 'a few Russian elements' (p. 25).

Although soundly conceived, the above-mentioned hypothesis is outweighed by careless argumentation. To begin with, it is not clear what kind of 'double perspective' is encoded in the title. Being a haphazard enumeration of both indigenous and borrowed features, 'the *suržyk* system' in chapter three is considered 'from a synchronic perspective'. At the same time, both 'dialectological' and 'diachronic' perspectives are applied in chapters four and five, which brings the number of perspectives to three. Additionally, Del Gaudio calls the language mix under consideration 'prototype [*sic*] *suržyk*' (pp. 19, 20), which is 'basic *suržyk* with milder connotations' [? – AD] (p. 19), and 'general' or 'generalized *suržyk* prototype' (pp. 31, 63). Perhaps as a consequence, the author struggles to distinguish between indigenous forms and 'real Russianisms' in *suržyk*. Among the Ukrainian forms treated as 'suržykisms' the author mentions *oce* (neuter) 'that' (p. 88) alongside 'the more Ukrainian *ce*' (p. 166), *deševše* 'cheaper' (p. 77), *čoho* 'why' (p. 85). On the other hand, the form *raxujet'sja* is not standard, as Del Gaudi believes (p. 132), but, to use grammaticalization terminology, a replica of the Russian *sčitajetsja*, cf. literary Ukrainian *vvažajet'sja* '(it) is considered'. No doubt, the book would benefit from the theory of grammaticalization, thus ushering in a 'new perspective' on treating otherwise elusive phenomena, impressionistically dubbed *fossilization* (p. 123) or *crystallized forms* (p. 139), cf. *grammaticalization* (*grammation*) and *grammatized forms* used in the grammaticalization theory.

What is most disconcerting, however, is the author's awkward English, permeated with stylistic mistakes, including *the Ukraine* (p. 142) and (*dialectal*) *chart* (p. 149) instead of *map*. Del Gaudio resorts to unusual terminology, such as *conservative speech parts* (p. 136) or *linguistic league* (p. 140) in place of *linguistic area* and offers numerous questionable translations, for example, *simple language* (p. 216) instead of *common* (*plain*) *language* for *prostaja mova*. He also consistently disregards conventional spelling and forms, e.g.*Volynjan* (p. 153) for *Volhynian*, or *Slobodan* area (p. 144) for *Sloboda* area.

In sum, notwithstanding its valid hypothesis, the book could hardly receive the full attention of serious scholars interested in Slavic language mixes.

Department of Modern Languages and Cultures ANDRII DANYLENKO
Pace University, New York

Sumarokov, Aleksandr. *Ody torzhestvennyia. Elegii liubovnyia. Izdanie podgotovil Ronald Vroon*. OGI, Moscow, 2009. [144] + 696 pp. Bibliography. Price unknown.

IN 1774, three years before his death in 1777, Sumarokov brought out at the Imperial Academy of Sciences' Press in St Petersburg two small booklets, one of thirty solemn odes and the other, entitled *Elegii liubovnyia*, of twelve elegies and two 'stanzas'. All the odes, ten of the elegies and one of the 'stanzas' had been published before either individually or in collections of his poems. However, Sumarokov did not republish these poems unchanged: in some he altered the wording, in others he rearranged the lines, and nearly all of them he shortened by removing whole stanzas. Professor Ronald Vroon's aim in studying these poems was to deduce from these changes the motives which led Sumarokov to make them.

The work begins with photographic reprints of the two booklets: the rest of the book, 696 pages in all, has the status of an appendix to the reprints. After a few preliminary pages, among which occurs a contents list for the entire work (pp. 5–[10] of the second sequence), this appendix contains, first, the texts of all the redactions of the poems which received their final form in 1774 (pp. [15–221]) and next, as a supplement, a small group of six odes and two elegies which had not found their way into the collections of 1774 (pp. [223–58]). Then follow commentaries, first, on the redactions of the poems included in the collections of 1774 (pp. [275–366], and, second, on the few odes and elegies previously omitted from them (pp. [367–83]). The commentaries, which include rich contextual and other elucidatory material, summarize in tabular form the origin of all the stanzas constituting each poem.

In this way the primary data, the poems themselves, are presented to the reader twice. First, he is shown the poems in their final forms in the reprinted collections. Then he is given their initial, usually much longer, forms with the fate of each of their stanzas, whether retained in the final forms of the poems or jettisoned, indicated in the margins and with other, mostly minor, changes recorded in footnotes. Professor Vroon points out that the versions of the odes in the posthumous collected works of 1781–82 are 'contaminated versions' in the sense that their editor Novikov alternated their original texts with their texts in *Raznyia stikhotvoreniia* of 1769 and *Ody torzhestvennyia* of 1774 (p. 392, n.5). These versions therefore can offer no evidence on Sumarokov's final decisions on the odes' texts, and Vroon rightly ignores them.

The final portion of the book consists of six substantial essays, in the first of which (pp. 387–[468]) Vroon discusses the significance of the textological changes detailed in the commentaries, quotes the explanations of them made by previous writers and then offers his own.

According to P. N. Berkov, Sumarokov removed stanzas containing exaggerated praise of 'crowned personnages', on the grounds that the latter had disappointed him. T. A. Bykova held that the reason for the removal of the stanzas was Sumarokov's dissatisfaction with Catherine's policies and with her failure to grant him the protection he felt he deserved. Iu. N. Tynianov, on the other hand, believed that the textual changes were a reaction in favour of Sumarokov's clarity and restraint against Lomonosov's hyperbolic language and use of metaphor, in a word his 'loudness'. To these explanations Vroon opposes the arguments that most of the discarded stanzas are not excessively servile, nor 'loud' in the Lomonosov sense; nor can the tactical considerations advanced to justify changes to the odes in praise of Catherine be used to explain the changes in those celebrating the deceased rulers Peter I and Elizabeth.

Further, the stylistic features blamed for the suppression of certain stanzas can be detected in others which were retained. Vroon's solution is to propose that Sumarokov's motive in rewriting his odes was his rejection of the principle of *beau désordre*, advocated by Boileau and, on Sumarokov's view, abused by Lomonosov (pp. 397–412).

The authors of the remaining essays broaden the scope of the work so as to consider various aspects of the literary, as distinct from the textological, features of the reprinted texts. Marcus Levitt examines the poems as examples of the poetic cycle, a literary form with roots in Ancient Greek and Roman literature. Kirill Ospovat focuses on the aesthetic ideas current in Elizabeth's reign and finds in Sumarokov's life-long polemic with Lomonosov an expression of the difference in socio-cultural orientation between the aristocratic courtier and the professional scholar (p. 528 and n.5). Viktor Zhivov, although citing Pushkin's reference to Sumarokov's barbaric and effete language, writes: 'However brief was Sumarokov's period as preceptor, it did take place, and his significance for the formation of the Russian literary language and its stylistic system was not a whit less than that of [his] rivals Lomonosov and Trediakovsky' (p. 556). The late Mikhail Gasparov deals with the rhythm, rhyme and stanza structure of the twenty-six odes in iambic tetrameters: the four in trochaic tetrameters are not included. He finishes with a comparison of the syntactic structures of Sumarokov's odes with those of Lomonosov (pp. 634–[638]). For Alexander Kamenskii 'the figure of Peter, the theme of Peter, undoubtedly played a unifying role in the whole cycle of compositions which the poet placed in his collection *Ody torzhestvennyia*' (pp. 642–43).

'The aim of the present work,' writes Vroon, 'is to investigate the multi-stage evolution of the texts of Sumarokov's odes' (p. 392). This aim he achieved in the first, analytical part of this volume and in the accompanying essay. The remaining five essays in no way detract from the integrity of the whole, because their focus remains on the two collections of 1774. The participants in this ingenious, subtle and scholarly study deserve warm praise for their contributions.

Imperial College London C. L. Drage

Aptekman, Marina. *Jacob's Ladder: Kabbalistic Allegory in Russian Literature*. Borderlines: Russian and East European-Jewish Studies. Academic Studies Press, Boston, MA, 2011. 250 pp. Illustrations. Notes. Selected bibliography. Index. $70.00.

It seems obligatory to begin any remarks about the study of Kabbalah with Saul Lieberman's old chestnut that mysticism is nonsense, but the history of nonsense is scholarship. Marina Aptekman's *Jacob's Ladder: Kabbalistic Allegory in Russian Literature* is scholarship — well-researched and historically extensive — attempts to explore the 'evolution of kabbalistic symbolism in Russian literature by explaining and presenting its origins and stages of development' (p. 33). Aptekman situates this development, from the 1780s through the 1920s, less with respect to the scant influence of Jewish Kabbalists on Russian writers, than to that of Western Christian Kabbalists (Masons in particular) whose ideas pervaded elite circles throughout various points in Russia's history. It is this latter influence that leads directly to the eventual association of Jews with both black magic and with foreign threats, resulting in one of Russia's enduring exports: the myth of a Judeo-Masonic international conspiracy. On the one hand, Aptekman identifies an evolution at work here: eighteenth-century Russian Rosicrucians embraced the kabbalistic allegory of *tikkun ha-olam* — the repair of the world to its primordial harmony — as part of their belief in moral and spiritual enlightenment; the Romantics of the nineteenth century believed this utopian repair depended upon the powers of poetic language, for which kabbalistic allegories and techniques served as an 'artistic science' (p. 226); the late Romantics shifted the balance of Russian Kabbalism away from collective ideology and towards the individual's quest for occult knowledge of creation; while the 'literary ideology of the Silver Age combined all these approaches, hence constituting the fourth and the last stage in the evolution of Kabbalah in the Russian literary imagination [...] in an attempt to create a new artistic ideology formed on occult creative principles and humanistic mystical goals' (pp. 226–27). On the other hand, Aptekman also detects a pattern in this evolution: the years drawing toward the end of the eighteenth and nineteenth centuries were marked by a messianic interest in the utopian, mystical aspects of Kabbalah; in the early years of each century, this fervour was replaced with a more occult Kabbalism, which gradually became the basis for the stereotyped image of Kabbalah as 'evil magic based on "scientific" numerological and linguistic principles — the image that is widespread in Russia even today' (p. 227).

Jacob's Ladder is more a cultural history and philological influence study than an inter-textual literary history or a work of criticism, and that is both its strength and weakness. It will find a welcome place on the shelf of anyone interested in the burgeoning field of Russian-Jewish literary affairs. But it often makes for dry reading, some of it poorly copy-edited. There is the philologist's (or dissertator's) tendency to survey too many writers and to spend too much time on lesser-known figures. For example, the author identifies an interesting Kabbalistic motif in Pushkin's *Queen of Spades*, but then refrains from close reading. Similarly, the second of two chapters on the Silver Age devotes much space to a middling Acmeist like Mikhail Kuzmin, but I am left wondering what Aptekman might say about the possible 'Kabbalism' of such classics as

Osip Mandel′shtam's 'Notre Dame' or 'Silentium'. The best moments of the book are those when Aptekman offers elegant insights that exceed what can otherwise feel like an obligatory and relentless review of the literature. In particular, her deeply thoughtful remarks on Vasilii Rozanov's seemingly mad and vicious intervention in the Beilis blood libel trial of 1911 perfectly capture the weird poignancy of 'Kabbalistic Allegory in Russian Literature', and so I will conclude with this passage:

> Rozanov's aim was definitely not the promotion of a pogrom. He analyzed kabbalistic 'magic' not as a politician but as a literary person who wanted to believe that Yushchinsky's murder served as an amazing proof that kabbalistic rituals did indeed exist and were as powerful and almighty as he wished them to be. He sincerely and emotionally hoped for the existence of mystery in nature: the mystery that we as simple non-initiated mortals could not perceive. As Alexander Blok once said upon learning about the tragedy of the *Titanic*, 'There is still Ocean.' However, in the political context of the right-wing years following 1905, Rozanov's articles were not acknowledged as literary or theological experiments in kabbalistic occult theology, but as clear and harsh anti-Semitic propaganda. (p. 180)

Eugene Lang College, The New School VAL VINOKUR
New York

Kheteni, Zh., Dukkon, A. and Kalafatich, Zh. (eds). *Gogol′ i 20 vek. Materialy mezhdunarodnoi konferentsii, organizovannoi doktorskoi programmoi ELTE 'Russkaia literatura i kul′tura mezhdu Vostokom i Zapadom', Budapesht, 5-7 Noiabria 2009 g.* Dolce Filologia, Budapest, 2010. 302 pp. Illustrations. Notes. Price unknown.

THIS collection of nearly thirty papers on Gogol′ in the twentieth century derives from what was clearly a stimulating and lively conference in 2009. Hungarian and Russian scholars predominate, though all the articles are in Russian. The volume is illustrated with witty line drawings by Lázsló Boris (1897–1924); incidentally, here, in a rare misprint worthy of Gogol′'s madman, his date of death is given as 1824. Another unusual feature of the volume is that the last half-dozen papers (four Hungarian and one Italian) are by postgraduates, and separated from the rest.

The article by Zsuzsanna Kalafatics, on the hardly new theme of the relationship of Gogol′ to Evgenii Popov, begins with the 'indisputable fact' that Gogol′'s work defined the basic trends of development in Russian twentieth-century prose (p. 122). It might have been safer to say that the absurdity he perceived everywhere is equally to be seen today. Be that as it may, the volume covers a wide range of topics. Some of the contributions are of a general nature, some specific, and one or two hardly reach the twentieth century at all, for instance Viktória Lebovics's piece on Gogol′ and Panteleimon Kulish (1819–97). Amongst the more general articles are Ágnes Dukkon on his reception in Hungary, and Elena Kabkova and Ol′ga Stukalova on the difficulties in interpreting his writings. On specific works may be mentioned Alessandra Cattani on the grotesque in 'Nevskii Prospekt', and Milána Czerják on 'Rim', and an interesting but somewhat whimsical article by Carla Solivetti and Artem Marchenko on the concept of *koleso* and *okolesitsa* in *Mertvye dushi*. Iurii Mann's perceptive piece on the fate of 'Portret' ends with a discussion of planned and actual settings of this story to music.

The early twentieth century saw an important rediscovery of Gogol′, and Tibor Baróti discusses laughter and tears at the beginning of this period; other contributions include Alla Gracheva on his concept of beauty in Russian modernism, Simon Sarolta on Gogol′'s role in European and Russian psychoanalysis of the time, and Danuše Kšicová on his place in the poetics and aesthetics of modernism. Also on the beginning of the century, but focusing on specific individuals are Rainer Grübel's very detailed article on Rozanov and Isabella Malej's piece on the same philosopher; Ol′ga Tabachnikova writes on Shestov's interpretation of Gogol′, Dóra Pöhle on Gogol′'s devil and Lermontov's *Demon* in understanding Merezhkovskii, Sándor Kristó on his 'little man' in the early work of Andreev, Katalin Szöke on inter-textual links with Remizov and Belyi, Mária Gyöngyösi on thematic connections between Blok and Gogol′ and, most esoteric, Sergei Kibal′nik on *Baklazhany* as a Gogolian meta-text by Sergei Zaiaitskii (1893–1930).

Slightly later in the century was the 1926 production of *Revizor* by GosTIM, discussed by Ol′ga Kuptsova, and the review of the eschatology of Gogol′ as reflected in the criticism and literature of the Russian emigration by Arkadii Gol′denberg as well as Dmitrii Tokarev's discussion of the 'Gogolian text' in Poplavkii's *Apollon Bezobrazov* (1926–32). Of the same period, but otherwise quite different, are two Russophile Italian writers discussed by Giuseppe Mussi: Vitaliano Brancati (1907–54) and Tommaso Landolfi (1908–79), including the latter's story, 'La moglie di Gogol' (1944), the eponymous wife being an anatomically detailed life-sized dummy. Judit Vertés discusses Vail′ and Genis's interpretation of Gogol′, and Anna Woźniak that of Abram Terts (Andrei Siniavskii). Apart from the already mentioned article on Popov, the contemporary scene is treated in Liudmila Safronova's piece on the postmodern text and Gogol′'s '*iazyk mozga*'.

The articles are presented democratically (apart from the postgraduates) in alphabetical order, but the magisterial piece by the editor, Zsuzsa Hetényi, stands out with its discussion of the very different images of Gogol′ found in twentieth-century criticism and literature, ending with some thoughts on his place in postmodernism.

This volume is never less than interesting and, at best, fascinating. It should find a place on many reading lists, as it will interest both teachers and students of Russian literature.

London ARNOLD MCMILLIN

Torri, Stefania. *Dostojewskij in der deutschen und italienischen Literatur. Eine komparative Studie (1881–1927).* Otto Sagner, Munich and Berlin, 2011. 264 pp. Notes. Bibliography. €30.00 (paperback).

STEFANIA TORRI has produced a meticulously arranged book (broken down into sections rarely longer than three pages), full of fascinating and little known information, some of which (particularly in the German section, which includes Austria) is important. Only the absence of an index is infuriating. But the reader comes away with a strange impression: as if a visitor describing London Zoo had spent hours with the small nocturnal mammals, ignored the big cats and left shortly after lunchtime. There is also a serious imbalance: Italy's reception of Dostoevskii was often weak and inconsequential, whereas Germany not only received, but diffused Dostoevskii. Just as Katherine Mansfield could not have been a Chekhovian had she not read Chekhov in German translations, so André Gide, the most Dostoevskian of European writers, read Dostoevskii in magnificent German translations of the 1880s and 1890s. Germany benefited from a number of bilingual German-Russian intellectuals — Johannes von Günter, Alexander Eliasberg, Fiodor Fidler, many of them St Petersburg teachers and academics — who prepared the ground and provided fine translations. Moreover, just as the French recognized Dostoevskii as a transformer of Balzac, so German readers could see Dostoevskii as a reinterpreter of Schiller: *The Brothers Karamazov* overtly reincarnates *Die Räuber*.

Torri ignores some of the most important *Kulturträger* such as Eliasberg, and devotes space to the undeserving. Her text and bibliography (organized chronologically, not alphabetically) single out a Dane, Georg Brandes and an idiot, 'Sir Galahad', the wisely anonymous author of the *Idiotenführer durch die russische Literatur* of 1925, but Torri's idea of literature excludes real writers, except for Herman Hesse and Stefan Zweig, and concentrates on critics writing in newspapers and journals. The strict time limits she sets herself are regrettable (in this monograph Gramsci is the only reader of Dostoevskii who falls into the 1930s). Only with Hitler and the devastation of 1945 does Dostoevskii make his impact, as nowhere else, on Germany. Thomas Mann's *Dr Faustus* plagiarizes the conversation between the intellectual (the composer Adrian Leverkühn) and the devil, right down to the devil's use of 'Du' and his shabby trousers, thus contradicting the tone of his later article

Dostojewski mit Massen. Joseph Goebbels, to judge by his diaries and radio speeches, must have imagined himself to be one of Dostoevskii's *Devils*, which gives Dostoevskii's political influence an importance barely adumbrated by Torri in her section on Dostoevskii 'als Auslöser nationalisticher Theorien'. But even before 1927, the Dostoevskian element is detectable in Thomas Mann's *Zauberberg*.

Germany, like Italy, did not receive Dostoevskii homogeneously: most monographs published between 1916 and 1925 emanated from Munich, a centre of émigré Russian culture and pro-Russian sensibilities since the 1830s. Russian philosophers and novelists, such as Nikolai Berdiaev and Dmitrii Merezhkovskii, published influential monographs, *Die Weltanschauung Dostojewskis* and *Ewige Gefährte* respectively, in Munich: Torri ignores them.

The Russian exiles and émigrés who settled in Italy (largely in Rome, but some in Sorrento) had different interests than those who gravitated to Munich: if not Marxists, they were futurists, aesthetes or Roman Catholics, and Dostoevskii was not central to their interests. Moreover, they had come as pupils, not teachers. Italian reception, unguided, more trivial, and relying on truly appalling translations, tended to sensational themes such as 'Dostoevskii and women', although socialists such as Gramsci mined the Russian author for new roles for the intellectual in society. Here, too, Torri avoids the big cats: of all Italian novelists, Italo Svevo (who read Dostoevskii in German) diffused Dostoevskian psychology most effectively: *La coscienza di Zeno* can be read as a benign version of *Notes from Underground*, and can be credited as a vector of the Russian novelist's techniques and outlook in Italian literature.

In short, Torri's book (particularly its Italian section) supplies information lacking elsewhere, and is clear, and even too unjudgemental. (It ends with a résumé in English, useful, but in need of editing by a native speaker.) But we urgently need a much bolder survey of Dostoevskii reception in Europe, extending at least to the 1960s, and tackling major Dostoevskian writers like Mann and Svevo as mediators and boosters of reception.

Department of Russian DONALD RAYFIELD
Queen Mary, University of London

Masing-Delic, Irene. *Exotic Moscow under Western Eyes*. Cultural Revolutions: Russia in the Twentieth Century. Academic Studies Press, Boston, MA, 2009. xviii + 245 pp. Notes. Bibliography. Index. $59.00.

IN its concern with questions of Russian national identity, place and perspective, *Exotic Moscow* shares some thematic common ground with recent works of scholarship such as Edith Clowes's *Russia on the Edge: Imagined Geographies and Post-Soviet Identity* (Ithaca, NY, 2011) and Katya Hokanson's *Writing at*

Russia's Border (Toronto, 2008). The volume further contributes to the field by complementing the approach adopted by *Under Eastern Eyes: The West as Reflected in Recent Russian Émigré Writing*, edited by Arnold McMillin (London, 1992).

Nine of the ten articles in *Exotic Moscow* are previously published works that have appeared within the last fifteen years. As the volume's introduction makes clear, the author has collected them here with the intent of creating thematic unification, namely through two formulations of opposed themes: the 'vitality of culture' and the stagnancy of civilization as well as the triad of civilization, barbarism and culture (p. xiii). As Masing-Delic notes, these frameworks help to define Russian identity both by mapping the relationship between Russia and the West and situating Russia within Eurasia. The essays consequently focus on critiques of culture and civilization that originate both within and outside the Russian literary tradition.

Exotic Moscow comprises three sections. The first, 'Dialogue', explores Russian literature in a comparative European literary and intellectual context, reading Turgenev through a Nietzschean lens and placing Goncharov's *Oblomov* and Dostoevskii's *Crime and Punishment* alongside Austen's *Emma* and Conrad's *Under Western Eyes* respectively. A study of 'Gorky, Gogol, Sologub, and the Mediterranean Model' shows how Gor′kii's *Skazki ob Italii* locates affinities and productive oppositions between cultures.

The second group of essays, 'Inner Divisions', reexamines fundamental questions of Russian identity. Drawing from the rich imagery of Russia as bride, a concept explored at length by Ellen Rutten in *Unattainable Bride Russia: Gendering Nation, State, and Intelligentsia in Russian Intellectual Culture* (Evanston, IL, 2010), these essays discuss the Pani Katerina figure of Gogol′'s 'Strashnaia mest′' as it has been reinterpreted or rewritten by Dostoevskii, Blok and Pasternak. 'Inner Divisions' is also concerned with the identification of 'others', locating oppositions such as intelligentsia and *narod*. It introduces the theme of barbarism and the idea of looking to the East through an examination of Tatars in Blok's work. Finally, section two addresses Pasternak's fragmented view of civilization.

The final third of *Exotic Moscow*, 'Saving the Heritage', analyses literary attempts at dialogue with the past and their invocation of the triad of civilization, barbarism and culture. Focusing primarily on the works of Vladimir Nabokov, 'Saving the Heritage' displays renewed attention to the theme of civilization and continued discussion of the Pani Katerina character. The chapters of this section address engagement with the past — a central theme in Nabokov's work — as well as contact points across cultures. The final chapter, a short essay on Valerii Briusov, aims to reconcile Russia and the West; thus it suggests an alternate way of understanding self and other as well as the relationship between the two.

Thematic, not chronological, considerations organize the volume. Though Masing-Delic acknowledges that the placement of the first and final articles might not be entirely natural or intuitive, she asks readers to consider the thematic architecture of *Exotic Moscow* and the more abstract links among the individual essays. (Broadly understood, the first section takes as its subject literary dialogues that transcend Russia's borders.) The second is more concerned with internal dialogues, while the third analyses both geographic transfers and dialogues across temporal boundaries.

The overall structure of the book is somewhat inconsistent. One article contains primary sources, references and notes, while the next three have notes only. A few chapters include bibliography and notes, but a separate bibliography also appears at the end of the text. The index is not thematic but contains only names and texts; a fuller index might have augmented the volume's usefulness.

Though the primary readership of *Exotic Moscow* will be scholars and specialists, graduate students will also find material of interest. The text could be excerpted for use in undergraduate courses addressing questions of Russian national identity through literature. Despite the distracting mechanical flaws of the volume, the groups of essays within offer thoughtful and nuanced, original analyses on a set of topics of persistent importance within the Russian literary tradition.

Sewanee: The University of the South ELIZABETH SKOMP

Moran, John P. *The Solution of the Fist: Dostoevsky and the Roots of Modern Terrorism*. Lexington Books, Lanham, MD, Boulder, CO, New York and Plymouth, 2009. x +135 pp. Notes. Bibliography. Index. $55.00.

THE SOLUTION OF THE FIST by John P. Moran is a concise and engaging discussion of the 'psychological' factors that lead to terrorism, a phenomenon which the author defines as 'violence (or threatened violence) in the pursuit of political change' (p. 2). Proceeding from the 'Narcissistic Personality Disorder Model' for understanding violent acts, as well as the research of psychiatrist James Gilligan, the author considers the role of similar factors in the fictional characters of Dostoevskii, whose subjective, value-based approach, he argues, is no less important or useful than a purely 'scientific' one in understanding the roots of terrorism. Toward that end the author devotes most of the book's six chapters to three of Dostoevskii's major texts, *The Idiot*, *Demons* and *The Brothers Karamazov*. Of these, attention centres predominantly on the political novel *Demons* (translated by the author as '*The* Demons') as a source for understanding the 'nihilistic terrorism' of Dostoevskii's day. In the book's final pages, the author demonstrates the similarity between Dostoevskii's views and more recent explanations for contemporary acts of terrorism, in light of which the author offers his own advice to governments in their 'counter-terrorism operations' to prevent it (p. 124).

The author contends that Dostoevskii's critique of reason, science and their 'deification' provides the philosophical starting point of *Demons*. Complementing Turgenev (in *Fathers and Children*) and Tolstoi (in *War and Peace*), to whom the author compares him, Dostoevskii aimed in *Demons* 'to demonstrate that the God of Reason, having displaced the Ancient Gods, creates the amoral and psychological conditions for terrorist violence and the political conditions for tyranny' or, in the words of Shatov in *Demons*, for the 'solution of the fist' (p. 21). Thus while the principal 'terrorist' in *Demons* is young Petr Verkhovenskii, it is in the 'rootless egalitarianism' (p. 51) of Petr's liberal father, Stepan, that the author locates the ideological origins of Petr's terrorism. Vain and disdainful toward traditional Russian beliefs and customs, Stepan's inability to transcend his own childish, 'Ptolemaic' world (p. 57) also leads to his son's neglect and estrangement. The force of 'shame' experienced by the neglected Petr — as well as by other characters in *Demons* — contributes significantly to a 'lack of self-love', the author explains, which 'propels him to lash out against the world so as to punish it' (p. 98).

Central to the analysis of Stepan's affliction is a notion of 'cosmopolitanism', which the author applies to any ideological or cultural trend that privileges 'worldly' or international values over local or national ones. Here the study makes perhaps its most original contribution to the study of Dostoevskii and *Demons*, in this reader's view, by revealing the novel's anti-'cosmopolitan' parallels with Rousseau's *La Nouvelle Héloïse* and, especially, Tocqueville's *Democracy in America*. Far better known as a source of Tolstoi's thought, Rousseau also proved relevant to Dostoevskii, the author demonstrates, for his critique of 'metropolitanism' (p. 32) and, more broadly, 'cosmopolitanism'. Thus the same Parisian intellectual culture and egalitarian values that repel Rousseau's St Preux also form the very foundation of Stepan's 'cosmopolitan' outlook in *Demons*. Similarly, the study examines the suggestive link between the notion of democratically centralized state tutelage, as envisioned by Tocqueville, and Petr Verkhovenskii's vision of equality through despotism. Together with his analysis of Fourier's writings (pp. 98–99), the author's discussion of Rousseau and Tocqueville provides a valuable supplement to his own analysis of Dostoevskii's fictional characters and their maladies.

The author's remarks on the political problem of modern terrorism provides the other extrinsic dimension of the book. Ultimately Dostoevskii's 'terrorists' in *Demons* share a meaningful affinity with modern terrorists, the author maintains, by virtue of the 'shame' from which they appear to suffer. Advising Western governments to 'speak softly and carry a big stick' (p. 122), the author suggests that a more concerted effort by cosmopolitan centres not to humiliate 'peripheral' cultures or express 'contempt' for them might reduce terrorism without compromising national security.

With its interdisciplinary approach, *The Solution of the Fist* should be of interest both to readers of Dostoevskii as well as to historians of terrorism. The compact format of the study and its clear exposition should make it especially appropriate for university courses that freely combine literature, history and/or political science. While some Dostoevskii specialists might regret the lack of more references to the substantial literary scholarship on *Demons* (particularly in Russian), *The Solution of the Fist* deserves to be recommended as a perceptive psychological reading of Dostoevskii's 'terrorists' and the causes of their destructive acts.

Department of Languages, Literatures and Cultures J. GOODWIN
University of Florida

Leving, Yuri. *Keys to 'The Gift': A Guide to Vladimir Nabokov's Novel*. Studies in Russian and Slavic Literatures, Cultures, and History. Academic Studies Press, Boston, MA, 2011. 534 pp. Illustrations. Tables. Notes. Bibliographies. Appendices. Index. $39.00 (paperback).

YURI LEVING's *Keys to 'The Gift'* represents a huge and ambitious undertaking. Leving justifies his effort at the outset as essential to *The Gift*'s English language audience, for the novel 'requires an especially meticulous and expansive scholarly guide'. Leving's claim might seem overstated — but not by much. For while it is possible for an educated reader of English to produce an acceptable, if tentative, first reading of the novel, that reading will certainly be even more blatantly gap-filled than one of many other Nabokov novels. Even for Russian readers, *The Gift* stands as one of Nabokov's self-consciously difficult novels, along with *Pale Fire* and *Ada*, and in contrast to deceptively accessible ones like *The Defense, Lolita, Pnin*, to name only the obvious. So for all readers *The Gift* begs openly for rereading, and also for the discovery of information outside its surface narrative flow. Leving's book strives to give a generous portion, something more than a heavy hint, of what is available to the curious reader who rereads and takes the textual experience outwards beyond the pages of the book. If readers want to follow the methodology enacted by Nabokov in his Cornell lectures, with their famous drawings of train compartments and dung beetles, this book will be of particular value.

The book is divided into seven chapters: Composition and Publication, Historical Context, Structure, Style, Commentary, English Translation, and Critical Reception. Each chapter is further divided into several sections: for example, the 'Structure' chapter includes entries for each major character, and sections for 'minor characters', 'setting', 'plot', 'timeline', 'themes'; the 'Style' chapter includes sections on 'transitions', 'form', 'points of view', 'sources', 'allusions' and 'intertextuality'. These sections (and comparable ones in other chapters) allow for coherent discussion of various issues each topic might raise and existing (or new) approaches to them, while allowing the book to be used easily in non-linear fashion. There are also four appendices: a translation of Nabokov's 1937 letter to Samuil Rozov and Leving's comment thereon (previously published in Russian); Nabokov's (through Véra) 1952 summary of *The Gift* for the London agent Curtis Brown (with commentary); a chronology of real and fictional events mentioned in *The Gift*; and a list of the thirty-three species of Lepidoptera mentioned in the novel. Leving calls the letter to Rozov 'probably one of the most valuable documents in the entire corpus of Nabokov's European correspondence [...]', offering 'deep insight into his intimate world and his artistic laboratory' (p. xv). In a similar vein, the 'Composition' chapter includes an extended passage from 'The Gift II' notebooks, not published before in English.

Keys to 'The Gift' provides a vast amount of information, much of it discovered by the many scholars who have worked on the novel, who are credited extensively. Leving also adds many significant finds of his own — historical, textological and documentary. In his summaries of leading approaches to the novel, he is thorough, objective and fair, yet not afraid to disagree respectfully with some critics or take sides in certain debates.

Chapter five, 'Commentary', means to instruct novices to literary criticism (perhaps advanced undergraduates or new graduate students) in the many possible approaches to elucidating the novel's hidden textures and material background. Offering examples of several types of commentary, Leving seeks to encourage future workers to join the still nascent task of annotating *The Gift*: he hopes for a future 'comprehensive annotated edition that will embrace all types of commentary' (p. 330). The chapter closes with an extended 'close reading' of the first several sentences, including manuscript and translation variants, with themes, motifs, subtexts, stylistic commentary explored in separate subsections. This section, about thirty pages of commentary for less than one page of text (although the section headings here are somewhat misleading, even confusing). Leving does not intend that *every* page of *The Gift* requires thirty pages of commentary in a critical edition; rather, his 'slow reading' is meant to demonstrate one pathway into the deep riches of the text (and its historical referents) for the curious reader. Leving suggests that this immersive reading of the opening lines sets the stage for a successful traversal of the rest of the novel. This section might be best viewed as a guide to teaching the novel in a certain way.

The process of translation into English by Michael Scammell with Nabokov's revisions, is presented with detailed reference to the correspondence between translator and author (or Véra). This method facilitates many new insights into

Nabokov's thought about the novel and its most important elements. Especially intriguing is his desire that Scammell achieve a neutral dialect somewhere between British and American English: Véra wrote that Nabokov 'does not mind if "*tram*" and "*streetcar*" appear on the same page' (letter of 5 July, 1961; Berg collection) (p. 385); yet Leving reports that this very juxtaposition was criticized in one review. Leving does not, as he might have, comment on *why* Nabokov may have wished for such an inter-dialectal tone.

The book is richly illustrated with period images (photography and reproductions of graphic materials, postcards, contemporary journalism and advertisements, manuscript pages, galley proof corrections, artworks mentioned in the novel, and more). Frustratingly and surprisingly for such an encyclopedic volume, there is no list or index of illustrations. There are also errors and gaps in citation of some images: for example, the same image is printed twice in illustrations 2–3 and 2–4, showing Chernyshevskii and Herzen in London, but illustration 2–4 purports to show Ivan Turgenev. The painting's caption credits 'a Soviet artist'. A little digging reveals that the painting was by Iu. N. Kazmichov, in 1952 (information which is included on the book's companion website — see below — although the image itself has been deleted as of this writing).

Supplementing *Keys to 'The Gift'* is an extensive and lush interactive website, www.keystogift.com, with further imagery (including relevant period maps), concordance, commentary and indexing of historical and interpretive material. Readers of this review are encouraged to explore that site for themselves.

For the most part, Leving refrains from interpretation, except in occasionally endorsing or questioning one critic or another. *Keys to 'The Gift'* does not offer a particular reading of the novel, or an interpretive solution to any of its riddles. Instead, it attempts to enable English-speaking readers to access conveniently much of the information they might need to make their own efforts at interpretation. The book is typographically clean, but not flawless. In addition to problems with image attribution and indexing, the prefatory 'Biography of the novel' (pp. xxii–xxvi) gives only partial details about the time of writing and dates (or at least issue number) of actual first publication of each of the several segments. Such information seems crucial for this 'at-a-glance' insert.

One might argue that a suitably educated person could construct a serviceable image of *The Gift*'s world. However, while the novel can certainly be read and reread profitably by those with only slight knowledge of Russian and émigré history, the curious will be able to add many layers to their experience of it with the help of Leving's book. For those wishing to embark on serious study of *The Gift*, Leving's *Keys* is a vital and invaluable starting place.

University of Tennessee, Knoxville STEPHEN H. BLACKWELL

Andryczyk, Mark. *The Intellectual as Hero in 1990s Ukrainian Fiction.* University of Toronto Press, Toronto, ON, Buffalo, NY and London, 2012. vii + 183 pp. Notes. Bibliography. Index. $40.00.

It is not unusual for authors to make writers the protagonists of their work. Nevertheless, as Mark Andryczyk's study demonstrates, in Ukrainian literature of the 1990s this practice became strikingly dominant. Most of the important prose works by Ukraine's most significant writers of this period featured intellectuals in the lead role, yet few critics have discussed the phenomenon. Andryczyk's study is thus both prescient and groundbreaking. It is not only his exploration of this particular facet of contemporary Ukrainian writing that makes this book important: this is, to date, the only monograph in English dedicated in its entirety to contemporary Ukrainian literature. More are bound to follow, but Andryczyk's study is more than worthy of its landmark status.

As Andryczyk points out in his introduction, the intellectual has long been both a driving force and a 'dominant prototype' in Ukrainian culture, particularly since the depictions of 'a socially engaged intellectual with a decidedly rural orientation and a strong dedication to serving the Ukrainian people' (p. 7), in the works of writers like Ivan Franko. Andryczyk charts the development of the Ukrainian intellectual through the revolutionary, urban-oriented verve of the modernist period, into the strictures of socialist realism, with particular attention to the intellectual climate of the 1960s and '70s, in order to establish clearly and concisely the context for the phenomenon that is the focus of the study. The book then divides its subject into three themes that the author sees as characteristic of representations of intellectuals in Ukrainian prose in particular and of Ukrainian culture in general: euphoria, chaos and community. After the Soviet Union collapsed, Ukrainian authors felt a sense of euphoria at their new-found freedom to express themselves as they chose (a unique position in the history of Ukrainian culture), yet were also overwhelmed by a sense of chaos, as the status and role of the writer-intellectual, and literature in general, were thrown into turmoil. Faced with this chaos and a continued sense of marginalization within their own country, intellectuals created a strong literary community within which they could pursue their vision of Ukrainian culture. Andryczyk notes that the 1990s were marked by 'uncertainty and contradiction', in which writers sought 'a balance between constrictive yet stabilizing structures and liberating yet chaotic freedom' (p. 142). This tension produced a literature that is restless, dynamic and endlessly inventive, as the author ably illustrates.

Andryczyk examines the intellectual as a literary trope through reference to seven leading Ukrainian writers (Oksana Zabuzhko, Iurii Andrukhovych, Iurii Izdryk, Iurii Gudz', Kostiatyn Moskalets', Ievheniia Kononenko and Volodymyr Dibrova, although several others are also discussed), a sample that is wide enough to give a sense of the diversity of contemporary Ukrainian writing, but focused enough to allow in-depth discussion of individual works. Indeed, a particular strength of the book are the author's close readings of his chosen texts, which combine perceptive analysis with an expert eye for detail and linguistic nuance.

The individual chapters of the book discuss many of the pressing questions that have arisen in Ukrainian literature of the post-Soviet period, such as Ukraine's post-colonial status, its relationship with Western and globalized culture, and the re-assessment of gender dynamics. To all of these problems, some of which have been discussed at length by scholars of Ukrainian literature, Andryczyk brings a fresh, original perspective backed up by extensive but judicious reference to primary and secondary texts. His analysis is always accessible, unencumbered by an over-reliance on literary theory, but using enough theory to lend the analysis depth and wider relevance.

Perhaps the strongest section of the book is that on community. Andryczyk convincingly demonstrates that Ukrainian authors utilize the figure of the writer in their works to create elaborate networks of intertextuality in order to establish a community of marginalized intellectuals. This, as Andryczyk shows through reference to postmodern identity politics, is a community that strives to be open to difference while pursuing the stability and structure needed to facilitate the survival of both literature and language in a situation of marginality. It is in this inherent respect for, and indeed reliance on, difference in the face of adversity that the true potential of Ukrainian literature lies. As Andryczyk puts it: 'For a country with such a fractured and diverse history, difference is a strength and a source of cultural creativity. A literature that recognizes and respects difference will be enriched as a result. Post-Soviet Ukrainian literature has the potential to develop in this manner' (p. 145).

Department of Slavonic Studies UILLEAM BLACKER
University of Cambridge

Renfrew, Alastair and Tihanov, Galin (eds). *Critical Theory in Russia and the West*. BASEES/Routledge Series on Russian and East European Studies, 60. Routledge, Abingdon and New York, 2010. xix + 220 pp. Notes. Bibliographies. Index. £85.00.

RENFREW and Tihanov introduce this collection as an attempt to historicize theory by tracing dialogic encounters between Russian and Western thinkers within specific cultural and historical contexts. As such, it is an important and much needed book.

Some questions arise in relation to the title. Perhaps no one would deny the fact that Russian theory (Formalism, Bakhtin, Lotman), treated as 'dissident', that is, not in tune with the official expectations of Soviet academics, contributed to the Western intellectual legacy. Is a politically neat separation between Russia and the West as indicated by the title adequate to describe a whole set of complex relationships, dialogues, divergences and convergences? The title also encompasses the promise of a monographic-scope overview, yet the chapters only offer perspectives into the works of separate thinkers. Though both Lotman and Shklovskii are listed in the introduction, considerable space is devoted to Shklovskii whereas Lotman is only mentioned twice in passing. The whole Tartu-Moscow school is presented apophatically, in a negative mirror of Alexander Etkind's critique of 'Russian semiotics', which is arguably akin to French structuralism and 'text-centred' theory. Instead of the outdated question, 'what is in the text?', Etkind observes that Slavonic studies would do better to ask 'what has this text done?'. However, those who have read Lotman's, Uspenskii's, Toporov's, Ivanov's and other Tartu-Moscow scholars' works would notice that Russian semiotics was culture-centred: it sought to discover how texts were functioning in culture and what impact they had on their readers. Finally, the question arises about the meaning of 'critical theory' and the intellectual and ideological agendas it attracts here.

Many chapters offer new perspectives on familiar phenomena, sketch new theoretical vistas or engage the reader in exciting theoretical dialogues. Alasdair Renfrew's chapter, 'The Resurrection of a Poetics', discusses three key issues in Russian Formalist theory: the issue of *skaz*, the question of the symbolic quality of the word and the problem of literary evolution. Renfrew draws on the Saussurean roots of Formalism yet, regrettably, leaves out other possible sources and reverberations (such as Bergson's philosophy of automatism, or German and Swiss phenomenological and hermeneutical formalist sources). He also highlights the significance of Kristeva's and Todorov's re-reading of Bakhtin as a problematization of formalist proto-structuralism, and a productive injection of the theory of discourse and genres in formalist poetics. Caryl Emerson and Inessa Mezhdubovskaya provide an engaging insight into Bakhtin's imaginary dialogue with Tolstoi and Dostoevskii on immortality and art, while emphasizing the importance of the Marburg connection in Bakhtin's intellectual biography. Galin Tihanov traces the formation of Gustav Shpet's philosophical aesthetics and its complicated position between philosophy and literary theory: while being distrustful of the claims of autonomous literary theory, Shpet presaged certain developments in Structuralism and semiotics. Thomas Seifrid explores organic metaphors in a broad range of theories of language from Herder and Humboldt to Husserl, Potebnya and, finally, Jakobson's eidetics. Michael Holquist elaborates on Jakobson's life-long adherence to a combined study of language and literature, which is particularly prominent in view of the present decline of philology. Holquist highlights that Jakobson's (and, in my view, Tynianov's) idea of merging synchrony and diachrony, fruitfully developed in his theories of markedness and simultaneity, reaches beyond Saussurian semiotics. Svetlana Boym juxtaposes Shklovskii's and Hanna Arendt's views on estrangement. An ambivalence inherent in Shklovskii's conception reverberates in the practice of the artist's double estrangement from Soviet reality as a strategy of survival, as well as in Arendt's two-folded conception of estrangement *from* the world and estrangement *for* the world. Alexander Etkind's chapter 'The Shaved Man's Burden: Internal Colonization' presents a part of what is now published as a book-length study, in which he develops Vasilii Klyuchevskii's idea of internal colonization as a specific form of colonialism in Russia. Carol Adlam discusses the contested standing of feminism in Russia, which is complicated by the subliminal association of Anglo-American feminism with the excesses of the Soviet agenda and, on the other hand, by the difficult history of Russia's own engagement with the issue of gender, starting in the eighteenth century. Mikhail Epstein's exciting chapter on the future of the humanities is inspired by Bakhtin's literary anthropology and the Kuhnian concept of the paradigmatic shift. Drawing on the Bakhtinian concepts of finalization and initiation, Epstein argues that all 'post-'s, such as postmodernism, post-humanism, post-Communism, are pregnant with 'proto-'s and have an inexhaustible potential for renovation. While envisaging the germs of such a renovation in the Bakhtinian idiom, Epstein suggests that tension between multiculturalism and universalism may be released through *interference*, ultimately opening into a transcultural dimension; that, instead of translation, *interlation* marks a new stage in linguistic contacts between various cultures; that the autonomous, immutable texts yield their way to dynamic and mobile *textoids* and *retextualizations*; that the principles of the dialogic cognition and interrogativity underlie the *rehumanization* of the humanities. Vitalii Makhlin's chapter, which concludes the collection, depicts the current moment as the end and negation of previous paradigms, as a moment of disorientation and uncertainty that encourages scholars to reach *beyond the text* in order to seek ways of differentiation and detachment from the past, and to overcome the force of historical inertia within the very experience of the past.

The volume does not provide a full or comprehensive overview of critical theory of the twentieth century. It is not always explicit enough about its own agendas. Yet it presents an important and gratifying attempt to place theory in the historical context and to bring it closer to the main humanistic and social concerns of the twenty-first century. It offers a thought-provoking and stimulating appraisal.

Department of Comparative Literature
University of Tartu

MARINA GRISHAKOVA

Longinović, Tomislav Z. *Vampire Nation: Violence as Cultural Imaginary*. The Cultures and Practices of Violence Series. Duke University Press, Durham, NC and London, 2011. x + 212 pp. Illustrations. Notes. Bibliography. Index. $79.95; $22.95.

VAMPIRE NATION is a timely, nuanced inquiry into contemporary cultural and political incarnations of neo-imperial vampires which, shifting shape and geographic locale, can code as destructive as well as beneficial. On the latter scale, these range from 'serbs' as sacrificial vampires that Western powers bomb and exterminate 'through radioactive and chemical contamination of the Balkan environment for decades to come' (p. 182), to the good vampires of *Twilight*, masking the violence that 'the new imperial configurations of power use' to 'consume the lesser ones' (p. 188). Tomislav Z. Longinović specifically explores how the rhetoric of the nation displaces its violence to the realm of cultural alterity, i.e. the shifting avatars of the vampire's blood and soil.

From Bram Stoker's *Dracula* to the 1990s Yugoslav wars, 'the serbs' — Longinović rejects the proper name to highlight their constructed, imagined collectivity — represent Europe's vampires as the underlying narrative of violence within one's own body, blamed for atrocities allegedly no longer tolerated by the civilized West. In the nineteenth century, the Gothic literary mirror that reflects the invisible ghost of the 'other' Europe steeps 'serbs' in an overload of bloody history, precluding them from entering modernity at the precise point when Eastern European nations develop cultural and political discourses of national independence. Longinović shows how this larger European dynamic of internal vampirism also figures as a perpetually reopened wound of masculinity in 'serbs'' post-Oriental condition. The scapegoating of converts to Islam during the Ottoman reign as vampiric traitors to the (European) 'serb' nation is invoked in literature, the resurrection of the Kosovo myth, and 1990s nationalist discourses.

The 1990s emergence of the repressed vampires of ethnic identities also dismantled Yugoslavia's multinational body; shifting emphasis from 'serb' nationalism, Longinović centres on Slovene collective imaginary that, combined with all others, abandoned the Orientalized Balkan state for 'Europe'. Positing Bosnia as the microcosm of the larger Yugoslav dynamic, Longinović also explores the fraught discourses of interethnic relationships in Ivo Andrić and Meša Selimović, whose novels as well as personal backgrounds mark the in-betweenness of Bosnia's cultural identifications, making them convenient targets for post-Yugoslav nationalists. *Vampire Nation* ends on a hopeful note, however, offering vampirism as a strategy of alternative memories and imaginaries to offset the ideological foreclosing effected by the rhetoric of national homogeneity. Readings of David Albahari's and Borislav Pekić's recalcitrant, volatile narratives are combined with reflections on Cyber

Yugoslavia, a virtual mock-nation, where traditional national signifiers are subverted through playful, parodic rewriting of memories of the common state.

This book appeals not only to scholars of Serbian and Yugoslav literatures, but also to anyone interested in cultural studies of (neo)imperial discourses, the rhetoric of the nation and American studies. Juxtaposing historical and contemporary cultural narratives, *Vampire Nation* abandons a linear argument in favour of a refreshingly multilayered texture, demonstrating why the 'serbs'' sense of victimization becomes an easily mobilized nationalist discourse in response to the (always present) possibility of foreign domination. The book's greatest strength is simultaneously its greatest weakness, however: each chapter tantalizingly combines various narrative strands, but often without sufficient elaboration. To mention a few examples, the book would have benefited from more in-depth discussion of the relationship between the 'serbs'' mythologized loss of Kosovo and historical discourses on masculinity (or gender in general), or from further analysis of the politically loaded parallel between 'serb' ethnic cleansing and the Holocaust. The tendency toward cursory discussion also leads to a bafflingly literal reading of NSK art as example of Slovene nationalism, without taking into account the many monographs and essays by and about NSK that seriously undermine such an interpretation (especially as NSK State in Time echoes the Cyber Yugoslavia project). Occasionally, *Vampire Nation* includes historical information without directing readers to consulted sources; some literary narratives are discussed in great detail but with few illustrations or quotes from the texts themselves (as in the section on Albahari).

Finally, while *Vampire Nation* brilliantly dissects the vampiric discourses of both 'serb' nationalism and neoimperial 'humanitarian' scapegoating, the frequent insistence that Western media, in their 'mendacious' reporting, 'staged the violence' (p. 41) in the Balkans that 'far exceeded' the real crimes committed by 'serbs' (p. 27) could unwittingly play into 'serb' nationalist discourses that hinge on downplaying the number of mass graves and general responsibility for the wars. Overall, however, employing psychoanalytic discourses to explore how the concept of vampirism figures in contemporary national imaginaries to justify violence opens up exciting new avenues of critical inquiry — a welcome theoretical extension of a concept that has become an overused, oversimplified pop-cultural cliché.

Department of English Language and Literature NATAŠA KOVAČEVIĆ
Eastern Michigan University

King, David. *Red Star Over Russia: A Visual History of the Soviet Union from 1917 to the Death of Stalin. Posters, Photographs and Graphics from the David King Collection.* Tate Publishing, London, 2009. 352 pp. Illustrations. Bibliography. Index. £30.00; £24.99.

PUT simply, this is a spectacular book — a stunning visual panorama of Soviet history from 1917 to 1953 with over 550 colour and black & white illustrations. Beautifully produced, it sells at a bargain price and deserves a place in every university (and secondary school) library, as well as in the bookshelves of all sorts of readers, certainly not just specialists.

Its author, David King, is a writer, photographer, graphic designer, editor and collector who has published widely on Russian and Soviet history in particular. His unparalleled private collection of primarily (but not only) visual sources on the Soviet era easily surpasses many prominent public collections and pieces from it have regularly been displayed at the Tate Modern. That long-term relationship has now facilitated the publication of this book (as well as a more recent and equally stunning volume, *Russian Revolutionary Posters: From Civil War to Socialist Realism, From Bolshevism to the End of Stalinism*, London, 2012).)

Red Star Over Russia is also a highly personal history. In an evocative introduction, King takes readers through snapshots of his own journey to making this book, from a childhood fascinated with things Russian and Soviet (and leftist politics) to his early visits to the Soviet Union and the development of his interest in both Trotskii as well as the material culture and art of the revolution. Anecdotes abound about famous and obscure individuals, travels across the globe and encounters in a range of liminal sites, from basements to airports, trains to bookshops. In sum, King successfully captures the feel of both the Soviet experience and his own fascination with it.

The volume then takes a combined chronological and thematic approach to the history of the Soviet Union through short, beautifully designed chapters. It opens with the fall of the Romanov Dynasty in 1917, tracing the revolutionary upsurge through carefully selected photographs of crowds and individuals, graphic art and decrees, and even five early covers of John Reed's *10 Days That Shook the World*. The journey then continues through the era of Civil War, considering its violence, hardship and utopianism alongside its posters, art and propaganda trains. This panoramic approach continues through the various eras of Soviet history concluding with Stalin's death, which is marked by three fabulous photographs: a group of factory workers listening to the announcement; a jungle-like view of Stalin's body lying in state, and a 1959 shot of Khrushchev celebrating with the stars of the American show event, 'Holiday on Ice' in Moscow (pp. 338–43). Along the way are short chapters on everything from bandits to kinomontage and textile design, from the death of Lenin and the many dimensions of the Lenin cult to the Show Trials and Stalin's victims. A particular strength is also the attention devoted to the many regions and peoples of the Soviet Union: this is very much a history of the Soviet Union as a multi-national (and imperial) project.

Though the visual is what drives this volume, King has also written a useful narrative of Soviet history that helps to contextualize the visual evidence. Furthermore, he provides translations of titles and slogans, a wide range of interesting and useful information (such as brief biographical or contextual material on the subjects of photographs or poster artists), anecdotes and interpretative readings of both form and content. He usefully notes, for example, that a couple of posters carried a warning in small print: 'Anyone who tears down this poster or covers it up is performing a counter-revolutionary act' (p. 88). In this way, the reader thus learns not only about the myriad themes of Soviet history but also about how to look at and 'read' these sources.

A brief review cannot do justice to this impressive volume. Credit must go to both King's knowledge, passion and striking design as well as to Tate Publishing for not skimping on production costs. In the end, one can both read *Red Star Over Russia* from cover to cover or simply open it randomly and explore a topic. Both methods may take the reader unaware: it is very easy to become engrossed and lose track of the time.

UCL SSEES SUSAN MORRISSEY

Smithgall, Elsa (ed.). *Kandinsky and the Harmony of Silence: Painting with White Border*. The Phillips Collection in association with Yale University Press, Washington, D.C., New Haven, CT and London, 2011. 135 pp. Illustrations. Tables. Notes. Selected bibliography. Index. $45:00: £28.00.

'WHAT more can we learn about Kandinsky by delving deeply into one masterpiece and reuniting it for the first time with its related studies?' (p. 10). This is the central question posed by Museum Directors Dorothy Kosinski (The Phillips Collection) and Richard Armstrong (The Guggenheim Museum) in their jointly authored Forward to this lavishly illustrated exhibition catalogue. Indeed, this publication makes a compelling argument for an exhibition devoted to a single 'masterpiece' and its related studies, although the evidence is in the paintings themselves, rather than in the essays in the catalogue.

The 2011 exhibition brought together Vasilii Kandinskii's *Painting with White Border (Moscow)*, 1913, owned by the Guggenheim; the artist's first oil sketch for the painting, owned by the Phillips Collection; and a second oil sketch owned by the Russian Museum in Saint Petersburg. The participating museums timed this exhibition with the 100th anniversary of the publication of Kandinskii's *Concerning the Spiritual in Art*, published first in Germany in 1912.

Given the curators' focus on a single painting, this reader found it frustrating to have to leaf through several images, and ten pages of text before actually finding *Painting with White Border (Moscow)*, 1913. Yet, the painting itself and the sketches under consideration appear several times throughout this beautiful catalogue, so there is ample opportunity for close looking. And close looking really is the justification for such an exhibit and its accompanying catalogue. For all the visual and aural din of most museum exhibitions, being given the chance to focus our normally scattered attention on a single work of art is a true gift.

Elsa Smithgall, a curator at The Phillips Collection, contributed the main essay for the catalogue, which is very good for its type. It introduces a general reader to the visual motifs found frequently in Kandinskii's painting from this period, especially the troika and St George slaying the Dragon. Smithgall delves into the source material for this imagery yet acknowledges Kandinskii's own insistence that his painting be experienced in a non-narrative, emotional way by an ideal 'receptive' viewer. While much of the relevant Kandinskii scholarship is nicely summarized, Smithgall's essay does not offer any new insights or critical perspectives on the painting or the artist. The astute museum-goer and reader would, I hope, see beyond Smithgall's endorsement of Kandinskii's own myth-making that art was 'born of the artists in a mysterious and secret way' (p. 32).

If anything, the presence of all the preliminary sketches and studies for *Painting with White Border (Moscow)* demonstrate quite the opposite: that Kandinskii's single-minded focus, and the labour intensive process, by which the artist arrived at the final painting after five months of work, had little to do with a process that was in Kandinskii's words 'foreshadowed by divine predestination' (p. 32). The detailed technical analysis along with the Pigment Analyses serve to further demystify the artist's creative process.

The Technical Analysis of the oil sketch revealed a painting underneath Kandinskii's sketch by Gabriele Münter, a German artist and Kandinskii's companion in Munich. The author of this brief essay raises some interesting questions about their working relationship, but they are not really answered as they are outside the scope of the exhibition and the catalogue.

The vast differences between the oil sketch for *Painting with White Border (Moscow)* and the final version reveal Kandinskii's shifting perspective on his native city. The oil sketch represents Kandinskii's experience of Moscow at the time of his extended visit in 1912: dark, moody, densely claustrophobic and very loud. Indeed the cacophony of voices heard in Moscow in 1912 — from the theatricalized debates of the Russian avant-garde to the anti-tsarist demonstrations after the Lena Goldfield Massacre — must have affected Kandinskii profoundly.

The 1913 painting, with its white border, does indeed shift the interpretative possibilities, especially in light of Kandinskii's own proscriptive text, *On the Spiritual in Art*, wherein the artist informs us that the colour white represents 'harmony of silence... pregnant with possibilities'. The 1913 painting becomes, then, an image of this ancient urban centre in the process of its very own transformation. The white border, in Kandinskii's words, 'effects our psyche like the silence of a great magnitude' (p. 33). Thus the final painting, while ostensibly depicting riotous Moscow, becomes a work that inspires meditation and even awe.

Whilst Smithgall's essay is directed to the general reader, the Technical Analyses published in the catalogue will be quite useful for scholars, curators and Kandinskii specialists.

What have we learned? The lessons of *Painting with White Border (Moscow)* are many, but perhaps not communicated by the contributors to the catalogue. Kandinskii's paintings appear chaotic and confusing. We must silence our minds in order to hear them speak one at a time.

Department of Slavic and Eurasian Studies PAMELA J. KACHURIN
Duke University

Neef, Sigrid. *Die Opern Nikolai Rimsky-Korsakows*. Musik Konkret, 18: Quellentexte und Abhandlungen zur russischen Musik des 19. und 20. Jahrhunderts. Ernst Kuhn, Berlin, 2008. xli + 418 pages. Notes. €59.95 (paperback).

Neef, Sigrid. *Die Opern Sergej Prokofjews*. Prokofjew-Studien, 7; Studia Slavica Musicologica, 45. Ernst Kuhn, Berlin, 2009. xviii + 326. Notes. Index. €59.95 (paperback).

DESPITE having produced some fifteen operas between 1868 and 1907, Nikolai Rimskii-Korsakov has never quite established himself in theatres in the West. The centenary of his death in 2008 was marked by precious few productions outside Russia, although that situation has been remedied to a limited and belated degree with performances of *Kashchei bessmertnyi* at the Buxton Festival and *Motsart i Sal′eri* at the Royal Opera House's Linbury Studio, both in 2012. The extent to which the composer himself is to blame for this state of affairs is not a question that directly interests Sigrid Neef (although in her introduction she does appear to concede that his stage works might lack something of the dramatic élan of Chaikovskii, Verdi or Wagner). Rather, Neef points to the role of traditions of reception — in both Russia and the West — that have tended to confine him to a colourful nationalist ghetto; as she pointedly puts it, Rimskii-Korsakov is 'Gut genug für Kinder, Nostalgiker und Slawophile' (p. xxii). However, Neef claims to detect a shift in contemporary society that might establish conditions more propitious to the success of the composer's operas. Noting that the modern world is faced with a profound environmental tragedy, she argues that Rimskii-Korsakov's pantheistic vision of our place in the natural order might be germane to our own present-day concerns. The extent to which this might be true is, perhaps, debatable. Productions by visiting Russian companies are still likely to stress local colour and pseudo-ethnographic curiosity, and Paul Curran's 2011 Covent Garden version of *Tsarskaia nevesta* turned a historical opera into a commentary on post-Soviet Russia as a mafia state. Yet Neef's deeply held and sensitively argued case is a welcome contribution to debates about the place of Russian music in the Western canon, and even if performers and directors have yet to pick up on the ecological potential of Rimskii-Korsakov's operas, her argument suggests parallels with the case of Chekhov, whose sensitivity to the perils of industrialization has become an important theme in the recent critical literature.

A second strain in Neef's introduction focuses on the potential for Rimskii-Korsakov's operas to speak to a renewed interest in questions of spirituality in a post-enlightenment age; for self-evident reasons, this aspect of the composer's work enjoyed little favour in the Soviet period and remains to be fully grasped today. The rest of Neef's introduction contains a number of further observations, whose pertinence can be traced both to her work as a thoughtful writer on Russian music and her practical experience as a former dramaturge at Berlin's Staastoper. She notes, for instance, Rimskii-Korsakov's major contribution to the redefinition of traditional operatic form, arguing that each of his operas fail to conform to inherited expectations of the genre, or combine them with elements of other genres (ballet, fairy-tale, Wagnerian *epos*). It is this failure to conform to the expectations of nineteenth-century grand opera, she implies, that might also constitute the basis on which Rimskii-Korsakov could be seen as a precursor to something newer and even more experimental. Similarly, the composer's preference for lighter, *mezza voce* singing, has meant that the subtlety of his works has often been mistaken for slightness (here, Neef makes favourable comparisons between recordings of sopranos from the composer's own era and the voice of Russia's current leading diva, Anna Netrebko).

Each of these topics could form the basis of a substantial study in its own right, yet Neef's introduction is brief and suggestive rather than thorough and documentary. The bulk of *Die Opern Nikolai Rimsky-Korsakows* consists of individual sections on the composer's operatic works. In each case, Neef details the authorship of the libretti, dates of composition (and in certain cases, revision), dates and venues of first performances, lists of dramatic personae, disposition of orchestral forces and even duration of performance, before going on to provide a summary of the action and a thorough commentary on aspects of the musical, historical and thematic content of each work.

Each section concludes with a discography and a brief bibliography; in the latter case, Neef's sources are principally Russian and German, and readers of English will also want to consult Richard Taruskin's revelatory essays for the *New Grove Dictionary of Opera*. It is something of a shame that the book contains no musical examples, less alone illustrations (given the particularly close relationship between Rimskii-Korsakov's operas and the visual arts, especially in the productions staged at Savva Mamontov's Moscow Private Opera).

Neef's study of the operas of Sergei Prokof′ev follows the same format (although she also includes a section on the Third Symphony that the composer fashioned out of music for the as then unstaged *Ognennyi angel*). Prokof′ev's operas have been more successful on Western stages than those of Rimskii-Korsakov. As well as tours by and co-productions with the Mariinskii Theatre, there is an established tradition of landmark productions; in the UK alone, one might mention stagings of *Liubov′ k trem apel′sinam* by Glyndebourne in 1982 and Opera North in 1988, English National Opera's 2001 *Voina i mir*, versions of *Obruchenie v monastyre* by Glyndebourne in 2006 and Scottish Opera in 2012, or the Royal Opera House's 2010 *Igrok*. Neef's introduction is more of an overview of Prokof′ev's evolution as an opera composer rather than the more penetrating and personal advocacy that characterized her writing on Rimskii-Korsakov, and her evocation of the Soviet cultural context that so complicated the production and reception of a number of these works (from *Semen Kotko* onwards) is relatively sketchy, replying primarily on memoirs and biography.

It seems unlikely that anybody would read either of these volumes from cover to cover, and readers hoping to search for specific pieces of information will find the lack of an index a distinct hindrance (although detailed lists of contents do facilitate navigation). Nonetheless, as introductions to an often neglected and underappreciated repertoire, both *Die Opern Nikolai Rimsky-Korsakows* and *Die Opern Sergej Prokofjews* have much to offer, and at their best contain insights that other scholars in the field might explore with profit in greater detail.

Wadham College, University of Oxford PHILIP ROSS BULLOCK

Joseph, Charles M. *Stravinsky's Ballets.* Yale Music Master Works. Yale University Press, New Haven, CT and London, 2011. xviii + 298 pp. Illustrations. Music examples. Notes. Bibliography. Index. £25.00.

IF you believe George Balanchine to be the greatest choreographer of the twentieth century, then this is the book for you; if not, you may be disappointed. Charles Joseph's *Stravinsky's Ballets* is a wide-ranging study of the music Stravinskii composed for ballet. It deals more or less with works made between 1910 and 1966, spanning just over fifty years of the last century, with substantial emphasis placed on the work Balanchine choreographed; over half the book is devoted to him.

Joseph offers some in-depth musical analysis of selected works but spends much less time on the choreography. Possibly because he regards Igor′ Stravinskii as the foremost composer of the twentieth century, Joseph gives priority to the music and there is little evidence that he can engage with dance. Even in the Introduction, he comments that it is a 'historically bereft genre' (p. xv), so not something with which a serious composer should engage.

There is, though, just an element of truth in this assertion. By the end of the nineteenth century, ballet in Europe was in the doldrums and it needed the magnificent productions of Serge Diaghilev's Ballets Russes to inject life into a fading and under-valued art form. So when Mikhail Fokin and Stravinskii's *The Firebird* wowed Paris in June 1910, a new era for ballet had begun. It is an important work, not just because it was Stravinskii's first composition for Diaghilev but also because it was a choreographic masterpiece.

No longer were tinsel and tutus adorning the stage, instead it was peopled with Russian princesses and characters from all over Russia's vast territory, dressed according to rank and ethnicity. Apart from the Firebird, the rest of the cast danced in soft shoes and each had a dance motif that acknowledged their cultural roots. Stravinskii had to allow for this diversity, which meant using some music from traditional sources. Joseph suggests that there is a mismatch between score and choreography and he expertly analyses the music but not the choreography. Providing a corresponding analysis might have dispelled this notion. The range of dance movement and expert handling of a large group is breathtaking and the seamless integration of narrative, character, music and costume changed ballet forever. Yet, although *The Firebird* and *Petrushka*, which followed in 1911, were musically radical, Europe was unprepared for what followed in 1913.

If *The Rite of Spring* (1913) signifies a major break with the past, then *Les Noces*, (1923) as Stephanie Jordan notes, occupies a 'unique position within dance/music history' (*Stravinsky Dances: Re-Visions Across a Century*, Alton, 2007). It has some of the most innovative and challenging choreography of the twentieth century. Bronislava Nizhinska's pared down, insistent motifs not only show great economy of means but also express the rhythms of the actions, such as the braiding of the Bride's hair. Like her brother, Vaslav Nizhinskii, Nizhinska could understand and analyse music and, when she rehearsed it with the Royal Ballet, company members remember her consulting the score on which she had marked out the choreography. Joseph devotes a scant eight pages to it, dismissing it merely as a hybrid. His limited understanding of dance is highlighted by his remark that Nizhinska's 'approach is breathtaking in its anticipation of Balanchine's *Apollo*' (p. 216), a comment he attributes to

Jordan. This is not what she wrote; she merely notes that the use of pointe work anticipates Balanchine's later ballets.

Joseph is at his strongest dealing with Balanchine's works, particularly in his discussion of *Agon*, though much of this material is drawn from his earlier book *Stravinsky and Balanchine: A Journey of Invention* (New Haven, CT, 2002). Yet he hardly mentions the four important works made by the choreographer, Frederick Ashton, to Stravinskii's music. Two of these receive a brief comment, though in a footnote, Joseph states that Ashton's *Scènes de Ballet* 'remains practically unknown to musicians' (p. 245). This overlooks the fact that the ballet has been seen and admired in the USA from the early 1950s.

Musicologists rarely deal with ballet and Joseph is to be congratulated. The book adds to the debate on dance and music and our knowledge of Stravinskii's music. It is not of course the first book on Stravinskii and dance; Jordan takes that honour, and with the centenary of *The Rite of Spring* this year there may well be more. Stravinskii's output of dance music is formidable and any book that encourages us to engage more fully with dance and music is to be welcomed.

Department of Dance GERALDINE MORRIS
University of Roehampton

Beumers, Birgit and Condee, Nancy (eds). *The Cinema of Alexander Sokurov.* KINO: The Russian and Soviet Cinema Series. I. B. Tauris, London and New York, 2011. xix + 262 pp. Illustrations. Notes. Filmography. Bibliography. Index. £16.99 (paperback).

IT was bound to happen; sooner or later an English-language volume devoted to Russia's 'most widely distributed' filmmaker (p. 1) would appear, reaching out to fans and keen followers of a cinema which exists beyond the action-infested, narrative-driven films that dominate the popular medium. In particular, Sokurov's *Russian Ark* (2002) has become an emblem of Russia's spiritual and intellectual cinematic survival following the break-up of the Soviet Union. Rather than offering a celebratory collection, reflecting Sokurov's popularity with art-house audiences and film scholars alike, these essays consider the curious position that Sokurov and his films occupy. On the one hand, Sokurov's filmmaking investigates the consequences of moving beyond the medium's limits, whilst on the other, it champions the moving image in its most auteurist, enigmatic and national essentialist forms.

The book is divided into five sections. Each focuses on an aspect of Sokurov's *oeuvre* or views a collection of his films from a particular perspective — documentaries, early feature films, power/family films, imperial connections and Russian (re)views. Although overlapping at times, these sections are well thought through, as is evident from the brief but solid introduction by the volume's editors, Birgit Beumers and Nancy Condee.

In the book's first section, Jeremy Hicks considers several of Sokurov's documentaries, or rather, reconsiders them in order to demonstrate the way in which Sokurov projects a double vision that can be detected only through repeated viewing, or through the filmmaker's persistent use of long-takes and subjective viewpoints. This double vision is situated within the fallen tradition of Soviet documentary filmmaking, which has little room to manoeuvre in the contemporary cinematic field of spectacle narratives. In the two following chapters, Eva Binder and Sabine Hänsgen seek to find stylistic parameters in either a reductionist cinema (pp. 35–36) or in postmodern minimalist filmmaking (p. 46). Although their analysis is convincing, these chapters fare less well in conveying Sokurov's objectives or his desire for this kind of aesthetics. An answer to this might be located in the collection as a whole, although what emerges is a strong preference for what one could call 'anti-cinema', that is, a cinema that does not want to be cinema. Sokurov's search for single author 'prophetics', it seems, runs counter to the industrial documentary film feature.

Nariman Skakov's close reading of *The Lonely Voice of Man* (1978) and its intertextual connections to Platonov's novel, as well as Tarkovskii's *Mirror* (1975), identifies Sokurov's feature debut as 'borrowing' from other texts in an 'aesthetic race' (p. 71) and in a rejection of linear narrative. Julian Graffy's emphasis on script development and the use of liminal spaces in *Day of Eclipse* (1988), also points to an anti-cinema in contradiction with itself. Sokurov's liminality occurs not as an 'either/or' dictum but as a 'both/and' space and, although *Day of Eclipse* can be viewed as Sokurov's most cinematic film until *Moloch* (1999), it essentially communicates that which it aims to reject, namely intellectual conformism. Anti-cinema, therefore, is not the rejection of cinema but its continuum through more cinema. Controversially, Robert Bird qualifies Sokurov's artistic ideas as old avant-garde traditionalism (p. 104). Sokurov isolates his viewer, he argues, through the obsolescence of images in a tradition that draws on Eizenshtein and Soviet montage rather than surrealism and absent narrative.

The absent parent features in Mikhail Iampolski's analysis of the family cycle, *Mother and Son* (1997) and *Father and Son* (2003), but here the absent becomes part of 'a cinema suspicious of words and of representation' (p. 120). Once again, Sokurov is seen to be moving away from a representational medium to a utopian cinema of non-representation. In the bio-pics, Denise Youngblood and Stephen Hutchings, each from a different approach — historical and auteurist respectively — come to the same conclusion: that there is a disruption of cause and effect which is elevated either to *ostranenie* or alienation. Hutchings argues that Sokurov seeks to transcend alienated cinema (p. 147) but, as he also suggests in the title of his essay, it is a 'failed' cinema. The question remains as to what Sokurov's cinema should transcend into, other than merely more cinema.

Failures, or accidents, are the focus of José Alaniz's excellent examination of *Russian Ark*. Taking the crowd or the control of the crowd as his springboard, Alaniz illustrates how Sokurov seeks absolute auteurist control over his images which, paradoxically, prove to be uncontrollable. The master filmmaker seeks to eradicate the cinematic effluence of the crowd and others, especially his German cameraman, because these cinematic 'bloopers' can 'turn Sokurov's traditionalist posturing into the stuff of farce' (p. 170). In the last two chapters of this section, Beumers and Condee offer their views on this traditionalist posture. If Youngblood was the historian of the power cycle, then Birgit Beumers is the art historian of *Russian Ark*, detecting disjunctions, omissions and eradications. Nancy Condee, on the other hand, digs deeper into the fabric of Sokurov's filmmaking by dissecting his use of allegory, arguing that, in *Aleksandra* (2007) in particular, even the simplest of plotlines carries the heavy burden of imperial metaphors (p. 196).

The book's objective is to account for Sokurov's cinema over several decades, and its final chapters give voice to Russian critics and co-workers. These are translated by Richard Taylor and are largely taken from two books on Sokurov edited by Liubov Arkus (St Petersburg, 1994 and 2006), as well as Aleksandra Tuchinskaia's website, 'The Island of Sokurov' (<http://www.sokurov.spb.ru/index.html>). In particular, I would like to highlight the sections by Yuri Arabov and Mikhail Trofimenkov: Arabov's account because it supports the general portrayal of Sokurov as moving from filmmaker to auteur supreme, and Trofimenkov's because it adds to notions of vanity and the static nature of man. These accounts neither uncover nor reveal 'secrets' from the 'inside', but rather confirm and advance the general perception of Sokurov's cinema as complex and wide-ranging, but also contradictory and conformist.

A favourite child has many names, and so does Sokurov: neo-conservative, minimalist, romantic cine-poet, traditionalist, pretentious mystic, megalomaniac controller, reductionist, sublime innovator and painter imitator. However, there is no denying that Sokurov, with his cinema of 'traditional experimentation', appeals to certain segments of both national and international audiences, which is no easy feat. This first, English-language study makes a significant contribution to the study of contemporary Russian cinema and addresses the cinema of Sokurov with a critical distance that is admirable and exemplary. Teachers, researchers and students alike will find in it useful material on art, cinema and the auteur.

School of Journalism, Media and Communication LARS KRISTENSEN
University of Central Lancashire

Meinander, Henrik. *A History of Finland.* Translation from the Swedish by Tom Geddes. C. Hurst and Company, London, 2011. xiv + 227 pp. Illustrations. Bibliography. Index. £25.00.

THIS is a fine work and its author, Henrik Meinander, has been well served by his translator from Swedish into English, Tom Geddes.

Things start with a geological event, the retreat of the ice-cap. But even then people seem to have been around, at least a few Neanderthals. After a cooler interlude of approximately a thousand years, everything began to get better again. The ice-sheet shrank once more. It left behind a lot of lakes for the Finns.

They came in quite early, bringing with them their Uralic language (though Kalevi Wiik's controversial book on this theme, *Eurooppalaisten juuret*, is not mentioned in the bibliography). Anway, Vikings from the West began to come in, too.

Since the author is a historian, he ploughs quite quickly into his title-theme. Carefully and concisely, his chapters reach forward. From the medieval and early modern world of Russo-Swedish political and religious conflict over the body of Finland, Meinander moves effectively into autonomy, independence, the wars of the last century, the post-Second World War accommodation with the Soviet Union, the acceptance of the European Union in 1995 and its constitution in 2004, and the brief period of economic prosperity that wavered indeterminately for a few years after. The present European mess has come too suddenly to be dealt with in this text, however.

Modern Finland is a Scandinavian country with many of its key institutions brought over by the connection with a once-powerful Sweden, which held the country till 1809. Most interesting too is Meinander's subsequent chapter on Pax Russica, in which he recounts the achievement of the crafty J. V. Snellman and his supporters in persuading Tsar Alexander II in 1863 to make Finnish an official language in Finland alongside Swedish. Tsardom felt that this might weaken the power of the Swedish (i.e. Western) language. In a way, this has gradually happened, as the number of Swedish-speakers decline in Finland. But it has not been to the advantage of either the Russian language or any Russian systems. What has occurred is that the tortuous Finnish language has become a Western language, in spite of its honourable past in the Urals and beyond. The victory has gone to the Swedish West, whose ideas now stand clear in the Finnish language.

It is to Meinander's credit that he mentions not merely the great sweeps of politics, but also the undercurrents in, for example, the music of Sibelius, or the toned-down politics of Rauli 'Badding' Somerjoki and 'Juice' Leskinen. The latter names cannot be found in the index — they are on page 179 — as some kind of confusion, alas, seems to have occurred between index and bibliography. Talking more specifically of political history, there are of course other political undercurrents that might have been mentioned. The author seems to take the Max Jakobson line with respect to the negotiations that preceded the Winter War with the Soviet Union. Was the initial offer of two large parishes in East Karelia in return for the Finnish territorial concessions only a trick as Max Jakobson seems to believe? Was it so much of a trick that it need not be mentioned by Meinander? In respect of later politics, Max Jakobson's own candidature for the post of United Nations Secretary-General is not alluded to, though many outside Finland have regretted the failure of this candidature. On the other hand, the succinct account in Meinander's book of Finland's advocacy of a Conference for Security and Cooperation in Europe is well done.

On more recent politics concerning Finland's entry into the EU, the ins-and-outs of the politicking in the Centre Party (formerly the Agrarian Union) might have provided the reader — had this been told — with a few more insights into the vagaries of Finnish public life. Never mind, since things are probably going to get tougher, and Meinander can deal with them next time.

University of Turku GEORGE MAUDE

Plakans, Andrejs. *A Concise History of the Baltic States*. Cambridge Concise Histories. Cambridge University Press, Cambridge and New York, 2011. xvi + 472 pp. Maps. Illustrations. Notes. Suggested readings. Index. £16.99: $27.99 (paperback).

THE Cambridge Concise History series gives helpful introductions to the histories of various individual countries (e.g. Hungary, Finland, and even Wales). The history of the Baltic states was the first book in this series that was dedicated to a region, i.e. to three countries (Estonia, Latvia and Lithuania). One may guess that separately the histories of these states would not have attracted broad enough interest to be included in this series. However, one can find another explanation for this in the book by Andrejs Plakans. It was only in the Soviet period after the Second World War that the eastern Baltic littoral became known as *Pribaltika*; a region rather than three separate republics (p. 378), and after 1991 'the west tended to imagine the three republics as a region or at least a region-in-the-making, referring to them as "the Baltics" just as in the old Soviet Union the littoral was most frequently simply *Pribaltika*' (p. 404).

The book demonstrates clearly that binding together the histories of three Baltic states is a challenging task, especially in the case of the history of Lithuania before the twentieth century. After all, 'Lithuania's historical memory contained a grand duchy, no less, while those of Latvia and Estonia could speak only of seven hundred years of subordinated peasanthood' (p. 448). One can conclude that Plakans has masterfully managed to offer an integrated historical survey of three Baltic states, although the distinct past of Lithuania is very often just presented in separate sub-chapters or paragraphs in the book. The author's Latvian background becomes very clear throughout the book as the history of Latvia is the most nuanced and exact. At the same time, the provinces of Estland and Ösel receive only scant attention.

The history of the Baltic states or the Baltic littoral, as the author prefers to call the region throughout the book, cannot be written without paying careful attention to ethnic relations. For more than eight hundred years language (whether German, Polish, Lithuanian, Latvian, Estonian, Russian, Swedish, Danish or Finnish) has been an indicator of political and social status. In addition to ethnic relations, Plakans concentrates on political and cultural history, somewhat less on economic history. Preference is clearly given to a smooth narrative and explanations of the events rather than the piling up of all possible facts and dates. This is undoubtedly the strength of the book.

Although the book does not overwhelm the reader with facts, there are regrettably too many mistakes in the basic dates given. The first human settlements in Lithuanian territory date from at least 11,000 BC (not 11,000 years ago: p. 3). In the listing of the Livonian towns in the Hanseatic League Viljandi and Pärnu are not mentioned (p. 61). The independence of Riga lasted until 1582, not 1682 (p. 87). The Academia Gustaviana (university in Tartu) was founded in 1632, not in 1631 (p. 249). Sweden invaded Poland-Lithuania in 1655, not in 1656 (p. 118). The facts that Russia was at war with Poland already from 1654 and that a large part of Lithuania and Livland was occupied by Russian forces in 1655 and 1658–61 are not mentioned at all. The Forselius Seminary was active in 1684–88 and therefore not founded in the eighteenth century (p. 249). Riga did not surrender to the Russians in 1709 (p. 122), but in 1710 (correctly given on p. 126). Catherine the Great became Empress of Russia in 1762, not in 1760 (p. 142). Hupel's *Topographische Nachrichten* appeared in 1774–82 (not in 1770: p. 132). Herder published his *Volkslieder* in 1778, not in 1787 (p. 150). The first Estonian weekly newspaper was not published in 1821–25 (p. 167) but in 1806 (*Tarto maa rahwa Näddali-Leht*).

In addition, one can find many misspellings (e.g. p. 328 'Isamalit', pp. 278 and 295: Jaan Tõnnison; p. 296: Jaan Poška instead of Isamaaliit, Tõnisson, Poska) and other imprecisions. In 1600 Charles was still only the Duke of Södermanland (until 1604) and not yet King Karl IX (p. 88). The emancipation law of Livland in 1819 was translated into Estonian practically in full the next year, not 'only a few sections' (p. 192). Furthermore, it did not forbid the movement of peasants across estate boundaries (p. 195) but allowed free resettlement within the parish and after a fixed period of years within the district and the whole province. The Estonian, Latvian and Lithuanian supreme councils did not announce their independence on the same day in August 1991 (p. 399). And Estonia introduced its own national currency in 1992, not with Latvia and Lithuania between 1993 and 1995 (p. 406).

However, it clearly appears that the author feels himself much more confident with the topics of modern history. And so the second half of the book dedicated to nineteenth- and twentieth-century history is more enjoyable to read than the first four chapters, which cover the period from archaeology to the end of the eighteenth century. The book concludes with an index that could surely be more helpful and thoroughgoing than it is but this was probably out of the author's hands.

Institute of Archaeology and History MARTEN SEPPEL
University of Tartu

Shore, Paul. *Narratives of Adversity: Jesuits on the Eastern Peripheries of the Habsburg Realms (1640–1773).* Central European University Press, Budapest and New York, 2012. x + 384 pp. Notes. Bibliography. Index. Register of geographical names. £50.00.

IN the words of Paul Shore, 'the Society of Jesus has inspired more debate, scholarship, and speculation than any other Catholic order' (p. 17). That this should be the case does not come as a surprise since the Jesuits burst on to the world stage in the mid-sixteenth century, and rapidly established themselves in the vanguard of Reformed Catholicism to which they gave a dynamic didactic impetus. On the day that the Pope approved the formation of the Society (27 September 1540), the Benedictines were already a thousand years old, the Dominicans and Franciscans over three centuries old. Within a century the Society had set up 800 schools on all the known continents. Their expansion gave rise to a close examination of their motivations and methods, and to a discussion of their setbacks in Japan, China and Ethiopia, but less attention has been paid to the fringes of the Habsburg Empire and the individual experience of Jesuit brothers and priests. Shore's book remedies that *lacuna.*

He brings to this study his authority as a scholar of the activities of the Society of Jesus in the eastern territories of the Habsburg Empire, having previously authored *The Eagle and the Cross: Jesuits in Late Baroque Prague* (St Louis, MO, 2002) and *Jesuits and the Politics of Religious Pluralism in Eighteenth-Century Transylvania: Culture, Politics, and Religion, 1693–1773* (Rome, Burlington, VT and Aldershot, 2007). In this present volume Shore looks further east and examines Jesuit goals, achievements and failures over a period of more than a century and a quarter in the eastern and northern fringes of the Habsburg Empire, in an area including Royal Hungary, but stretching to Moldavia,

Ukraine, Serbia and Wallachia. Using an impressive array of primary sources in several languages, the author discusses the experience of challenge and adversity amongst some of the Jesuits of the Empire from the moment of 'high tide' of the Society, in the fourth decade of the seventeenth century, to the Society's suppression by papal brief (*breve)* in 1773. That experience emerges, in the documents generated by the brothers and priests, 'as a complex mixture of subjective and individually varied reactions to events' (pp. 19–20).

Shore explores the subjective, recorded responses of Jesuits to a variety of situations, amongst them adversity, doubt, miscommunication and failure. His exploration is aided significantly by our growing understanding of the different ways in which Jesuits collected, categorized and recorded information. In this regard, Shore raises questions which exercise every conscientious historian when confronting his or her sources. In the case of Shore's Jesuits a grasp of what individuals understood themselves to be doing sometimes remains elusive, since they kept their records in a language that was not their native tongue (and as the documents themselves reveal, of which some Jesuits had a tenuous command) and in composing them followed established formulae and epistolary forms that could obscure their own motives and sentiments (p. 20). Furthermore, they were acting in regions in which the ethnic mix included Hungarians, Romanians, Germans, Ukrainians, Serbs, Armenians, Gypsies and others, and in which religious diversity encompassed, among others, Orthodox, Greek Catholics, Roman Catholics, Calvinists, Lutherans, Unitarians and Muslims.

The cases in which a Jesuit found himself operating as an individual were more numerous than those encountered by members of most other Catholic orders. This stemmed from the responsibility (particularly when on isolated missions) placed upon him to make decisions, often without recourse to his superiors, who might live hundreds of miles away. The book examines the life and work of such figures in towns such as Košice, Trnava, Belgrade, Banská Bystrica, Kláštor pod Znievom, Sárospatak and Levoća; thematically, it has chapters entitled 'Sex and Demons' (chapter five), and 'Theatre and Suffering' (chapter seven). In the former, cases in which Jesuits conducted exorcisms on women who imagined sexual contact with a demon (or demons) are recounted, In the latter, the significance attached by the Jesuits to the *theatrum*, in the sense of public performance or display, is discussed. These involved not only the production of staged dramas in smaller communities, especially in schools, but extended to flagellant processions of laypersons organized by Jesuits. One such procession took place in Temesvár (Timişoara) during Holy Week in 1727.

It is regrettable that in a book which examines the periphery of an empire, in which myriad names of little-known localities are invoked, there is no map. Furthermore, it would have been helpful to the reader to have some idea of the populations of the regions covered — here the Habsburg censuses would have helped. Nevertheless, Shore's study shows us that Jesuit culture in the Habsburg East thrived on adversity, an adversity most evident in the 'clear-cut if infrequent moments when a Jesuit was given the choice between renouncing his identity or death' (p. 308). If one is looking for a grand project of eighteenth-century Habsburgs that, as Shore writes, 'echoes the ambition of "Unus non sufficit orbis" a century earlier', then the search will be in vain. ('One World is Not Enough', a reference to the motto on the *Imago primi saeculi*, an opulent volume printed a century after the establishment of the Society, with contributions from its writers and artists, with poems in Latin, Greek and Hebrew, and many intricate and emblematic engravings. The line is from the Latin poet Juvenal's Tenth Satire: 'unus Pellaeo iuveni non sufficit orbis'.) Yet the presence of the Jesuit communities of the area is perceptible, as Shore shows, in collective literary and material products. His book is a invaluable source for our understanding of interplay between culture and religion in this part of Europe.

UCL SSEES & Georgetown University, Washington, D.C. DENNIS DELETANT

Davies, Brian. *Empire and Military Revolution in Eastern Europe: Russia's Turkish Wars in the Eighteenth Century.* Continuum Studies in Military History. Continuum, London and New York, 2011. ix + 364 pp. Map. Notes. Select bibliography. Index. £65.00.

THE publication of Brian Davies's *Warfare, State and Society on the Black Sea Steppe, 1500–1700* in 2007 (London and New York) was a major event in military history, announcing as it did the publication of a comprehensive *oeuvre* on Russian expansion in the Black Sea basin. This second volume takes the story forward for most of the eighteenth century, from 1700 to the war of 1768–74, and announces a third volume which will treat the establishment of Russia's hegemony during the reign of Catherine II, from 1768 to 1791. This second volume is not an easy read; it is dense and replete with factual material, but to anyone interested in the subject it offers a magnificent panorama of the country's expansion. The reader will return to it again and again, not only to appreciate what good scholarship must be, but also as an inexhaustible source of information.

The book begins with a survey of the geopolitical situation about 1700 in the Balkan frontier, the Ukrainian lands (with an excellent section on social developments in Little Russia) and the Polish-Lithuanian Commonwealth. Davies shows here (and elsewhere in the book) a remarkable knowledge of geography, and more maps would have helped. The next chapter (all six chapters are about fifty pages long, which shows how Davies exercises a tight control over his material) examines Peter I's reforms of the army and the impact of the Russo-Swedish War in the southern theatre up until the battle of Poltava. Chapter three examines the Prut campaign and the Persian war. Chapter four returns to the organization of the army and Münnich's reforms of the 1730s. Chapter five (a bit longer) is devoted to the Turkish war of 1736–39, and chapter six wraps up the story with a survey of the geopolitical situation from 1770 to 1774 (even though the war of 1768–74 will be part of the third volume). To put it differently, Davies devotes fifty-nine pages to the organization and reforms of the army, forty-three pages to the war of 1736–39, and forty-two pages to the Russo-Swedish operations between 1706 and 1717. These sections are embedded in a rich tissue of geopolitical developments in the Balkans, the Ukrainian lands and the Polish Commonwealth. A well-organized book indeed, which keeps the reader's attention focused on the essentials.

The book is so rich in details that it is hardly appropriate to quibble about a few things. One wonders what the author meant when he writes that the Right Bank Ukraine was 'nominally' under Crown control (p. 29), when in fact it was part of the *Korona*, i.e., of Poland proper. The reasons for the liquidation of the Zaporozhian Cossacks may be more complex than is asserted on page 258. When Charles XII turned to Russia, he found 'the most favorable opportunity' by invading through Ukraine (p. 36), while in fact he was forced to take the southern route because of a shortage of supplies, as Davies himself recognizes on page 92. But the book also raises larger questions which Davies will perhaps address in the third volume.

Military historians sometimes forget that wars do not simply take place but are fought for a purpose. We are never told why the Russians fought the Turks — and they did thirteen times, more often than they fought any other power. Surely there was more to it than a Turkish declaration of war, which is usually how these wars began in the eighteenth century. The United States did not fight Nazi Germany because Hitler declared war: that would be a purely legal argument. The United States fought because it recognized that the occupation of the European shore of the Atlantic Ocean by a hostile power was a threat to its vital interests. War against the Crimean Tatars was a defensive war — against the threat represented by the khanate since the sixteenth century. But the Turks? Were those wars of aggression fought for geopolitical, religious, and/or commercial reasons? Davies remains silent.

He might also have discussed the strategic dilemma faced by the Russian high command over the priorities to give to their offensives: the Danube or the Crimea. Golitsyn aimed at the Crimea, Peter at the Danube, Münnich focused on the Crimea until the last year of the war (and wasted so many lives in so doing), which was settled in Bessarabia on the Prut; Rumiantsev would focus on the Danube, defeat the Turks there, and then turn on the Tatars and crush them, ending the dilemma. Davies, with his remarkable knowledge of Russian army organization and the geography of the terrain, would have enriched his discussion if he had emphasized the importance of this issue.

His book includes the words 'Military Revolution', a concept he discusses on pages 274–83. Rather than seeing this revolution merely as the introduction of new weapons, he sides with Jeremy Black's understanding of the word — a shift in the balance of military power from Asia to Europe. This was certainly the case, not only among the maritime powers, but also between the Russians and the nomads, who had terrorized the fringes of Russian settlement for centuries. One wonders whether the Russian political and military establishment was aware of it, in the same way as, say, we nowadays sense a shift in the balance of economic power from the West to Asia. This may be a difficult question to answer, but it deserves to be raised. And if they were aware of it, the question of strategic objectives immediately comes to mind. The Russians were fighting wars in order to take advantage of this shift in the balance of military power, and their strategy was geared to reach certain objectives. What were they? We may find the answer in volume three.

This is not to detract in any way from this reviewer's admiration for Davies's achievement. We now have a splendid work of reference and analysis to understand the geopolitical situation in the Black Sea basin during much of the eighteenth century. Readers must look forward to the appearance of the next volume.

Davis Center for Russian and Eurasian Studies J. P. LeDonne
Harvard University

Butterwick, Richard. *The Polish Revolution and the Catholic Church, 1788–1792: A Political History.* Oxford University Press, Oxford, 2012. xxii + 369 pp. Maps. Tables. Notes. Select bibliography. Glossary. Index. £65.00.

The Four Years' Sejm of 1788–92 radically reconfigured the government of the Polish-Lithuanian Commonwealth, culminating in the Constitution of 3 May 1791. In this 'Polish Revolution', Richard Butterwick writes, 'an assembly of almost entirely Catholic nobles' instituted a set of policies that would tax clergy at a rate double of that of the nobility, would secularize the estate of the Bishop of Cracow, and 'rearrange dioceses so that equal episcopal salaries would be paid for equal episcopal work' (p. 6). With this book, Butterwick seeks to explain why these decisions were made, how they differed in their origin and result — for example, with regard to the closing of monasteries — from reform and revolution in other Catholic countries in the eighteenth century. In seeking to answer these questions, Butterwick provides a detailed and painstaking reconstruction of the Commonwealth's political history from the beginning of the 'Polish Revolution' in 1788 to the counter-revolutionary Confederation of Targowica, which, supported by the Russian invasion of 1792, dismantled the Constitution of 3 May 1791.

Butterwick's mastery of the primary and secondary literature is evident on every page. Though he writes that the book is not for specialists in Polish-Lithuanian history (p. vi), it does tacitly assume familiarity with Polish history in the eighteenth century. While the book possesses a thorough index, the narrative of political intrigues and various parties and factions can be hard to follow for those without a solid grasp of the major players of the period. Insightful and important conclusions are presented at the end of long sections. Affinities with other Catholic reform movements, especially in Joseph II's Habsburg Monarchy, are pointed out, but not developed enough in this book to appeal to those outside the orbit of Polish-Lithuanian historiography.

Nonetheless, the book makes a persuasive case that the noble republicanism of the Polish Revolution was not hostile to Catholicism as such, but that it sought a series of 'patriotic' reforms that, in the long run, proved more enduring in strengthening the role of Catholicism in the Polish national imagination than has been previously thought. In contrast to the consequences of the French Revolution, the Polish revolution 'could have become the basis for an evolutionary transformation of state and society in the nineteenth century' (p. 328). It was not the revolution, but the counter-revolution and partition that broke these links. The historiographical image of the Polish Revolution as inimical to Catholicism was a result of the fallout of this counter-revolution and subsequent polemic.

Butterwick makes his case in three parts. Part one opens with the death of the bishop of Cracow. The question of succession to Poland's wealthiest see brought into sharp focus questions of Church wealth, inequality among the episcopate, as well as the usual political intrigues surrounding nominations to an important diocese. The tide of noble republicanism that was swept in with the new Sejm culminated in the secularization and seizure of the bishopric's estates. The overwhelming desire of the nobility to expand the army and free the country from Russian influence made the question of the Church's wealth and the taxation of the clergy especially acute. Butterwick discusses the ways in which polemical pamphlet literature in the public sphere defined and shaped political possibilities. The second part of the book discusses how the king worked to avoid a schism with Rome, and in the process was able to re-assert some of his influence and authority, courting the support of moderate nobles. The author argues that the nobility's essential respect for Catholicism's dominant role meant that they too did not want to break from Rome, even as many of them pursued policies of toleration and limited ecclesiastical reform. The third part examines the place of the Church in the aftermath of the Constitution of 3 May. Many of the clergy greeted the new order as a 'providential' Revolution: 'the Catholic clergy propagated and sacralized the Revolution, and in so doing confirmed the dominant status of Catholicism' (p. 272). Although a new wave of polemic, spurred by fears of the Church's fate in France, threatened to weaken the new order, the newly strengthened bonds between throne, altar and the people were undone not from within, but 'by counter-revolution and partition' (p. 328). Butterwick concludes that 'the Revolution left intact just enough of the Church's dignity for the myth of unity between Church and nation to put down, in the rich soil of Providentalist euphoria, the roots of its future luxuriant growth' (p. 331).

Wesleyan University Michael Printy

Lachowicz, Teofil. *Polish Freedom Fighters on American Soil: Polish Veterans in America from the Revolutionary War to 1939.* Translated by Albert Juszczak. Two Harbors Press, Minneapolis, MN, 2011. 495 pp. Notes. Addenda. Bibliography. Index. $26.95 (paperback).

Teofil Lachowicz's indispensable, albeit hermetic almanac of the Polish ex-combatant experience in the United States is divided into two chronological parts: first, the period between the War of Independence and the First World War and secondly, the interwar years up to 1939.

The first part of the book is based almost exclusively on secondary sources, some of them hard to find. The second draws on a wealth of primary sources chiefly from a single, exhaustive collection — that of the Polish Army Veterans' Association of America (PAVA) held in New York City and Orchard Lake, Michigan — but also material from the Piłsudski Institute in New York, the Hoover Institution at Stanford University and the Archive of New Acts in Warsaw. The monograph sadly fails to include any English-language primary sources and hardly any non-Polish secondary ones. Its first part concerns veteran personalities; the second describes various veteran organizations, most particularly PAVA.

To set up the story, the author briefly recounts the exploits of personalities such as Tadeusz Kościuszko and Kazimierz Pułaski during the War of Independence. Many others, often obscure and forgotten, surface in the author's chronological list of personalities. Most get an honorary mention; a few merit a mini-biography.

Although Lachowicz's statistics are, regrettably, scattered and inconclusive, a few thousand Polish veterans had settled in the USA by the 1880s. Most of them came voluntarily, but several hundred had been forcibly deported by the

Habsburg authorities during the mid-nineteenth century. Only a few returned to the Old Country or, at least, to Europe, to fight again or retire at home. Many stayed behind to sample fully the American experience.

Amongst those who stayed, some were lucky and did well for themselves, but most ex-soldiers had a tough time. They generally experienced indifference from federal and state authorities who often limited themselves merely to declarations of sympathy. On exceptional occasions they were backed by political resolutions which were, in theory, aimed at relieving the hardships of the Polish veterans but which in practice failed to deliver, such as the unrealistic congressional Ohio land grant project of 1834.

The Poles' encounters with the denizens of the United States usually reflected the latter's utter ignorance of Poland and its plight. On the other hand, the former military men, many of whom were noblemen, were largely ill-equipped to take advantage of America's individualistic freedom. They also found themselves at the bottom of the social ladder. Some complained that the blacks enjoyed a status superior to them because of their lack of command of the English language: 'We are worse than the Negroes, under whom we work in domestic service situations. We are placed under their supervision because they know the native language' (p. 15).

After a while, the veterans set up a number of organizations, most of them ephemeral, like the Polish Committee in New York. Some veterans were also active in establishing major fraternities, including the Polish National Alliance (PNA) and the Polish Roman Catholic Union of America (PRCUA), which eventually provided the framework for PAVA. Most ex-military Poles remained unorganized, however. Some assimilated quickly; others simply wandered the continent.

The fate of the wanderers was chequered. Some experienced kindness from native Americans in Ohio in 1834; others died at their hands, like the band of Polish ex-military brothers who left Louisiana for Texas in 1835. Others fought them in the ranks of the American army, for example during the Seminole wars between 1834 and 1842. Overall, however, only a few Poles joined the US military during the nineteenth century with the exception of the Civil War, when numbers of Polish volunteers markedly increased. Poles fought in every American conflict but often paid the highest price. The Petrussewicz brothers were killed by Mexicans at Fort Goliad in 1836, for example, while Gustaw Szulc was hanged by the British following his participation in the ill-fated American military incursion into Canada in 1838.

Statistically, after 1863, Polish veterans were not representative of the American Polonia. After the 1870s, arrivals from Poland were dominated by economic migrants, mostly peasants. Military and political figures were exceptional. However, those peasants and their offspring (and here the author unfortunately fails to include any references to Thaddeus and John

Radziłowski's work on Polish-American consciousness) became American Poles. During the First World War about 20,000, spurred by patriotism, fought for Poland, and subsequently in the 'Blue Army' under General Józef Haller, while nearly 40,000 American Poles joined the US armed forces.

The 'freedom fighters' of 1914–21 were inspired by the Polish veterans of 1830 and 1863, as well as by their patriotic priests. Polish-American troops played a significant role in the conflict in Ukraine and contributed to the victory against the Bolsheviks, even though they were shabbily treated by Józef Piłsudski. This was in response to the Polish-Americans' solid support for Roman Dmowski and Ignacy Paderewski, which reflected not only their preference for nationalism over socialism but also the logical embrace of the Entente over the Central Powers, which was in congruence with the United States' war-time policy. Thus, American Poles remained patriots of both the USA and Poland.

Once the conflict in Europe had ended, most of these fighters returned home to America; a few stayed behind or later re-emigrated. Although designated as 'Americans' in Poland and evacuated home by the White House in 1921, the soldiers of the 'Blue Army' were denied veteran status in the United States and all rights to government assistance that went with it. This was based on the spurious grounds that Poland did not exist as an allied state when the men had volunteered, regardless of the fact that in 1917 they had gone into action in France as allied units, or that the political leadership of the 'Blue Army' was uniformly recognized by the leaders of the Entente, including President Woodrow Wilson, as a de facto Polish government. Unlike Belgian veterans resident in the US, Polish ex-combatants had, for example, no access to federal health care. On arriving home the Polish Americans had to rebuild their lives on their own and find a way to re-integrate into a society crippled by post-war recession.

To maintain the spirit of camaraderie from the trenches, the 'freedom fighters' founded PAVA. This was a fraternity *par excellence*. Its main objective was to look after the welfare of its members but it also participated in cultural, educational and political events. These included defending both Poland and America in print and deed, in order 'to repel anti-U.S. and anti-Poland propaganda', as reaffirmed in their statutes of 1937.

The main function of PAVA was self-help. Most of its funds, collected from subscriptions and supporters' contributions, most notably by Ignacy Paderewski and the clergy ('among the larger donors the names of priests predominated', p. 193), helped to sustain widows, orphans, war invalids and down-on-their-luck veterans, and Lachowicz's account of their plight is harrowing. There were several deaths by starvation and suicide among homeless veterans, such as Piotr Malinowski in 1922, and the Great Depression created more victims. 'About 45 persons' died in the interwar period, all of them unaffiliated veterans

(p. 190). During this time, PAVA played an important, albeit ancillary role. It was a relatively small outfit, having by 1939 only about 4,500 members, since most veterans failed to enrol (p. 146). Nevertheless, it took care of its members and often extended free membership to the needy who turned to the 'freedom fighters' for help. The PAVA Women's Auxiliary Corps, for example, under ex-combat nurse Agnieszka Wisła, distinguished itself in this endeavour.

Teofil Lachowicz's history of the Polish-American 'freedom fighters' demonstrates that, inspired by a spirit of nationalism and camaraderie, American Poles not only fought for Poland's independence but were also able to take care of their own, by their own means, when their victorious troops returned home.

Institute of World Politics MAREK JAN CHODAKIEWICZ
Washington, D.C.

Uyama, Tomohiko (ed.). *Asiatic Russia: Imperial Power in Regional and International Contexts*. New Horizons in Islamic Studies. Routledge, London and New York, 2012. xv + 296 pp. Maps. Notes. Index. £80.00.

THIS informative collection of essays, generated from an international symposium at the Slavic Research Center at Hokkaido University, explores the history of Russian expansion into the Muslim world. Its main aim is to establish 'a dialogue between Russian studies and Oriental studies' in the tradition of *Russia's Orient: Imperial Borderlands and Peoples, 1700–1917* (edited by Daniel Brower and Edward Lazzerini, Bloomington, IN, 1997). The key term, 'Asiatic Russia (*Aziatskaia Rossiia*)' is a direct translation from its vernacular version, which has political implications for this region.

The book is divided into four themes covered in thirteen papers. The first theme is Russian expansion into the East and the Tatars' role as intermediaries during this mission. Ricarda Vulpius compares Russia's eighteenth-century civilizing mission with British colonization policies in India. Although there may be some similarities, it proves unproductive to compare these two contexts, and particularly to apply the same concepts (colonization, colonial) to describe these policies. Hamamoto Mami contributes to this theme with historical accounts of Kargala, which was Russia's trading centre in Central Asia, whilst Gulmira Sultangalieva's essay describes the Tatars' intermediary role in relations between the Russian Empire and the Kazakhs.

The book's second theme is the institutional formation and demography of the conquered regions. Matsuzato Kimitaka details the complexities of the governor-generalship and its relations with the ministries of the empire. Anatolii Remnev describes the agrarian policy of moving Russian peasants to Siberia and Central Asia and the political implications of resettlement. He argues that russification was an important aim of this and other Russian expansionist policies. Sergey Abashin shows how numbers were manipulated in order to satisfy the interests of both Russians and local leaders of certain ethnic groups in Central Asia, skilfully mapping out the politics of numbers.

The volume's third theme relates to Russia's relations with her eastern neighbours — China, Iran and Tibet. Noda Jin discusses the accounts of Russian-Chinese trade relations, which were conducted through Central Asia. Robert Crews focuses on politically- and economically-driven disputes between Russia and Iran, highlighting the complexity of these relations. Kimura Satoru explores the hostility between Sunni and Shi'i Muslims in Bukhara where, after the defeat of Bukhara in 1868, Shi'i Muslims were favoured by the Russians for their cooperation during the conflict. Finally, Nikolay Tsyrempilov examines Adgvan Dorzhiev's role in Soviet-Tibetan relations.

The volume then turns to national and religious movements in Central Asia. Salavat Ishakov and James Meyer consider Muslim political movements in Turkestan and Orenburg respectively, whilst Uyama Tomhiko deals with Kazakh national movements.

This volume claims to present the Russian empire as neither a 'prison of nations' nor as a protector and civilizer, but rather to emphasize the interaction between Russian administrators and local authorities. The essays demonstrate that, whilst Russia used its military strength to suppress resistance, it was also aware of its weaknesses, and was prepared to compromise and enter into agreements with local elites.

In his introduction, Tomohiko Uyama claims that the book offers an unbiased account of Russian expansion into the East by utilizing both Russian and non-Russian sources, yet most of the contributors rely heavily on an elitist view of the processes they describe. For example, Remnev provides a one-sided view of Russia's population movements, focusing on the government's silencing of the disputes on the ground. What it meant to be resettled by force has, however, been compellingly portrayed by Pavel Polyan (*Against their Will: The History and Geography of Forced Migrations in the USSR*, Budapest and New York, 2004), who cites the correspondence of those resettled as well as their complaints to the Soviet government. Although the periods covered in both accounts differ by seven to ten years, the patterns are similar. Nevertheless, this volume will be of interest to anyone studying the dynamic historical accounts of Russia's policies in the East, and particularly Central Asia, until the times of the Soviets.

Max Planck Institute for Social Anthropology R. TURAEVA
Halle, Germany

Sked, Alan. *Radetzky: Imperial Victor and Military Genius.* I. B. Tauris, London and New York, 2011. xxiv + 262 pp. Maps. Illustrations. Chronology. Notes. Index. £25.00.

ALAN SKED is an acknowledged expert on Field Marshal Johann Joseph Wenzel von Radetzky, having published his first monograph (1979) on Radetzky's role in saving the Habsburg Monarchy in Italy in 1848–49. In this less than full-length biography, he brings a lifetime's study to the illumination of a subject the importance of which, he persuasively argues, has been long obscured. Sked describes Radetzky as a 'genius', although this is perhaps more a question for a philosopher than an historian. What is clear is that Radetzky was, in Sked's words, 'a rare bird for his times' (p. 112), certainly in the Habsburg armed forces: an innovator, capable of thinking outside the box, who believed in action and the offensive instead of caution and delay. The military history of the Habsburg Monarchy from the Theresian reforms onwards suggests that, however efficiently administrative reforms were carried out, there always remained a problem with generalship. Radetzky represents the exception to this rule. If Sked is right, and it was Radetzky's plans which guided the Leipzig campaign in 1813 and the invasion of France in 1813–14, then Radetzky has a good claim to be a figure of world historical importance, because his contribution brought about the fall of Napoleon in an astonishing eight months, and made possible the Vienna settlement of 1815, which shaped the rest of the nineteenth century.

Born three years before Napoleon, and a serving officer from 1784, Radetzky was 'Napoleonic, almost *avant la lettre*' (p. 218): offensive in mentality; a believer in planning and knowledge of the terrain; flexible; quick to move; able to concentrate his forces and use artillery effectively; but also clear on the need for an educated officer corps, humane treatment of the rank-and-file, and the general importance of *esprit de corps*. A chapter on the 'educator of armies' makes a good case for Radetzky's importance in professionalizing the Habsburg army after 1815, although, since he spent most of this period in command of the Italian provinces, it is not clear that his sensible approach to training was universally adopted. Radetzky also held surprisingly progressive views for someone of his class and position, in that he believed in constitutional government, at least up to 1848; thereafter he became a regretful apologist for absolutism. An opportunity is perhaps missed for comparing Radetzky's unusual views on the need for a genuine *Landwehr* or people's militia, with those of the Prussian military theorist Carl von Clausewitz, who in the same period argued that war was 'the business of the people'. Or, as Radetzky put it in 1828, 'a nation standing completely under arms has never yet been fully subjugated' (quoted, p. 102). It would be fascinating to know whether Radetzky was influenced by Clausewitz, or whether, as Sked appears to assume, he arrived independently at these insights into the importance of mass motivation. On the revolutionary year of 1848–49, Sked makes the point that Radetzky, by saving the situation in Italy, enabled the Monarchy to recover its nerve and face down revolution in Hungary. Had Radetzky '*not* triumphed, the European balance of power would have been overthrown' (p. 115), and a general European war in the mid-century would have been virtually inevitable; so for the second time this one individual, and in his early eighties, had played a role of world historical significance. There is a depressing coda on Radetzky's rule over Lombardy and Venetia down to 1857. Sked is judicious here, acknowledging the genuine unpopularity of Austrian rule, and the essentially reactionary nature of Radetzky's task.

The originality of the book, however, is let down by inattention to detail. Sked has a confusing habit of telling things backwards, sketching in a long-range summary of events, and then backtracking to take up a more detailed narrative. This is particularly noticeable when, having dealt with the climactic campaigns against Napoleon, he then devotes two pages to a summary of Radetzky's marriage (in 1798!), his numerous children, and the stress caused after 1815 by his wife's inability to manage the family finances. Surely the fact that Radetzky could cope with these personal difficulties, while also reaching the pinnacle of his profession, has some relevance to the overall picture? The critical apparatus, too, is thoroughly distracting. The bibliography is incomplete, in that it does not list all the sources consulted, as the notes make clear. The notes are inconsistent and confusing: some information is needlessly repeated, while other references are gnomic in the extreme; names are misspelled, dates of publication are omitted, and there is an undergraduate habit, in the text, of inserting the references for quotations before, rather than after, the quoted material. The text has been poorly edited: some passages are littered with misspellings, with French names and accent marks faring particularly badly. Finally, the publishers do Sked a disservice by clustering the ten maps at the front of the book, rather than dispersing them throughout the text, where in a military history they would be most illuminating. The maps themselves are on too small a scale, and too crowded, to convey much; certainly they do not serve the text well.

Grant MacEwan University, Edmonton IAN D. ARMOUR

Jianu, Angela. *A Circle of Friends: Romanian Revolutionaries and Political Exile, 1840–1859*. Balkan Studies Library, 3. Brill, Leiden and Boston, MA, 2011. xvi + 382 pp. Illustrations. Notes. Bibliography. Index. €109.00: $154.00.

THE most recent book on the events surrounding the 1848 revolution in Wallachia is Angela Jianu's *A Circle of Friends: Romanian Revolutionaries and Political Exile, 1840–1859*. Its novelty is the emphasis laid not so much on the political proceedings in 1848, but on personal lives and individual evolutions then and later on. This is why the 'story' in this book does not end with the toppling of the revolutionary government in Bucharest, but goes on with the ten-year-long exile of C. A. Rosetti and Ion Brătianu in Paris, of Dumitru Brătianu in London, and occasionally of Ion Ghica and the Golescu brothers and cousins in the Ottoman Empire.

Angela Jianu's book is a brilliant solution to the question of retelling the story of the 1848 revolutionaries, with the merit of contextualizing a considerable mass of documents up until now largely neglected by scholars, as they seemed irrelevant for Romanian national history. The author takes interest in the *petite histoire* of this group, as she focuses mainly on the post-revolutionary period and also on 'uninteresting' family ties, loves and friendships. Angela Jianu investigates family papers, letters, personal diaries, literary memoirs, Masonic archives and ancient Parliamentary files in France and Britain concerning the 'circle' around the liberal revolutionaries from Bucharest. The importance of the restoration of this history lies in the unexpected vicinities encountered in Rosetti and the Brătianus's exile. Academics and public intellectuals such as Jules Michelet and Edgar Quinet, diplomats like Effingham Grant or Robert Colquhoun, British MPs such as William Gladstone and Elias Regnault, French *hommes politiques* like Lamartine and Jean Abdolonyme Ubicini are cited not just as useful tools in the political struggle, but also as friends, husbands, brothers-in-law and (sometimes estranged) allies. Personal relationships were crucial in times of persecution for securing a steady course of joint political action and, as this book demonstrates, reciprocal dislike between D. Brătianu, Golescu-Arăpilă and Lajos Kossuth may have been one of the causes of the failure to create a common European revolutionary movement in the 1850s around the future hero of a united Italy, Giuseppe Garibaldi.

Angela Jianu also argues that a Romantic vision of things, celebrating love and friendship as universal solutions, was inherent not only to the Romanian revolutionaries' political project, but also to their character. However, this frame of mind was one of the reasons for the errors they made in their later, governmental phase, when their generous idealism failed to keep pace with the realities at hand and the result was a 'culture of discourse' that would be more accurately described as deceitful propaganda. Angela Jianu's account has the merit of insisting on other 'lesser', but still very important events, such as the fatherly feeling which guides C. A. Rosetti, the recent father of a daughter named Liberty, in the political upheaval of June 1848; the savage persecution of liberals by the Russian army in the wake of the Walachian revolution; the 'inner exile' that Michelet is forced to endure alongside Rosetti's family after the French imperial restoration of 1852; Edgar Quinet's Romanian pseudonym when crossing the border into Belgium, and the agitation for the Romanian cause in the British Parliament fuelled by the agile Dumitru Brătianu.

I have two reservations about this very interesting book. First, it fails to bring together all its separate narratives, as a consequence of its mainly French and British archival finds concerning C. A. Rosetti and Ion Brătianu. The rather large sections on the Golescus's life during their Turkish exile or on Dumitru Brătianu's efforts in London, whilst containing new and pertinent information, do not contribute to the story of the Paris-centred exiles. Nevertheless, as Hayden White argued, history should not be obliged to conform to a clear and simple narrative pattern.

Secondly, Angela Jianu's hypothesis that the experience of exile 'made the more reflective of this cosmopolitan group realize that individual and national identities are fluctuating entities which can be given or constructed, assumed or relinquished, invented or reinforced', has to be amended. No matter how many pseudonyms the exiles use, their nationalism remains solid, 'classical', as shown by all their discourses and ideological stances, then and later on. Leaving this minor correction aside, Angela Jianu's book is a refreshing inquiry into the background of major historical events, illuminating their causes and hidden motivations.

University Alexandru Ioan Cuza, Iași DORIS MIRONESCU

Becker, Elisa M. *Medicine, Law and the State in Imperial Russia.* Central European University Press, Budapest and New York, 2011. x + 399 pp. Illustrations. Notes. Bibliographical references. Index. £35.00.

THIS impressive book opens new paths of consideration for our understanding of the evolution of Russia's professions. Elisa Becker approaches her story from a very rewarding and challenging angle: examining the development of medical disciplinary authority in autocratic Russia across the entire imperial period, she focuses on an occupational group that by its very definition — given in Peter the Great's Military Statute from 1716, which defined the state physician as forensic physician — assumed a pivotal position at the intersection of autocratic policies, and both the legal and medical professions. Becker takes the challenge to bridge the gap between heretofore isolated histories of either Russian medicine or Russian law in order to scrutinize the mechanics by which the emergence of the two closely intertwined professions was inherently linked to the transformation in legal structures in the reform and post-reform period. Ultimately, the book departs from many common assumptions, in particular concerning the relationship and interaction between the autocratic state and its medical and legal professions.

One of the many strengths of the book is the author's emphasis on continuity within the changes brought about by the judicial reform. As Becker lucidly demonstrates, the inquisitorial system by which Peter the Great created and defined Russian medicine as state service in fact institutionalized considerable medical authority and autonomy within Russia's legal-administrative system up to 1864. Legislative and procedural arrangements, founded on Peter's broader objective to structure society under the guiding ethos of logic and rationality, ascribed preponderant weight and status to medical evidence over any other types of testimony (except confession). In practice, physicians were exempt from any objections by other judicial players and enjoyed judge-like authority in court. What is more, as jurists and physicians made continuous and joint efforts to define the occupational and intellectual lines between medicine and law, medical authority in fact expanded from the legal to the administrative level during the first half of the nineteenth century. Analysing pre-reform forensic medicine, Becker compellingly illustrates the unique and distinct circumstances that, in particular during Nicholaevan rule, granted the physicians an enormous (albeit not unlimited) autonomy, occupational authority and social influence within the political culture of autocratic Russia.

Against this background the judicial reform, as Becker aptly puts it, 'meant physicians' fall from infallibility' (p. 88). While inquisitorial procedure had valorized written medical evidence as perfect proof, the introduction of adversarial procedures put evidentiary weight on the physician's oral 'persuasiveness', his 'credibility' and 'trust' which had to be gained by the judge. Questioning the physicians' professional rights and authority, the new approach to judicial judgement also radically changed the relationship between physicians and lawyers: physicians now had to defend themselves against those with whom they had common occupational interests since Peter I. Having lost their legal protection physicians were forced to redefine their professional role if they wanted to maintain the influential status they had hitherto enjoyed.

With analytic rigour and a gift for lucid writing Becker traces the intellectual, cultural and political debates that evolved around defining the new procedural rules, including the forensic-medical statutes and thus the physician's official legal role-to-be. As the reader witnesses the coexistence of multiple layers of both institutional, legal, medical and intellectual traditions and innovations, Becker elegantly reveals how physicians and jurists as well as top governmental officials, academic scholars and, finally, public spectators and publicists took an active part in developing a multitude of competing views about the new place of medical knowledge. Already in view of the impending reform, physicians had shifted their self-perception from administrative bureaucrat to scientific expert as advocated by foreign models and texts. Illuminating the complex process of reception and adaptation of Western European intellectual sources and institutional models, which came to overlap with Russia's judicial institutions, Becker demonstrates how the newly imported category assumed its particular meanings and utility in the physicians' attempt to maintain medical authority. Russian physicians sought to gain professional autonomy not in opposition to the state but by working from within the state's legal-administrative structures, with which the physicians' occupational work and interests, after all, were intertwined. At the same time, prominent reform-minded legal officials inside the government regarded scientific expertise as crucial to the success of the judicial reform. Extending her analysis into the post-reform period, Becker elucidates how leading lawyers once again realigned themselves with their medical colleagues when entering the twentieth century not with the intent to regain autonomy but rather to transform the state along rational and scientific principles.

Becker's book, which is an expanded dissertation, is a formidable scholarly work, to which this short review cannot do justice. Her work is based on a wide range of research and, likewise, on a thorough knowledge and impressive command of a broad spectrum of historiographical and theoretical literature. The bibliographical references are meticulously thorough, detailed and informative. This book will appeal not only to historians of Imperial Russia but also to specialists in the history of science, law and medicine, as well as to historians of the comparative history of the professions.

Zürich CHARLOTTE HENZE

Dennison, Tracy. *The Institutional Framework of Russian Serfdom*. Cambridge Studies in Economic History. Cambridge University Press, Cambridge and New York, 2011. xx + 254 pp. Map. Glossary. Figure. Tables. Notes. Bibliography. Index. £60.00: $99.00.

TRACY DENNISON has performed a valuable service in challenging superficial notions of Russian peasant society that can be found in many works. She calls this the 'peasant myth': the idea that Russian peasants under serfdom lived in large, complex households which were part of cohesive communities that equalized their land allotments, and whose economic decisions were motivated not by markets but by an aversion to risk and a 'moral economy'. The principal villain of the piece, for Dennison, is Baron von Haxthausen, who 'discovered' the peasant commune and related aspects of peasant life on his visit to Russia in the 1840s, and propagated the 'myth'. Also criticized are those who have fallen for the 'myth', including the Slavophiles, Herzen, the officials who drew up the statutes of 1861, Tolstoi, the Populists, the SR party, Chaianov, James C. Scott, and a number of historians with whose work she engages, in a scholarly manner, throughout the book. In particular, she challenges views that the ways Russian peasants conducted themselves were a result of a 'collectivist peasant culture', which she believes to have been the prevailing interpretation. She briefly considers the role of geographic factors. Instead, however, she sets out to demonstrate that, in line with recent work by development economists and economic historians it is 'institutions [that] are the fundamental determinants of social and economic outcomes' (p. 17).

In order to challenge 'the peasant myth', she presents a rigorous and sophisticated analysis of the Sheremetev estate of Voshchazhnikovo in Iaroslavl′ province, in the central industrial region, from the late eighteenth century to 1861 on the basis of the estate records. She finds that peasants on the estate lived in smaller, simpler households and married later (and some never married) than the 'myth' would have us believe and studies of other estates have shown. Peasants on the estate, like many in the region, farmed the land, but also engaged in various non-agricultural activities, and paid *obrok* to their owner. Some owned their own manufactories and employed other serfs. There was considerable socio-economic stratification among the peasants, which was institutionalized by the Sheremetevs, who required richer peasants to pay higher dues. Thus, there was no reason to equalize land allotments. Instead, Dennison finds that land redistribution served to redistribute the burden of obligations attached to the land, and to exclude poorer households from access to land altogether. Further chapters present evidence that peasants on the estate were involved in markets for land and labour, credit transactions, and had a more sophisticated attitude to retail and consumption than Russian peasants in this period are often given credit for.

An important element of her argument is that the ways peasants in Voshchazhnikovo ran their lives were in response to the particular ways the Sheremetevs managed their estates: 'The specific local manifestations of serfdom […] were, in many respects, dependent on landlord-specific policies and regulations; not all landlords managed their estates in the same way' (p. 91). Thus, institutions, i.e. the ways in which the Sheremetevs enforced serfdom on their estates, matter. Dennison compares and contrasts her conclusions with those of Peter Czap and Steven Hoch, who studied estates in the central black-earth region, and also Rodney Bohac who studied another estate in the central industrial region. The estates studied by all three were owned by the Gagarin family, who issued different instructions to their serfs, and thereby shaped their behaviour in different ways. She also makes comparisons with the Lieven estate of Baki, also in the central industrial region, studied by Melton.

Do we need to rewrite the history of rural Russia? Among the strengths of Dennison's book is that the author is an accomplished economic historian who is familiar with the literature on other societies and has located her analysis of a Russian serf estate in a wider, comparative framework. She is right that some general works have persisted in presenting a superficial picture of Russian peasant society. Her book, moreover, is timely. It is a generation since Bohac, Czap, Hoch and Melton carried out their estate studies. On the other hand, there is a risk of throwing out the baby with the bathwater (or perhaps replacing the wooden plough with an imported foreign model). To the extent that some Russian peasants, in part on the instructions of their landlords, did live in large, complex households, hold their land in common and redistribute it more equally, and take decisions based on a collective assessment of risk, it was peasants who lived on large seigniorial estates and performed *barshchina* in the largely agricultural central black-earth region, not the region Dennison studied. As she indicates in the text, historians have long recognized diversity in Russian peasant society before 1861, and considered factors other than a presumed peasant culture in influencing their decisions. Throughout history, peasants have taken decisions that may seem irrational, such as strip farming, but which, as McClosky argued, have their own (non-cultural) rationale. In correctly emphasizing the importance of institutions and the practices of individual landlords over some notion of peasant culture, it may be, however, that Dennison has understated the significance of regional variations in the rural economy.

Much of Dennison's 'reinterpretation', however welcome, is not altogether surprising to historians who have carried out archival research on rural society in Russia in the period under consideration, and have also found a more varied, more complex and multi-faceted peasant society, many of whose members knew the land was not 'God's', were quite happy to buy and sell it, act selfishly without regard to the interests of their neighbours, and would not have recognized the 'peasant myth' Dennison sets out to demolish. Moreover, as Cathy Frierson argued in *Peasant Icons: Representations of Rural People in Late Nineteenth-Century Russia* (New York, 1993), educated Russians constructed a number of conflicting myths of the peasants, and had largely abandoned that of the communal peasant by the end of the nineteenth century. Nevertheless, all historians of Russia and peasant societies are urged to read Dennison's book. It is to be hoped that we will not have to wait another generation before someone else takes up the challenge of writing a micro-history of a Russian (or perhaps a Ukrainian) peasant community based on local records.

Department of History, University of York DAVID MOON

Klier, John Doyle. *Russians, Jews and the Pogroms of 1881–1882*. Cambridge University Press, Cambridge and New York, 2011. xxiv + 492 pp. Maps. Illustrations. Notes. Appendix. Glossary. Bibliography. Index. £70.00: $110.00.

THE anti-Jewish pogroms of 1881–82 in the Russian Empire have always attracted considerable scholarly attention. Jonathan Frankel described them as 'a decisive turning point' in modern Jewish history: 'From then on can be dated the gradual but unbroken emergence of the new movements that [...]

would transform the structure and content of Jewish politics' ('Crisis as a Factor in Modern Jewish Politics, 1840 and 1881–1882', in *Crisis, Revolution, and Russian Jews*, Cambridge, 2009, p. 16 — originally published in Jehuda Reinharz [ed.], *Living with Antisemitism: Modern Jewish Responses*, Hanover, NH, 1987, pp. 42–58).

Besides this, the pogroms of 1881–82 became a linchpin of two, perhaps the most important myths about modern Jewish history, widely spread both in scholarly works and in Jewish collective memory. The first myth claims that Russian officials were responsible for anti-Jewish violence and the second explains the enormous Jewish emigration from Russia in the late nineteenth and early twentieth centuries as a flight caused by the immediate danger of violence.

The myth of governmental conspiracy behind the pogroms was seriously questioned by Hans Rogger in 1971 ('The Jewish Policy of Late Tsarism: A Reappraisal', in *Jewish Policies and Right-Wing Politics in Imperial Russia*, London, 1986, pp. 28–33 — originally published in *Wiener Library Bulletin*, 25, 1971, pp. 42–51), and later completely refuted by Michael Aronson (*Troubled Waters: The Origins of the 1881 Anti-Jewish Pogroms in Russia*, Pittsburgh, PA, 1990). Aronson's *Troubled Waters* convincingly showed that the authorities did not instigate anti-Jewish violence and their inability to stop the pogroms quickly or to prevent them altogether was caused by shortage of manpower, incompetence and ineffectiveness. However, Aronson's works were written in the time when Western researchers could not access Soviet archives and he also did not use the Russian press (ibid., p. 8).

Profound interest in Russian archives and especially in the Russian press singled out the late Professor John Doyle Klier. His magisterial work on the 1881–82 pogroms, largely based on archival materials and press reports, was awaited with great interest by the scholarly community. Unfortunately, John Klier died on 23 September 2007, at the age of sixty-two, before the completed manuscript had become a book. It was brought to print — one must add, in superb form — by his wife Helen and colleagues François Guesnet and Lars Fischer. In this way the historiography has been significantly enriched by the appearance of an excellent work which discusses the 1881–82 pogroms and the full spectrum of immediate responses to them.

Part one of Klier's book describes the events of 1881–82 and proves again Aronson's thesis that 'Russian officials neither desired, encouraged, nor tolerated pogroms' (p. 384). Nonetheless, Klier revises Aronson's opinion that 'the violence was spread mostly by migrant unemployed laborers' and homecoming peasants (*Troubled Waters*, p. 232). and shows evidence from the statistics on arrested *pogromshchiki* that they were mostly from the Pale of Settlement and that 'the majority were probably local people' (p. 51).

Extremely fascinating is Klier's placing of the 1881–82 pogroms in comparative perspective and in a broader theoretical framework of ethnic riot.

He regards the pogrom violence as 'filled with meaning' and asks 'what were mobs trying to say when they attacked Jews?' (p. 67). His main answer is that 'the popular conviction of non-Jews that Jews [...] were somehow inferior to them offers a key to decipher the psychology underlying the pogroms. They were, in important respects, about status in village and town' (p. 76). He also stresses that, as in many other ethnic riots, 'violence is used as a weapon of social control' (p. 83) and its continuation is facilitated by 'authoritative social support' (p. 86): 'Neither the Russian governing elite nor society *wanted* pogroms, but they believed that they *understood* them and they certainly *empathized* with them' (p. 86, emphasis in the original). It is noteworthy that usage of very modern theories reaffirmed, although on a different level of understanding, the main thesis, which was put out by liberal defenders of Jews in the 1880s and afterwards, until the very end of the Russian Empire: the discrimination of Jews by Russian law caused non-Jews to view them as inferior, while the criminal inactivity of authorities allowed physical violence.

Part two is devoted to the reaction to pogroms by non-Jewish actors: officials at all levels, from local police to the tsar and his ministers; Russian society, from Judeophobe conservatives to socialists, as well as public opinion abroad. Klier pays special attention to the development of the ideas which brought about the notorious May Laws of 1882 and the failure of the minister of internal affairs Nikolai Ignatiev to promulgate more severe restrictions. Klier also questions the effectiveness of the May Laws, which limited Jewish settlement in the countryside in order to protect peasants from Jewish exploitation. Contrary to the complaints of the Jewish press (and Jewish historiography), which described the Laws as causing economic ruin, Klier cites the Judeophobe press and official reports which stated that the effect of the Laws, in short perspective, was minimal. It should be added that the effectiveness of the May Laws was minimal in the long perspective too and, according to statistical sources, the number of Jews in the countryside continued to be high (see, for example, Boris Brutskus, *Statistika evreiskogo naseleniia*, St Petersburg, 1909, p. 4).

Part three deals with Jewish responses to the pogroms: the reaction of the press, and the development of politics and philanthropic actions. Among other topics Klier presents the actions of the Baron Gintsburg Circle of Jewish notables. For one hundred years Jewish historiography repeated the statement of the proto-Zionist activists of 1882 that the plutocrats in St Petersburg lost their central role in Jewish politics as a consequence of their inability to cope with the crisis (see, for example, Jonathan Frankel, *Prophecy and Politics: Socialism, Nationalism and the Russian Jews, 1862–1917*, Cambridge, 1981, pp. 52–98). This thesis has been already refuted by Benjamin Nathans, who described the change in tactics of the St Petersburg elite in the following period (*Beyond the Pale: The Jewish Encounter with Late Imperial Russia*, Berkeley, CA, 2002, pp. 186–98). Klier, on the other hand, provides a detailed description of the strategy and methods intensively employed behind the scenes by the

Gintsburg Circle in 1881–82 in order to prevent future pogroms and to subvert anti-Jewish measures proposed by Ignatiev. Although these activities did not achieve their goal, it is impossible to argue any longer that this circle was inactive or acted reluctantly under the pressure of the adherents of emigration.

The major product of the Gintsburg Circle was a 250-page memorandum written by Emanuel Levin that fully formulated arguments which produced the myth of the authorities' conspiracy in the pogroms. The epilogue thus investigates the emergence and development of this legend both in Russia and abroad, especially in Great Britain.

John Klier has left an outstanding work which presents the issue of the 1881–82 pogroms in its entirety and in a rich variety of perspectives. There is no doubt that *Russians, Jews, and the Pogroms of 1881–1882* will become a standard work in Jewish and Russian historiography. The book's illustrations, mostly of anti-Jewish character, deserve a separate mention, as they add significantly to the strong impression which this excellent and elegantly written book makes on the reader.

Hebrew University of Jerusalem VLADIMIR LEVIN

Kocho-Williams, Alastair. *Russian and Soviet Diplomacy, 1900–39*. Palgrave Macmillan, Basingstoke and New York, 2012. 215 pp. Figures. Tables. Notes. Select bibliography. Index. £55.00.

'As already reported', the British ambassador to the Soviet Union, Sir Esmond Ovey wrote in 1930, 'the natural instinct of a Bolshevik statesman is to be exceptionally rude to any country with whom he is negotiating. To him and to his colleagues, this seems to be the highest form of diplomacy'. Explaining why (or whether) this was so is the essence of this book by Alastair Kocho-Williams, senior lecturer at the University of the West of England.

Kocho-Williams begins with the assertion that Russian diplomacy before the Revolution and Soviet diplomacy thereafter were in many ways similar, despite the disparate ideologies underpinning them. Bolshevik Russia needed to interact with the existing international order, and this international order had its own norms of diplomatic practice. The degree to which Bolshevik Russia had to abide by these normative practices and the way in which accepting them involved a return to the usual diplomatic practices of tsarist Russia make up the body of this work which, the author explicitly states, is not meant to be a study of foreign policy. His focus is on the personalities of the principal participants in the practice of Russian and Soviet diplomacy as well as on the institutions that carried out that function.

To achieve this, Kocho-Williams begins with a look at pre-Revolutionary Russian foreign policy, itself a sub-set of the 'old diplomacy' practised by the

Great Powers before 1914. He begins with capsule biographies of three of the last tsarist foreign ministers: V. N. Lamsdorf, A. P. Izvolskii and S. D. Sazonov. Here, he points out that the former was a typical *chinovnik*, while the latter wished to reform the Ministerstvo inostrannykh del (MID). Here, Kocho-Williams's research parallels that of John W. Steinberg's study of the Russian general staff, where similar divisions between traditionalists and reformers occurred. Kocho-Williams then outlines from which social groups the MID was recruited and then discusses the career paths of those who entered the service as well as the structure of the MID itself. Here, his study is useful and parallels the work done on the British Foreign Office by such people as Zara Steiner and Thomas Otte, whose *The Foreign Office Mind* (Cambridge, 2011) sets the standard for such examinations. This is useful, and Kocho-Williams's look at the Russian diplomats fits nicely into an earlier work by Otte, his comparative examination of European diplomacy 1850–1914 (in Markus Mösslang and Torsten Riotte [eds], *The Diplomats' World*, Oxford, 2008).

After an examination of Russia's wartime diplomacy, Kocho-Williams turns his attention to the Bolshevik revolution and its impact on how Russia pursued its diplomatic ends. The Bolsheviks initially felt that diplomacy was part of the bourgeois baggage that they would make irrelevant, but found that they needed to interact with other states through traditional means. While the MID was reconfigured as the Narkomindel, much remained the same. The real struggle was with the tsarist diplomats in place throughout the world, the bulk of whom refused either to serve their new masters or to be replaced.

However, replaced they were and the Narkomindel in the 1920s was shaped largely by G. V. Chicherin. Kocho-Williams's discussion of Chicherin is very good, showing how a man who had been born into the classes who dominated the MID (and, in fact, began a career there) but became a revolutionary himself, realized that the Narkomindel had to conform to the outward norms of European diplomacy if the Soviet state were to maintain stable relations with the external world. As a result, Soviet diplomats, despite superficial differences adopted the styles in dress, manner and social conventions generally of their equivalents from other states.

This changed in 1930. The new Soviet foreign minister, Maxim Litvinov, had long criticized what he viewed as Chicherin's bourgeois style. Litvinov ended the centralized approach that had characterized Chicherin's reign, but imposed a new discipline on Soviet diplomats and, in line with the broader changes in the recruitment of personnel into key positions in the revolutionary state, after 1934 recruited from those who had few ties to the pre-Revolutionary world. The focus of Soviet diplomacy became security not revolution, and Litvinov pursued this policy energetically, following a style of diplomacy not dissimilar to that of other European states. However, like the rest of Soviet society, the Narkomindel became the victim of Stalin's paranoia about the external world, and Soviet diplomats tended to isolate themselves from foreigners, lest their behaviour lead to being purged as anti-Soviet elements (there is a helpful section on the impact of the Purges on Soviet diplomats). Litvinov's influence shrank and he was finally replaced by someone far less sophisticated but judged to be far more politically reliable, Viacheslav Molotov.

This is a useful book, although not without flaws. It is rather short (some 156 pages of text) and this means that many issues are treated rather superficially. The documentary basis is sound — valuable Soviet primary material and a sprinkling of documents of individual Russian diplomats found abroad — along with a multi-lingual bibliography. The meat of the book deals with the sections on Soviet diplomacy in the 1920s and 1930s, where the author adds to our knowledge with his discussion of the structures of the Narkomindel and its personnel. However, his examination of the pre-1914 MID is not as enlightening and would have benefited from looking at Dominic Lieven's *Russia's Rulers under the Old Regime* (New Haven, CT, 1989). Kocho-Williams builds the book around the issue of how revolutionary states behave with regard to observing international norms and the degree to which they find it necessary to conform. His conclusion is not startling: Soviet Russia found the international practice of diplomacy to be unbending and was forced to behave in a way acceptable to the existing order. However, Soviet politics affected the degree to which this was possible. This is not new. What is valuable is his consideration of the personnel of the Narkomindel, although this does not add considerably to the work of Sabine Dullin, in particular her *Des Hommes D'Influence: Les Ambassadeurs de Staline en Europe, 1930–1939* (Paris, 2001). However, perhaps what he has done is enough to gain at least a partial explanation for why 'Bolshevik statesmen' behaved in the way that Ovey observed.

Department of History KEITH NEILSON
Royal Military College of Canada

Pinnow, Kenneth M. *Lost to the Collective: Suicide and the Promise of Soviet Socialism, 1921–1929*. Cornell University Press, Ithaca, NY and London, 2010. xi + 276 pp. Notes. Bibliography. Index. $49.95: £31.50.

KENNETH PINNOW's *Lost to the Collective* explores the meaning of suicide in the early Soviet period. Relying extensively on archival sources and publications by social science professionals (psychiatrists, physicians, statisticians and forensic experts, among others), Pinnow asserts that 'responses to suicide reflected the way that the individual and society [...] were imagined and constructed through a mixture of rhetorical strategies and concrete politico-scientific practices' (p. 3). He situates these strategies and practices within the context of the emergence of Soviet social science, arguing that suicide studies provided a way for professionals and Red Army officials to measure the extent of the revolutionary transformation. In so doing, Pinnow explores Soviet understandings of the individual personality and its position within the collective, the development of scientific and statistical studies of society, the role of the state, and Soviet notions of modernity, progress and health. His arguments complement and reinforce other recent studies of social science professionals in early Soviet society, including Dan Healey, *Bolshevik Sexual Forensics: Diagnosing Disorder in the Clinic and Courtroom, 1917–1939* (DeKalb, IL, 2009), Daniel Beer, *Renovating Russia: The Human Sciences and the Fate of Liberal Modernity, 1880–1930* (Ithaca, NY, 2008) and Sharon Kowalsky, *Deviant Women: Female Crime and Criminology in Revolutionary Russia, 1880–1930* (DeKalb, IL, 2009).

Suicide remained problematic for the new Soviet regime as it represented a repudiation of an individual's collective responsibility and ultimately of revolutionary values that stressed individuals would reach their full potential once the boundaries between private and public had been destroyed. Suicide thus raised the question of how best to integrate individuals into society. Indeed, the social isolation of the individual that led to suicide was deemed 'unhealthy, unnatural, and dangerous' (p. 16). Soviet authorities placed as much responsibility for suicides on the collective milieu as on the individual who committed the act, emphasizing the importance of mutual surveillance to identify problems before it was too late. Moreover, suicide provided an avenue for the state (collective) to intervene in private life, as a way to identify potentially bad influences and unreliable or counter-revolutionary elements. Pinnow argues that suicide studies helped to establish a 'medicopolitics that promoted the comprehensive care of the individual as an integral component of the collective's existence and well-being' (p. 228). Thus, suicide narratives contributed to constructing the meaning of individual and collective responsibility.

Throughout the book, Pinnow traces the emergence of Soviet social science and the professionalization of its practitioners as they developed strategies for studying suicide. Before the Bolshevik Revolution, physicians and psychiatrists used suicide studies as a means to diagnose social ills. After the Revolution, these same professionals expanded and organized their efforts, establishing a standardized questionnaire for collecting information about suicides (including age, marital status, party membership, occupation, nationality and education, among others) from across the empire. They attributed suicide both to socioeconomic and physiological factors, highlighting physical deformities (e.g., degeneration) as well as social influences (nervousness, weakness, etc.) as contributing factors for suicide. Their efforts were one element of a broader movement to gather moral statistics — rates of crime, suicide, deviance, abortion, etc. — in order to define knowledge and record the transformation of Russian society. Suicide studies were thus part of a larger pan-European project to quantify social life. In the Soviet context, this quantification was imbued with political importance, as suicide statistics became 'part of an effort to measure the assimilation of new values, to identify and eradicate the remaining pockets of illness, and to generally know how far away the Soviets remained from achieving the socialist utopia' (p. 229). Ultimately, Pinnow stresses the centrality of information collection to the construction of the modern Soviet state.

Lost to the Collective is a well-written, richly documented, and compelling study of early Soviet society. It is refreshing to have the notes placed at the foot of each page rather than at the end, a practice that has become all too rare in today's publishing world. As the notes make clear, Pinnow situates his arguments within a wide variety of recent historiographical trends, from discussions of health, crime and degeneration to studies of professionalization to interpretations of individual narratives. He presents his points effectively and traces the relevance of his subject through the early Stalin period, but he lacks a clear conclusion that might draw out more explicitly some of the implications of suicide for understanding the modern state, and he also fails to engage with some recent relevant arguments, including my own, that would reinforce his conclusions. These minor critiques aside, Pinnow has made a significant contribution to our understanding of the complexity of early Soviet society. His book will appeal to scholars and graduate students of Russia and the Soviet Union, as well as those interested in notions of modernity and the modern state, the role of statistics and social science in the study of society, the development of Soviet society and professionalization, narrative in the Soviet context and the Soviet individual. It deserves to find a wide audience.

History Department SHARON A. KOWALSKY
Texas A&M University-Commerce

Haynes, Rebecca and Rady, Martyn (eds). *In the Shadow of Hitler: Personalities of the Right in Central and Eastern Europe*. I. B. Tauris, London and New York, 2011. xii + 332 pp. Notes. Index. £59.50.

As the invocation of Hitler in the title suggests, the focus of this volume is not on the traditional Right, but primarily on fascists. Nevertheless, the volume contains a broad spectrum of personalities: those of the nationalist Right, such as the champion of modern Polish statehood Roman Dmowski (chapter authored by Andreas Kossert) and Ukrainian radical nationalist icon Stepan Bandera (David Marples); the authoritarian Right, such as wartime Romanian dictator Ion Antonescu (Dennis Deletant) and Yugoslav Prime Minister Milan Stojadinović (Dejan Djokić); genuine fascists such as Hungarian Arrow Cross leader Ferenc Szálasi (Martyn Rady) and Romanian Iron Guard leader Corneliu

Codreanu (Rebecca Haynes); Nazis such as Sudeten German leader Konrad Henlein (Mark Cornwall); as well as those who achieved notoriety through collaboration with the Third Reich during the Second World War such as Croatian Ustasha death-squad leader Jure Francetić (Rory Yeomans), the head of the independent Slovak state Msgr Jozef Tiso (Thomas Lorman) and Serbian politician Dimitrije Ljotić (Jovan Byford). Side-by-side with these infamous figures, the volume also features little-known personalities such as Hungarian 'anti-feminist feminist' Cécile Tormay (Gwenyth Jones) and Austrian Nazi Edmund Glaise von Horstenau (Georg Christoph Berger Waldenegg). Of the seventeen selected cases, most are individuals who came to prominence in the 1930s and during the Second World War, but the volume also includes a couple of personalities whose political career began in the late nineteenth century and are presented as sources of inspiration for Nazism: Austrian German radical nationalist Georg von Schönener (Steven Beller), admiringly cited in Hitler's *Mein Kampf*, and Theodor Fritsch (Egbert Klautke), the 'godfather' of German antisemitism. Plus one charismatic personality who seems geographically somewhat out of place in this volume: Italian poet and political revolutionary Gabriele D'Annunzio (John Woodhouse).

The most represented nation in this collection is Hungary, with three personalities featured, the third being Hungarian Prime Minister Gyula Gömbös (Miklós Zeidler). Finland is justifiably included in the volume with an insightful and succinct contribution by David Kirby, which unlike the other chapters does not focus on a particular individual but gives a well-rounded overview of the radical right in interwar Finland. Conspicuously absent, however, are the Baltic states. Artur Sirk, the leader of the Estonian War of Independence Veterans' League, one of the most successful European radical right movements that never came to power, and Latvian Thunder Cross leader Gustavs Celmiņš, an antisemite who ended up in a Nazi concentration camp, are two personalities from the region who would certainly deserve an introduction in English. One could quibble about the selection of personalities, but there is no question that this volume offers a rich palette of representative figures whose individual biographies collectively provide insight into the political development of the countries of modern Europe.

The doyen of fascist studies, Roger Griffin, contributes an introductory essay highlighting the cultural production of personalities during the first half of the twentieth century as an aspect of modernism. In her introduction, Haynes notes the shared core traits of those portrayed: a strong emphasis on the nation, anti-Communism, antisemitism, and rejection of democracy. A common thread is that the 'Right' presented in this volume was not conservative, but revolutionary in its nature. Many of the figures, though devout Catholic or Orthodox Christians, created their own political religions and made liberal use of Christian imagery in their rhetoric, especially of martyrdom and salvation. Though Hitler looms large in the title, most of the personalities in the book evolved their political views and careers independently, but had to accommodate themselves to great power realities during World War Two, which invariably meant alignment in various degrees with the Third Reich.

In sum, this collection of political biographies enriches and expands our knowledge and is rewarding reading for students of the region, fascism and nationalism. Furthermore, it helps bring Eastern Europe back from the periphery into the mainstream of modern European history.

University of Tartu A. Kasekamp

Apunen, Osmo and Wolff, Corinna. *Pettureita ja Patriootteja. Taistelu Suomen ulko- ja puolustuspolitiikan suunnasta 1938–1948*. Historiallisia Tutkimuksia, 244. Suomalaisen Kirjallisuuden Seura, Helsinki, 2009. 482 pp. Maps. Notes. Bibliography. Index. €38.00 (paperback).

The title of this work means 'traitors and patriots'. Actually, it is substantially rather a compendium about different kinds of patriots than traitors. The setting is the fate of Finland in the Second World War and after.

Osmo Apunen and Corinne Wolff's book deals with a politics which, when it came to it, preferred Germany to Russia, joining Germany in a so-styled Continuation War (1941–44) ostensibly to get back the lands lost to the Russians in the Winter War (1939–40). In the heady days of the second conflict, however, a slice of extra Russian territory, say East Karelia, would not have come amiss to the Finnish leaders, a matter that disturbed many of the rank-and-file of the Finnish army. But in the end a third conflict had to occur in a Lapland war (1944–45), when the Finnish army (often of youngsters) had to turn on the Germans and drive them out.

The authors, towards the end of their text, have the honesty to quote J. K. Paasikivi and his doubts about the wars (though, in fact, when the Continuation War started Paasikivi supported it). However, the authors do not mention that in 1939, prior to the start of hostilities, it crossed the mind of the Finnish foreign minister, Eljas Erkko, to exchange key Finnish islands in the Gulf of Finland for two enormous parishes in East Karelia — Repola and Porajärvi. He even discussed this with the German minister to Finland, Wipert von Blücher, shortly after the Nazi-Soviet Pact had been signed on 23 August 1939. In the first negotiations, the Russians were prepared to offer the parishes, whilst there was even more concessionary thinking on the Finnish side: Marshal Mannerheim felt that with respect to the Finnish Karelian Isthmus the Russians had a case in asking for an adjustment of the frontier. But somehow these ideas were lost. Quickness was of the essence and the Finns were not quick. They dawdled and the Soviet military pushed itself forward.

But if the Finns had made *and taken* these concessions in time, would it have made any difference? This is 'the what if' of history and Apunen and Wolff do not explore this type of historical thinking. Instead the reader is presented with 'the what was' of history. The text sometimes speaks of a clever sleight-of-hand, a politics that produced the survival of a state: the Finns fought the Russians until the Germans were ready to help, then in 1944 the last springs of German aid enabled the Finns to force an armistice on the Russians, who could then get on with the drive to Berlin, which was really what they wanted to do. Less than four years later, all was ready for the FCMA treaty between Russia and Finland.

In this research compendium there is, however, another politics bursting to break through the politics of war. It is the old politics of Western constitutionalism based on negotiation, compromise and hope. Not that the principal Western Powers, the one (Britain) having declared war on Finland, the other (the United States) having reduced its diplomatic representation to a pittance, were able, according to the authors, to bring the country out of the war. For, avowedly, both Western Powers had committed themselves at Casablanca to the doctrine of unconditional surrender.

Nevertheless, by March 1943 a Finnish peace activist, Laurin Zilliacus, could claim that half of the Finnish Parliament were supporters of the opposition to the war. What served this *Loyal Opposition* was the country across the water, Sweden. To Sweden travelled the more prominent members of the Opposition, and also those like Väinö Tanner and Eero Wuori, the trade union leader, who kept their links with the war government. In Sweden, these visitors often saw the Soviet eminence, Madame Alexandra Kollontai, the old revolutionary, a friend of Finland, who had maintained her earlier ideals. In fact, she gave the visiting Finns too great a set of expectations, beyond the scope of her narrow-minded colleagues in Moscow, proposing as late as February 1944 the possible exchange of Petsamo for Viipuri in a forthcoming armistice agreement. The Swedes, in the person of Erik Boheman, the leading official of the Swedish Foreign Office, also played this game of Russian generosity, suggesting that Finland might well be able to keep Viipuri and the Saimaan Canal. This was sweet-talking, even if it buoyed up Finnish hopes, but it was not *all* sweet-talking. By November 1943, Kollontai tried to dash the Finnish aspirations to be allowed to retain East Karelia — something a war ought to have won for Finland?

Occasionally, the tale is told in a minor key, when Arthur Deakin of the TUC arrives in Stockholm on a secret mission in the middle of the war, and then in his cups blabs it all round. Or when that dapper Anglophile, Risto Ryti, prime minister at the time, expresses the hope to the German minister that Germany would conquer England as quickly as possible. But these touching incidents were as nothing compared to the truth coming out about Katyn which, according to Apunen, helped to prevent the complete withdrawal of US diplomatic relations from Finland.

University of Turku GEORGE MAUDE

Rochlitz, Imre. *Accident of Fate: A Personal Account, 1938–1945*. With Joseph Rochlitz. Life Writing. Wilfred Laurier University Press, Waterloo, ON, 2011. xiii + 223 pp. Maps. Illustrations. Glossary. Appendix. Index. $29.95 (paperback).

ALMOST two decades ago Ernst Pawel published a memoir of his teenage years spent as a Jewish refugee in Yugoslavia from 1934 to 1938, entitled *Life in Dark Ages*. Just as the Pawel family was emigrating to the United States, another Jewish boy, Imre Rochlitz, was seeking refuge in Yugoslavia. But this is where the similarities between these two accounts of Jewish refugee teenagers fade away. With *Accident of Fate* we have a first-hand record of the much darker period between 1938 and 1945 which, as Rochlitz insists, he survived by pure chance. And very convincingly, after one discovers that over these few years Rochlitz was imprisoned several times, forced to dig mass graves at the Jasenovac death camp and fought alongside fugitive Partisans. It is not, however, Rochlitz's tribulations that distinguish this book, but his sombre observations and unbiased perspective. As a foreign Jew in Yugoslavia, Rochlitz was an outsider, but being young, having learnt the language and being in possession of an amiable character, Imre easily became the Yugoslav Mirko. This peculiar double-sidedness gives Rochlitz's memoir invaluable significance for the historiography of Yugoslavia's wartime fratricide.

Born in Budapest in 1925, Rochlitz grew up in a relatively poor but well integrated Viennese family. His carefree childhood and dreams of becoming an actor were abruptly interrupted by the Anschluss. With only one month left on his Hungarian passport, Imre managed to escape to Zagreb, but the relative calm there was short-lived. After the destruction of Yugoslavia and the establishment of the Ustashe state of Croatia in April 1941, his family was on the run again. Even though he was the youngest, Imre was the first to end up in the Ustashe death camp of Jasenovac at the age of seventeen. Starved and frozen, he was tortured, utterly dehumanized and, like any other camp inmate, awaited death as a relief from suffering. But in yet another 'accident of fate', Imre was released on the intervention of none other than the Nazi Plenipotentiary General for Croatia, Edmund von Glaise-Horstenau, following the intercession of one of Imre's uncles who was an Austrian First World War veteran. Aided by false documents, Rochlitz escaped to Italian-occupied Dalmatia. Interned first in Kraljevica and then on Rab island he encountered many surviving

Yugoslav Jews. However, Italian capitulation in 1943 brought about the demise of this prison paradise, and with the remains of his family Imre fled to the Partisan-liberated territories. Young and able-bodied, he enlisted and was soon promoted to the rank of lieutenant even though he spent most of his time in a makeshift Partisan veterinarian hospital. Besides their common enemy, Rochlitz shared little with the Partisans and felt uncomfortable in their 'terrain of suspicion, paranoia, and arbitrary justice' (p. 141). In a final accident of fate, Rochlitz fled to Bari, but not before participating in fighting in Kordun, part of the mountainous Krajina region of Croatia, and in the rescue of a number of allied pilots (their names are listed in the appendix).

For Pawel and many sceptical readers, autobiography is a 'blend of fact and fiction that reveals by concealment and conceals by revelation'. The value of Imre Rochlitz's memoir is that it does not attempt to conceal the ordinary. Thus we find rare and rather unpleasant descriptions of how biological needs were met in death transports and camps, or of matters of hygiene during prolonged guerilla resistance. There are also vivid descriptions and scrutiny of the Partisans' sex lives, or lack thereof, which remains a taboo for Yugoslav veterans and a controversial subject in historiography to this day. Equally valuable are Rochlitz's stories of how food was procured and provisioned, as well as everyday pastimes and entertainment in zones of war. Finally, he describes how the Partisans perceived the Jews, how they treated dissent and Otherness, and how they navigated between allies and enemies to emerge as sole victors, although at a high price.

Throughout, Rochlitz proves himself to be a shrewd, incisive and very critical observer. He spares no harsh words for his own Jewish upbringing in Vienna, in this most famous of all Jewish communities, which was riddled with tensions, disunity and vanity. Once in Croatia Rochlitz is disdainful of the sickening, murderous Ustashas and the brutality of the Partisans. Drunken British envoys also receive their share of criticism. Only the Americans get away easily, if one discounts the story of his friend in Bari, Junius Scales, who was subsequently sentenced to six years' imprisonment as the first and only American ever convicted simply for being a Communist Party member. Most importantly, Rochlitz takes every opportunity to express his gratitude to the fascist Italian military's refusal to comply with Germany's plans for the Final Solution and its eventual rescue of many Yugoslav (as well as Greek and some French) Jews — a subject featured in his son Joseph's 1987 documentary, 'The Righteous Enemy'.

Imre's son also helped with this book which so impresses with its thoroughness of historical detail, its meticulous research and contextualization, illustrated with authentic photographs, and reprints of original documents and maps. This is a book both for scholars and the general reader, but especially for young readers who find the horrors of the Holocaust so hard to imagine. While gruff at times, Rochlitz's recollections are never ill-hearted. Behind his criticisms we find a deep, unchallenged humanity and an inspiring passion for life.

UCL SSEES Bojan Aleksov

Swain, Geoffrey. *Tito: A Biography.* Communist Lives. I. B. Tauris, London and New York, 2011. xi + 219 pp. Notes. Index. £56.50.

Josip Broz Tito was once considered one of the greatest statesmen of the twentieth century, a war and post-war hero who defied both Hitler and Stalin, and who reunited Yugoslavia and helped gather 'third world' countries around the Non-aligned movement. Until a recent revival of interest, nearly forgotten, Tito was a Communist revolutionary, an enigmatic guerrilla leader and a charismatic statesman whose life- and leadership style, in his later years, resembled that of a monarch. It is perhaps no wonder he generated interest and fascination among scholars, politicians and Hollywood celebrities in almost equal measure. Richard Burton, who played the Partisan leader in a Yugoslav state-sponsored Second World War epic, Elizabeth Taylor, Sophia Loren, Orson Welles and Yul Brynner were among international celebrities Tito entertained (he had a fascination with film, as recently shown by Mila Turajlić in her excellent documentary, *Cinema Komunisto*, Serbia, 2010). Tito did not write memoirs, but granted extended interviews to a select group of Yugoslav and Western authors, including Phyllis Auty, who once taught South Slav history at SSEES. The Yugoslav road to socialism offered a 'third way' that appealed to Western intellectuals and politicians; those on the left could point out that not all Communist leaders were like Stalin, while those on the right that Stalin did not control all Communists. This was possibly the reason why books about Tito tended to be somewhat lacking in critical approach, sometimes even when written by academics.

The best 'in this rather hagiographical genre' (p. 1) was a study by Auty (*Tito: A Biography*, London, 1970), argues Geoffrey Swain, the author of this new and, according to the jacket description, 'first post-communist biography of Tito' (a somewhat exaggerated claim given that in English alone the following works have been published since the fall of Communist regimes in Eastern Europe: Stevan K. Pavlowitch, *Tito, Yugoslavia's Great Dictator: A Reassessment*, London, 1992, Richard West, *Tito and the Rise and Fall of Yugoslavia*, London, 1994 and Neil Barnett, *Tito*, London, 2006). Published as part of the I. B. Tauris series 'Communist Lives' edited by Matthew Worley, this is a seriously researched and well-written book that makes an important contribution to the historiography of former Yugoslavia, generally weak in the biography genre. Geoffrey Swain, one of the leading historians of Eastern Europe, joins a recent trend among scholars in former Yugoslavia who are rediscovering Tito. Although Swain apparently did not look at Tito's recently released papers, he consulted the Central Committee archives and read published primary sources as well as numerous secondary sources in English, Serbo-Croat and Russian. The result is a concise but readable political biography that is likely to become an important reference point for students of Yugoslav history and East European Communism more generally.

Born Josip Broz in 1892 in Kumrovec, a small Austro-Hungarian village (in present-day Croatia, on the border with Slovenia), in a large and relatively poor family of a mixed Croat-Slovene background, Tito's early years did not necessarily suggest a revolutionary career. Even when Broz was arrested and tried in a high-profile 'bomb affair' of 1928, which earned him a five-year prison sentence, he was still not one of the leaders of a small party, hit by regime oppression and internal factionalism. It took another decade, and Stalin's purges of the almost entire Yugoslav Party leadership, for Tito to become the leader, installed by Stalin, initially in a caretaker capacity. Swain tells the story of Tito's emergence as the leader of the Yugoslav Party extremely well, and although he is obviously sympathetic to Tito and the Partisans, he provides an effective brief account of occupied Yugoslavia. The bulk of the book (more than two thirds of the main text) is concerned with Tito as the leader of post-war Yugoslavia, and it is here that Swain's expertise in the Cold War period becomes obvious. He tells the story of the central role Tito played in the establishment of a Communist regime in the aftermath of the war, the split with Stalin in 1948, and subsequent search for a Yugoslav type of socialism built around the concept of the self-management of the proletariat, a non-aligned foreign policy and, of course, Tito's personality, with authority and clarity. Swain proposes an original and thought-provoking interpretation of events in Yugoslavia in 1968 as a lost, and perhaps final, opportunity for Tito to offer a truly reformed concept of socialism and, crucially, of the Yugoslav state.

Swain positions himself between largely hagiographical works such as those by Auty, and more critical works, such as Nora Beloff's *Tito's Flawed Legacy* (London, 1985), but admits his is a 'sympathetic biography' (p. 2). He argues that Tito's experiment was a worthwhile exercise, despite its ultimate failure a decade after his death in 1980. Essentially, the book largely confirms the previously dominant interpretations of Tito as 'the last Habsburg' (as A. J. P. Taylor famously described him), and a capable leader whose policies represented a short-term success, but, ultimately, a long-term failure (Pavlowitch). Swain's book is refreshingly free of the politicized agendas of some previous works on Tito (and on former Yugoslavia more broadly). It will be read alongside Pavlowitch's shorter and less sympathetic biography and Milovan Djilas's insightful *Tito: The Story from Inside* (London, 1981). Together with these works, Swain's book should provide an excellent platform from which to further pursue related questions such as Tito's personality, both private and political; the evolution and nature of his leadership style; conflict with dissidents such as Djilas and potential opponents within the Party such as Ranković; re-examination of the Non-aligned movement and Yugoslavia's place in it; and the long-term causes of Yugoslavia's disintegration. Several factual errors and typos notwithstanding (e.g. Prince Paul was not King Alexander's son, but his first cousin (p. 24); the correct spellings are Sutjeska and Zelengora (p. 47), while Josip Kopinič's name is sometimes Serbocroatianized to 'Kopinić'), this is a welcome addition to the historiography of modern Eastern Europe and is highly recommended to anyone interested in Tito, Yugoslavia and East European Communism.

Department of History DEJAN DJOKIĆ
Goldsmiths College, University of London

Ewing, E. Thomas. *Separate Schools: Gender, Policy and Practice in Postwar Soviet Education.* Northern Illinois University Press, DeKalb, IL, 2010. xii + 300 pp. Illustrations. Tables. Notes. Bibliography. Index. $42.00.

AMONG the less-well-known details of Soviet history is an eleven-year educational experiment in which most schools in urban centres throughout the Soviet Union were separated by gender. Following a relatively short trial of separate secondary schools in Moscow in spring 1943, in July 1943 the Soviet leadership ordered that separate schools be created across the country for the start of the new school year on 1 September 1943.

In this thoroughly researched and carefully argued study, E. Thomas Ewing assesses the implementation of separate schooling, the content and context of separate boys' and girls' schools, policy debates and the ultimate return to coeducational schooling in September 1954. He assesses the role of schools, teachers and educators in Soviet society, making this a rich resource for any study of the Soviet Union in Stalin's later years.

Ewing lays out his argument carefully and provides extensive analysis of published and unpublished sources in exploring the development and experience of separate schools. A variety of discussions and policy proposals relating to single-sex schools took place in the late 1930s and early 1940s, primarily in Moscow. Ewing believes that pre-war experiments in Moscow schools and policy discussions provide evidence that the policy change was not solely due to wartime contingencies. However, he concedes that 'The exact process by which Soviet leaders decided to separate schools remains obscured by the lack of reliable records as well as the complexities of the Stalinist decision-making process, especially in wartime conditions' (p. 33).

The change in national educational policy was announced on a limited basis in July 1943, and most school officials and teachers had just two-to-three weeks to prepare. Ewing estimates that 'between three and four million Soviet children, approximately 13 percent of total enrollment, attended separate schools each year from 1943 to 1954' (pp. 56–57). Rural schools and elementary schools were generally not separated; rather, the policy focused on secondary schools in urban centres. In 1943, the policy specified seventy-one cities in the Russian Republic, and ninety-six cities were later added to that number. The highest proportions of separated schools were found in Moscow (97 per cent) and Leningrad (93 per cent) in 1952, well after the Second World War had ended. Coeducational schools remained part of the landscape, and Ewing asserts that incomplete data hamper the researcher in identifying the full scope of this educational experiment.

The core of Ewing's analysis comes in chapters that focus on teaching and learning in separate schools, the experience in girls' and boys' schools, and debates over repealing the policy and returning to fully coeducational schools. Boys' schools are described as tough places where discipline was often weak, while girls' schools were seen as 'clean, warm and calm'. While some teachers did well in boys' schools, Ewing observes that many experienced teachers transferred to girls' schools, leaving less experienced teachers to teach in boys' schools. Although the educational experience in girls' schools was positive, ultimately the concerns over poor discipline in boys' schools, overcrowding, and the perceived need for boys and girls to interact more frequently fuelled the debates prior to the change in policy in 1954, one year after Stalin's death.

Ewing's analysis of the development of separate schools, the debates over policy, the role of gender in Soviet society, and the ultimate end of the policy is judicious and balanced. His extensive source base includes published sources, unpublished letters, school inspector reports, correspondence, and other documents from numerous archives across the Soviet Union.

Many readers will find something of value in this volume. Students of Soviet history will benefit from this study of gender politics and schooling under Stalin. Letters to the editor written by students and teachers and debates among teachers and school officials provide useful windows into the dynamics of life and public debate during late Stalinism. Those interested in single-sex schooling will find a fascinating case study that pays careful attention to gender roles and expectations in modern society.

For the most part, Stalin and Communism take a back seat in this assessment, as Ewing places Soviet educational policy and practice in the foreground. One main weakness of this approach is the limited attention to the broader political processes of late-Stalinism. A second weakness is a tendency to minimize the changes that took place during the eleven-year experiment. At times the period is treated as unchanging, without much differentiation between the war years and post-war years. Despite these minor flaws, *Separate Schools* makes numerous insightful additions to the history of education in the Soviet Union.

Center for International Studies and Department of History, Wake Forest University, NC STEVEN T. DUKE

Roxburgh, Angus. *The Strongman: Vladimir Putin and the Struggle for Russia.* I. B. Tauris, London and New York, 2012. xiv + 338 pp. Illustrations. Notes. Index. £20.00.

ANGUS ROXBURGH, the author of this book, was the distinguished Moscow correspondent for the *Sunday Times* in the mid-1980s and for the BBC in the El′tsin years. Between 2006 and 2009, he was also adviser on press relations to the Putin administration and he devotes a chapter to his time in Moscow attempting to improve Putin's public image. He is keen to emphasize, however, that the Kremlin rarely took his advice and sounds nothing less than appalled by some of Putin's more recent publicity stunts, such as swimming butterfly in an icy Siberian river and riding on a Harley Davidson at a bikers' rally.

The book is a tie-in with the recent BBC Two series, 'Putin, Russia and the West', for which Angus Roxburgh was a senior consultant, and viewers of the series will recognize many of the anecdotes and quotations in the book. There is, for example, the tale of the US Secretary of State, Condoleezza Rice, and the Soviet Defence Minister, Sergei Ivanov, slipping out of a performance of the *Nutcracker* to view the more avant garde Eifman ballet company in rehearsal, but still having time to return to their seats in the Mariinsky Theatre before the lights went up. Condoleezza Rice later said, 'personal relationships do matter [...] I came to trust that Sergei Ivanov was someone who was going to deliver on what he said he would do, and I think he believed the same about me' (p. 45). My own favourite anecdote, however, is when Putin allows his pet dog to sniff around Angela Merkel's legs despite knowing the German Chancellor's fear of dogs. At moments like this, it is hard not to be impressed by Putin's devotion to the Machiavellian art of politics.

It is perhaps the nature of the two media that overall the book provides a fuller and more nuanced account of the Putin era than the TV series. In chapter one, for example, Roxburgh has the space to provide the historical context which can help explain Putin's continued popularity in Russia. For whilst El′tsin tended to be viewed in the West as a staunch if unpredictable defender of freedom, democracy and the market, most Russians remember his time as President as one of impoverishment, rising crime and national humiliation. As Roxburgh makes plain, Putin understood this popular sentiment well and took it upon himself as the new President to make the people proud to be Russian again.

Roxburgh is equally good in explaining Putin's growing disenchantment with the US after early attempts to seek some kind of partnership with Washington after 9/11. There were many reasons for this disenchantment, but NATO expansion and America's promotion of the coloured revolutions in the Soviet successor states seem decisive. In Putin's eyes, Washington was seeking by every means possible to expand into areas long perceived to be of vital economic and strategic importance to Russia. There might have been some justification for Putin viewing Washington's promotion of democracy as a potential threat to his administration, but the claim that the West was also involved in terrorist atrocities, such as the Beslan school siege in September 2004, always sounded outlandish. Whether Putin really believed them or not, he certainly used such fears to legitimize his policy of further reducing Western influence in Russian affairs.

There are fascinating insights to be had throughout the book, but I found the concluding chapter on the relationship between Medvedev and Putin particularly interesting. Roxburgh argues that there were real political differences between the President and Prime Minister. Lacking a power base of his own, however, Medvedev was never in a position to challenge Putin's pre-eminence, and he was forced, humiliatingly, to relinquish the presidency to allow the strongman's return. It is, one feels, more in sorrow than anger that Roxburgh ultimately accepts the consensus view that Putin has taken Russia back towards authoritarianism. Putin, however, faces a less quiescent population as he prepares for his third term as President, and it will be interesting to see how far he is forced to change both his politics and his leadership style as a result.

School of Political, Social and International Studies MIKE BOWKER
University of East Anglia

Ališauskienė, Milda and Schröder, Ingo W. (eds). *Religious Diversity in Post-Soviet Society: Ethnographies of Catholic Hegemony and the New Pluralism in Lithuania.* Ashgate, Farnham and Burlington, VT, 2012. xiv + 212 pp. Illustrations. Tables. Notes. Bibliographies. Index. £50.00.

THIS collective volume presents the research of seven ethnographers and one historian, focusing on the religious landscape in Lithuania. It took shape following a workshop at the Vytautas Magnus University in Kaunas in 2008, funded by the Volkswagen Foundation, at which the overarching question was whether Antonio Gramsci's concept of hegemony could fruitfully be applied to the Lithuanian religious scene. Several of the chapters return to this question, almost uniformly giving a positive answer, maintaining that the historical role and dominance of the Roman Catholic Church forces any religious discourse in Lithuanian society to use Catholic language or at least refer extensively to the Catholic Church. Some of the authors even show how their New Age, Buddhist or Pagan interlocutors do not see the Catholic Church as a competing faith, but as the framework within which they may live according to their specific faith.

The nine chapters primarily address four different research questions. These are, first, the theoretical assessment of Lithuania's religious landscape and, second, the historical role of majority and minority religions in Lithuania. The third focus is on the interaction between official Catholicism and the beliefs and traditions of the common Lithuanian, and the fourth on the self-perception and institutional self-assessment of non-Christian religious currents in present-day Lithuania. None of the chapters exclusively treat only one of these foci, although the first and second chapters closely correspond with the first and second research problems.

Ingo W. Schröder, in the conceptual first chapter, sets out a theoretical framework within which the reader should or could place the following case studies. Referring to Gramsci and Pierre Bourdieu, Schröder identifies three processes at work in contemporary Catholic majority societies: 'First, there is the erosion of the unified majority religion by the increasingly individualistic understanding of what this religious identity means. [...] Second, there is the closely related trend toward secularism — not toward the disappearance of religion but toward the loss of church authority in people's everyday lives. [...] Third, a proliferation of "other" religions takes place, even if it hardly shows in the statistical figures' (pp. 31–32). Schröder contradicts the paradigmatic understanding of religion in Eastern Europe as a special case by claiming that this is a universal trend in Catholic majority societies. The second chapter, by the renowned Lithuanian church historian Arūnas Streikus, provides a historical overview of Lithuanian religious history since the nineteenth century. It is refreshingly little concerned with issues of internal church life, but rather concentrates on the relationship between the dominant Catholic Church and the various religious minorities.

The next three chapters focus on the third research question identified above. Lina Pranaitytė-Wergin's chapter provides a picture of a Catholic village, although her findings seem somewhat trivial. Schröder focuses on the urban environment in the fourth chapter, where he convincingly argues that the Catholic Church has retained its role as the monopoly provider of religious services, whereas it has lost its appeal to the general public. An interesting chapter by Gediminas Lankauskas on the 'syncretic rapprochement' between Catholic and charismatic Evangelical Christians shows how the oppositional attitude that has prevailed since 1990 has in recent years been replaced by mutual recognition and occasional co-operation. According to Lankauskas, this has occurred as a means of countering a trend towards what he calls 'post-Christian spirituality'.

The last four chapters, providing case studies of non-Christian religious actors, are very diverse and sometimes seem unwilling to focus on the theme of the rest of the book. Michael F. Strmiska recounts the links between Lithuanian Paganism and India, whereby the author cannot conceal his own sympathy for the Pagan movement. His conclusion that the links between Lithuania and India 'may prove a spiritual crossroads of great importance to the further development of modern-day Paganism' (p. 147) betrays a lack of distance from his object of study. Egdūnas Račius's study of Muslims in Catholic Lithuania oscillates between the wish adequately to analyse the historical presence of Muslim Tatars in Lithuania, and an attempt to characterize post-Soviet Lithuanian converts to Islam. The two contributions on the New Age and Neo-Buddhism are more concise. Donatas Glodenis analyses the identity and aspirations of the White Lotus Movement in Lithuania, with much theoretical insight and an elaborate analysis. However, the obscure nature of the movement and the fact that its religious aspects petered out after 2002 makes the analysis seem rather marginal. The strongest chapter in this section of the book is without doubt Milda Ališauskienė's analysis of the New Age milieu in post-Soviet Lithuania. Ališauskienė convincingly shows how the actors in this milieu, although operating outside official Roman Catholic doctrine, do not see any problems of incompatibility. Moreover, one of its leaders, Vytautas Kazlauskas, is genuinely concerned about the survival of the Catholic Church.

All in all, this is a good collection of studies looking at contemporary religious life in Lithuania outside the dominant Catholic Church. The need constantly to define a position in relation to the Catholic Church is made overly clear in all the contributions, and thus affirms the use of the Gramscian term 'hegemony' in relation to the Lithuanian religious scene. Nevertheless, as Schröder concludes, most people in Lithuania officially endorse the dominant Catholic Church, while practising a *bricolage* religiosity. The Lithuanian case is thus not all that different to the secularized West.

Department of Religious Studies S. Rimestad
University of Erfurt, Germany

Headley, Stephen. *Christ after Communism: Spiritual Authority and Its Transmission in Moscow Today*. Orthodox Research Institute, Rollinsford, NH, 2010. vii + 559 pp. Illustrations. Notes. Bibliography. Glossary. $25.95 (paperback).

Stephen Headley has written an extraordinary book. The following two questions have directed his research: i) where does Christianity come from in post-Communist Russia, and ii) what is its place in a non-secular modern society? Headley answers these by presenting the biographies of numerous priests and church elders (*startsy*), some of whom were killed by the Stalinist regime and later canonized by the Russian Orthodox Church (ROC). In this, he draws on his experience as an ROC priest who has served in Western Europe for thirty five years and who has spend an almost equally long time studying religion and prayer in Indonesia from an anthropological perspective. He is thus able to work comparatively and to combine an insider's perspective with an outsider's view. Unfortunately, he does not draw up a definition of non-secular modernity nor does he explain why he believes that this concept can be applied to post-Soviet Russian society.

After a discussion of the importance of memory in general and for the ROC in particular Headley proceeds to an analysis of Pavel Lungin's film *Ostrov* (2006), in which he highlights how spiritual authority can be created in post-Soviet Russia. This is followed by an interpretation of the *Basic Social Concept* and the *Code of Moral Principles and Rules of Economic Activity*, which was adopted by the Eighth World Russian People's Council in February 2004 (chapter five) as well as by almost hagiographic descriptions of the lives of those who have helped to revive the traditions of icon painting and church singing after the millennium celebrations of the baptism of Rus′ in 1988.

The second part of this book consists of an ethnographic description of three Orthodox parishes in Moscow which is based on the author's fieldwork between 2006 and 2009. Here, the biographies or memories of those priests and elders who either maintained or recreated these communities feature prominently. Headley thus shares with his readers the knowledge that most of the long-term members of these parishes would have. By approaching the topic in this way, he succeeds in shedding light on the lifestyle of devoted Orthodox believers and clerics and provides detailed insights into how the ROC works at the grassroots.

Headley is convincing in that it was certain extraordinary people who have kept the Russian Orthodox faith, its customs and traditions alive during the Soviet period. He presents their lives and achievements in an engaging and highly readable way whilst clearly identifying himself as an Orthodox theologian and cleric. This, however, does not mean that he does not criticize the Moscow Patriarchate when he sees fit. As he mentions on several occasions, he has deliberately chosen not to take the neutral approach that most other sociologists of religion would have opted for. He explains this by arguing that a neutral approach would have entailed the risk of obscuring the hierarchy of values which the communities observed by him have embraced (p. 476).

While this decision seems reasonable and undoubtedly has some merit it has apparently prevented Headley from making a more direct connection between his primary material and his central research questions. In other words, more discussion of the collected data and more thorough conclusions would have been desirable. This inclination also appears to have resulted in the underlying assumption that most Russians were devoted Orthodox believers, which is certainly not the case. Although the author clarifies in the final chapter that he is aware of this (p. 517), he appears to have neglected these circumstances in most of the preceding pages. Apart from this, the reader would have benefited from a more careful choice of title and chapter headings. In my opinion, it would have been helpful if the book's focus on personal histories had been made more explicit in the title and if the table of contents had made it clear that two documents rather than one are discussed in chapter five.

Nevertheless, this monograph makes a valuable contribution to the academic literature on the post-Soviet ROC by providing insights into certain aspects of the everyday life of parishes in Moscow, which are most probably transferable to other urban settings. The author's background also has advantages in that he is able skilfully to bridge the gap between a Western audience, which might or might not be familiar with the Orthodox religion, and Russian Orthodoxy. His book is therefore of interest to a wide readership, including Orthodox theologians who are unfamiliar with Russia's past and present. Furthermore, Headley is consistent in his critical portrayal of the USSR's anti-religious policies and its often devastating effects on the lives of individuals and communities. He achieves a good balance as he refrains from skipping over or embellishing this difficult period of Russia's past whilst avoiding the temptation to overemphasize it.

Department of Religious Studies KATJA RICHTERS
University of Erfurt

Keman, Hans and Müller-Rommel, Ferdinand (eds). *Party Government in the New Europe*. Routledge/ECPR Studies in European Political Science, 79. Routledge, London and New York, 2012. xxiii + 256 pp. Figures. Tables. Notes. Bibliography. Index. £75.00: $125.00.

THIS new collection offers a state-of-the-art survey of research on the place of parties in democratic governance in Europe taking in both established West European democracies and newer democratic systems in Central and Eastern Europe (CEE). Despite far-reaching social and geopolitical changes over the past two decades, patterns of European party government have proved surprisingly resilient. Although public dissatisfaction and electoral volatility have increased in Western Europe — driving the emergence of new parties — established parties have maintained their central position in government. Newer party systems in CEE have also been characterized by high (if reducing) volatility, but here too a small number of established parties have dominated government. Paradoxically, Keman and Müller-Rommel note, CEE's more fluid party systems thus suffer less of a 'gap in representational quality' than those of Western Europe where there is growing mismatch between the pool of parties represented in parliament and a subset of governing parties.

Political science has often (implicitly) viewed the essential role of party competition as generating governments. However, as Ian Budge and Michael D. McDonald argue, this has often deflected attention from the nature of the democratic majorities which underpin them. More specifically, they address the question of whether — and how — elected governments' majorities should overlap with the position of the median voter or with the electorate of the largest party. Running a series of simulations, they find that there is often considerable tension between the two varying according to the format of party system and the speed and scope of policy change under a new government. Slower rates of policy change make it more straightforward to reconcile the two models of 'democratic congruence'. Such findings, Budge and McDonald note, are particularly relevant to CEE, where lack of voter-party identification makes simplified party competition models of this kind a closer fit with reality. This is confirmed in a chapter by Fernando Casal Bértoa and the late Peter Mair examining party system institutionalization in the region through the stability and distribution of cabinet positions: CEE party systems, they conclude, have institutionalized less than those in earlier waves of democratization, becoming, if anything, *less* institutionalized over the last decade.

Social policy specialists have long seen party competition as a key determinant of welfare outcomes, with the strength of left parties in particular regarded as leading to higher trade union membership and more egalitarian welfare states. Klaus Armingeon tests this proposition on the new democracies of CEE using the concept of necessary conditions. While Armingeon finds no instances of social democratic welfare regimes without strong left parties in the region, many CEE cases clearly fit the West European paradigm uncomfortably. As F. G. Schmidt notes, addressing broadly the same question, additional factors such as the national legacies of Communist rule are clearly in play. Schmidt's analysis of patterns of party government and social policy in CEE identifies two distinct groups: the Visegrad countries and Slovenia, where as in Western Europe the party-political coloration of governments matters and Bulgaria, Romania and the Baltic states where it does not. Paul Penning's analysis of social benefits across Western Europe adds a further level of sophistication: using Charles Ragin's QCA technique he finds that the left/right complexion of governing parties matters for policy only *in combination* with factors such pre-existing benefit levels, integration into global markets or corporatism.

Reviewing the literature on models of democracy, veto players and the legislative process, Detlef Jahn concludes that a new typology of government decision-making is needed. He proposes a two-dimensional measure combining efficiency and social consensus. Assessing OECD states through an expert survey, he finds that no democracies outside Scandinavia combine efficiency and consensus. Interestingly, however, the four Visegrad states fall across three clusters, although the specific measures chosen to operationalize the dimensions and the small number of expert respondents suggest that further research is needed.

Party Government in the New Europe is an engaging collection which gives a lucid overview of a well established but still evolving research agenda. Although it narrows 'party government' to party *influence* on policy — more precisely to the influence of *governing* parties on policy — it is highly effective in pinpointing some central underlying issues in European party democracy. The book is arguably less successful in integrating the comparative study of Western Europe and CEE. Arguably only four of the book's chapters are genuinely pan-European in scope. Moreover, faced with the usual awkward patterns of difference and similarity, few really advance between a strategy of simply juxtaposing the two halves of Europe or viewing CEE through the prism of Western Europe.

UCL SSEES SEÁN HANLEY

Stewart, Michael (ed.). *The Gypsy 'Menace': Populism and the New Anti-Gypsy Politics*. Hurst and Company, London, 2012. xxxviii + 382 pp. Notes. Bibliography. Index. £18.95 (paperback).

THIS edited volume examines the rise of anti-Roma prejudice across Europe and paints a bleak picture for the 10–12 million-strong Roma/Gypsy community, demonstrating how and why the wave of populism sweeping Europe has constructed Roma as an ethnic 'other'. The volume explains how anti-Gypsyism has been unleashed by the rise of populism, nationalism and anti-immigrant sentiments, and further exacerbated by the impact of European Union integration and the global economic crisis, which have been felt acutely in the newer democracies of Central and Eastern Europe. This cocktail has conspired to transform Roma in the eyes of many from merely a 'nuisance' or a 'problem' into an 'unbearable thorn in the side of the struggling nation' (Stewart, p. xxxvii). The volume houses fifteen chapters which cover a range of empirical contexts as well as analytical insights. Whilst Stewart provides a coherent and interesting analytical framework, not all contributions speak to this. Unsurprisingly, with so many chapters, there are divergences in quality and coherence to the main arguments of the book.

Chapter one (Stewart) lays out the conceptual framework which draws upon the work of two scholars: Douglas Holmes and his arguments concerning 'integralist' populist politicians and the building of political imaginaries of the nation; and Mabel Berezin whose work explores how people are dissatisfied with existing socio-economic and political structures and search for new political, social and cultural spaces. János Zolnay provides an overview of discriminatory practices in education and the labour market in Hungary in chapter two. The third chapter by Georgia Efremova really speaks to the conceptual framework and examines 'redemptive' anti-Gypsy politics in Bulgaria. Building on integralist insights, she reveals how Roma are reformulated as a disease which has contaminated the nation. Chapter four (Karel Čada) looks at public attitudes towards Roma and right-wing political discourse targeting Roma in the Czech Republic. Giovanni Picker goes beyond the obvious and highlights how the left has elaborated similar discourse to the centre and the far right when targeting Roma for political gain in Italy in chapter five. Chapter six (Ilsen About) links the expulsion of Roma in France in 2010 to historical categorizations of *Gens de voyage* in the nineteenth and twentieth centuries. The seventh chapter by Kata Horváth provides a fascinating discussion of negotiating difference internally (between Gypsies) and externally (in relation to non-Gypsy Hungarians) and the impact of naming this difference on belonging and visibility. Chapter eight (Gwendolyn Albert) focuses on particular events in political life (riots, elections) to show how Czech society is polarized between those who are 'inadaptable' (Roma) and those who are decent (everyone else), and discusses the ascription and impact of victimhood. Colin Clark and Gareth Rice use the concepts of fear, violence and public space to understand the intimidation of Roma families in Belfast, Northern Ireland in 2009 in chapter nine. Stephánia Toma draws upon quantitative research to uncover the explanations put forward for supposed inter-ethnic conflict between Roma and ethnic Hungarians in Romania in chapter ten. Chapter eleven (Stefan Benedik, Wolfgang Göderle and Barbara Tiefenbacher) demonstrates the complexity of interactions in the production of knowledge about Roma in Austria. This fascinating chapter highlights migration, gender, the issue of presence, as well as the negative impact of NGO intervention. Lídia Balogh documents the rise of hate crime in Hungary, focusing on two Hungarian villages in chapter twelve. Chapter thirteen (Britta Schellenberg) is short on detail. Rather, it lists strategies to combat right-wing populism but fails to engage with the shortcomings of the anti-racist movement. Chapter fourteen (Cecília Kovai) is refreshing and well written and addresses kinship, belonging and visibility in Hungary. Finally, Andraś Pap takes a legal perspective and laments the shortcoming of human rights legislation in Hungary to protect Roma in chapter fifteen.

Many of us who work on Roma do so because we want to understand why Roma are so persecuted. In order to really get to grips with this question it is imperative to appreciate the impact of prejudice. Indeed, any policy intervention at the local, regional, national or international level is destined to fail unless parallel processes of combating anti-Gypsyism are cultivated.

Whilst Stewart has gone some way to highlighting the impact of this across Europe, and I think this volume does push the debate forward in terms of why anti-Gypsyism is on the rise, it does not really get to grips with combating extremism, even though several chapters claim to do so. The intellectual dexterity of the conceptual framework is certainly useful. I would have liked more focus on one of the central themes of the book though — presence — which is not adequately drawn out. The majority of the contributions highlight one of the ultimate paradoxes for Roma: in order to address prejudice and challenge negative stereotypes they must be visible in public life however, as soon as they are present in the public sphere they are subject to exogenous categorization, stereotyping and marginalization. The volume is a welcome addition to the burgeoning literature on Roma and ought to be read by anyone interested in populism, the extreme right, discourse, ethnicity, presence, migration and nationalism.

School of Applied Social Science AIDAN MCGARRY
University of Brighton

Publications Received

Chodakiewicz, Marek Jan. *Intermarium: The Land between the Black and Baltic Seas.* Transaction, New Brunswick, NJ and London, 2012. $59.95.

Dralyuk, Boris. *Western Crime Fiction Goes East: The Russian Pinkerton Craze 1907–1934.* Russian History and Culture, 11. Brill, Leiden and Boston, MA, 2012. €96.00: $133.00.

Easter, Gerald M. *Capital, Coercion, and Postcommunist States.* Cornell University Press, Ithaca, NY and London, 2012. $26.95 (paperback).

Ezrahi, Christina. *Swans of the Kremlin: Ballet and Power in Soviet Russia.* University of Pittsburgh Press, Pittsburgh, PA, 2012. £27.95.

Fagan, Geraldine. *Believing in Russia – Religious Policy after Communism.* Routledge Contemporary Russia and Eastern Europe Series, 41. Routledge, London and New York, 2013. £90.00.

Green, Yvonne. *After Semyon Izrailevich Lipkin: 1911–2003.* Smith/Doorstop Books, Sheffield, 2011. £9.95 (paperback).

Herzen, Alexander. *A Herzen Reader.* Edited and translated by Kathleen Parthé, with a critical essay by Robert Harris. Northwestern University Press, Evanston, IL, 2012. $34.95 (paperback).

Hicks, Jeremy. *First Films of the Holocaust: Soviet Cinema and the Genocide of the Jews, 1938–1946.* Pitt Series in Russian and East European Studies. University of Pittsburgh Press, Pittsburgh, PA, 2012. $28.95 (paperback).

Jones, Stephen. *Georgia: A Political History Since Independence.* I. B. Tauris, London and New York, 2013. £35.00.

Kavaliauskas, Tomas. *Transformations in Central Europe between 1989 and 2012: Geopolitical, Cultural, and Socioeconomic Shifts.* Lexington Books, Lanham, MD, Boulder, CO, New York, Toronto and Plymouth, 2012. $70.00: £44.95.

Khapaeva, Dina. *Nightmare: From Literary Experiments to Cultural Project.* Translated by Rosie Tweddle. Russian History and Culture, 10. Brill, Leiden and Boston, MA, 2013. €112.00: $156.00.

Kollmann, Nancy. *Crime and Punishment in Early Modern Russia.* New Studies in European History. Cambridge University Press, Cambridge and New York, 2012. £70.00: $115.00.

Kurunmäki, J. and Strang, J. (eds). *Rhetorics of Nordic Democracy.* Studia Fennica: Historica, 17. Finnish Literature Society, Helsinki, 2010. €32.00 (paperback).

LaPierre, Brian. *Hooligans in Khrushchev's Russia: Defining, Policing, and Producing Deviance during the Thaw.* University of Wisconsin Press, Madison, WI, 2012.$29.95 (paperback).

Leving, Yuri (ed.). *Anatomy of a Short Story: Nabokov's Puzzles, Codes, 'Signs and Symbols'.* Continuum, London and New York, 2012. £19.99 (paperback).

Maguire, Muireann (trans.). *Red Spectres: Russian 20th-Century Gothic-Fantastic Tales.* Angel Classics. Angel Books, London, 2012. £12.95 (paperback).

Maguire, Muireann. *Stalin's Ghosts: Gothic Themes in Early Soviet Literature.* Russian Transformations: Literature, Thought, Culture, 4. Peter Lang, Bern, Oxford and New York, 2012. £45.00 (paperback).

Marin, Irina. *Contested Frontiers in the Balkans: Ottoman and Habsburg Rivalries in Eastern Europe.* I. B. Tauris, London and New York, 2013. £54.50.

Mendras, Marie. *Russian Politics: The Paradox of a Weak State.* Comparative Politics and International Studies Series. Hurst & Company, London, 2012. £25.00.

Norman, Will. *Nabokov, History and the Texture of Time.* Routledge Transnational Perspectives on American Literature, 19. Routledge, London and New York, 2012. £85.00.

Norris, Stephen M. and Sunderland, Willard (eds). *Russia's People of Empire: Life Stories from Eurasia, 1500 to the Present.* Indiana University Press, Bloomington and Indianapolis, IN, 2012. $35.00: £23.99 (paperback).

Pallot, Judith and Piacentini, Laura. *Gender, Geography, and Punishment: The Experience of Women in Carceral Russia.* With the assistance of Dominique Moran. Oxford Geographical and Environmental Studies. Oxford University Press, Oxford and New York, 2012. £55.00.

Pettifer, James. *The Kosova Liberation Army: Underground War to Balkan Insurgency, 1948–2001.* C. Hurst & Company, London, 2012. £29.99.

Rethage, Wilma. *Strukturelle Besonderheiten des Russischen in Deutschland. Kontaktlinguistische und soziolinguistische Aspekte.* Specimina Philologiae Slavicae, 165. Otto Sagner, Munich and Berlin, 2012. €36.00 (paperback).

Richters, Katja. *The Post-Soviet Russian Orthodox Church: Politics, Culture and Greater Russia.* Routledge Contemporary Russia and Eastern Europe Series, 35. Routledge, London and New York, 2013. £85.00.

Segel, Harold B. *The Walls Behind the Curtain: East European Prison Literature, 1945–1990.* Pitt Series in Russian and East European Studies. University of Pittsburgh Press, Pittsburgh, PA, 2012.$35.00 (paperback).

Sikimić, B., Hristov, P. and Golubović, B. (eds). *Labour Migrations in the Balkans.* Studies on Language and Culture in Central and Eastern Europe, 18. Otto Sagner, Munich and Berlin, 2012. €29.80.

Viellard, S., Troubetzkoy, L. and Aslanoff, S. (eds). *La lettre et l'esprit: entre langue et culture. Études à la mémoire de Jean Breuillard. Revue des* études *slaves*, 83, 2012, 2–3. Centre d'études slaves et Institut d'études slaves, Paris, 2012. Price unknown.

Voinovich, Vladimir. *A Displaced Person: The Later Life and Extraordinary Adventures of Private Ivan Chonkin.* Translated from the Russian by Andrew Bromfield. Northwestern University Press, Evanston, IL, 2012. $21.95 (paperback).

Abstracts

Aleksandr Ivanov and Nikolai Gogol′: The Image and the Word in the Russian Tradition of Art as Prophecy by Pamela Davidson
The Russian image of the artist as a prophet is generally regarded as a verbal construct, developed through literary tradition. This paper introduces a new perspective: the role of the visual arts. Focusing on the relationship between Aleksandr Ivanov (1806–58) and Nikolai Gogol′ (1809–52), it argues that Ivanov's visual treatment of prophecy (in 'The Appearance of the Messiah to the People', 1833–57) interacted with and influenced Gogol′'s literary approach (in *Dead Souls*, 'The Portrait', *Selected Passages from Correspondence with Friends*). Tensions over the relative value of the image and the word in creating new forms of religious art and competition over assuming the role of leading prophet led to a crisis point in their relationship around 1848.

Londoners and Outlanders: Polish Labour Migration through the European Lens by Kris Van Heuckelom
This article covers a series of prominent tropes and shifts that characterize the cinematic portrayal of immigrant workers from Poland in contemporary European film, with a special focus on the on-screen treatment of Polish jobseekers moving to the United Kingdom in the post-accession period. As a comparative and contextual analysis of recent London-set films such as Ken Loach's *It's a Free World* (2007) and Dominic Lees's *Outlanders* (2007) indicates, Polish characters are gradually climbing up the social ladder within Fortress Europe, getting rid of their label of prototypical labour immigrants, whereas the empty space is taken up by immigrants from outside the Schengen zone.

The Intertwining of Religion and Nationhood in Interwar Yugoslavia: The School Celebrations of St Sava's Day by Pieter Troch
The celebration of St Sava's Day in schools during the interwar period expressed the policy of the Yugoslav state authorities to reconcile religious diversity among its population with national unity by highlighting the parallel national character of Yugoslav Catholicism, Orthodoxy and Islam. These celebrations, however, generated strong opposition from leaders of the religious communities in Yugoslavia. Crucially, the criticism was not directed against the Yugoslav national programme in education as such, but revolved around the fundamentally different ontologies of the nationalizing state and religious thinkers. For the former, religious symbolic resources like St Sava served the purpose of the nation, for the latter the meaning of St Sava could not be detached from Orthodoxy. The divergence between religious thinking and the national program of the Yugoslav state authorities explains the parallel shift among religious thinkers in Yugoslavia away from Yugoslavism to the Croatian Catholic, Serbian Orthodox and Bosnian Muslim nationalization of religion.

The Peculiar Prosperity of Psychoanalysis in Socialist Yugoslavia by Mat Savelli
This article traces the history of psychoanalytically-oriented mental health care in the Socialist Federal Republic of Yugoslavia. Like many other places in Central and Eastern Europe, psychoanalysis in post-war Yugoslavia faced a host of barriers to its long term survival. Rather than retreating or dying out, psychoanalytic ideas came to greatly influence Yugoslav psychiatry, both by informing treatment modalities and by providing a theoretical framework for understanding mental illness. The article outlines exactly how this transformation came to pass by documenting the threats posed to psychoanalysis and then analysing how these challenges were overcome.

Caught between Germany and Russia: Memory and National Identity in Poland's Right-Wing Media Post-2004 by Ewa Stańczyk

This article explores representations of Germany and Russia in the Polish print media by investigating how the memory of both World War Two and the years of Communism in particular fuelled media discourse in the period between Poland's accession to the European Union in 2004 and the tragic crash of the presidential plane near Smoleńsk on 10 April 2010. By concentrating on selected cover stories published between 2005 and 2009 by the then right-wing weekly news magazine, *Wprost* (*Straight Talk*), this article also seeks to examine ways of constructing and articulating Polish collective memory and national identity.

THE SLAVONIC & EAST EUROPEAN REVIEW

The Slavonic and East European Review, the journal of the UCL School of Slavonic and East European Studies, is published quarterly by the Modern Humanities Research Association (MHRA). Issues are numbered serially, the four annual issues constituting a volume. Up to and including 1965 an even-numbered issue (published in December) together with the following and odd-numbered issue (published in June) constituted a volume.

Scholarly contributions are invited on all subjects related to the field of Slavonic and East European Studies. Articles should be between 8,000 and 12,000 words, although contributions falling outside this range may also be considered. Book reviews should be no longer than requested. Other contributions (marginalia, obituaries, summary notes) should aim at a corresponding and proportionate brevity. Original documents are specially welcome. No correspondence is published in the *Review*.

Contributions should be submitted in English in a form ready for publication and in the final state intended. Contributors should study the leaflet, 'Guide for Contributors', obtainable on request from the Deputy Editor, SEER Office, UCL SSEES, Gower Street, London WC1E 6BT (seer@ssees.ucl.ac.uk), or online at www.ssees.ucl.ac.uk/seer.htm. All contributions must adhere to the *Review*'s house style.

Contributions and other editorial communications should be sent to the Deputy Editor. While the editors take every possible care with regard to typescripts, they advise authors to retain duplicate copies. The editors do not consider themselves responsible in the event of the loss of a contribution.

Online access to *The Slavonic and East European Review* for individual members of the Modern Humanities Research Association is included in the annual subscription. Further information about the activities of the Modern Humanities Research Association and individual membership can be obtained from the Honorary Secretary Dr Barbara Burns, School of Modern Languages and Cultures, University of Glasgow, Hetherington Building, Bute Gardens, Glasgow G12 8RS, UK, or from the website at www.mhra.org.uk. For institutional subscription rates and information, please contact JSTOR (http://about.jstor.org/csp). Orders and enquiries relating to back numbers (from Vol. 48 to date), should be directed to Periodicals Service Company (http://www.periodicals.com).

ISSN 0037-6795 (print); ISSN 2222-4327 (online)